Contents

Bárður Snæfellsás sculpture
LAUREN PIASECKI/SHUTTERSTOCK ©

Plan Your Trip
Iceland's Top 10

CHRISTIAN GEHRIG/500PX ©

Reykjavík

Embrace the world's most northerly capital

Historic Reykjavík combines colourful buildings, quirky people, eye-popping design, wild nightlife and a capricious soul in an endearingly compact package. For all its new-found fame and creative cosmopolitan air, Reykjavík remains an overgrown village at heart, where walking is still the best way to get around but world-class arts, culture and museums abound, and quality bars, restaurants and coffee houses appear on every street corner.

Top left: Harpa (p57); Top right: Laugardalslaug (p61)

DENNIS VAN DE WATER/SHUTTERSTOCK ©

The Golden Circle

Geysers, waterfalls and the world's oldest parliament

Only a couple of hours' drive from the capital, the Golden Circle is beloved of tour groups but should be visited by all: even after you've ticked off the mega-attractions of spurting Geysir, the dramatic waterfall Gullfoss and Þingvellir, site of Iceland's original parliament, there is much to explore. Save time for rock climbing, rafting, soaking in geo-pools and exploring a 6500-year-old explosion crater. Strokkur geyser (p75)

SMIT/SHUTTERSTOCK ©

The Diamond Circle

A diamond in the northern rough

It may be trading on the Golden Circle name, but the route dubbed the Diamond Circle, encompassing stunning Mývatn lake and Dettifoss waterfall, is the undisputed gem of the rugged northeast. Explore the vents, fumaroles and craters in the moonscape around Krafla, circumnavigate the lake and experience the power of nature at Dettifoss (pictured; p104), one of Iceland's most spectacular waterfalls.

Jökulsárlón

A ghostly procession of luminous-blue icebergs

This surreal scene (handily right next to the Ring Road) is a natural film set: in fact, you might have seen it in *Batman Begins* and the James Bond film *Die Another Day*. The ice calves from Breiðamerkur-jökull glacier, an offshoot of the mighty Vatnajökull ice cap. Boat trips and kayaking among the bergs are popular, or you can simply wander the lake-shore, scout for seals and exhaust your camera's memory card.

Heimaey

An island formed by volcanic power

An offshore archipelago of craggy peaks, Vest-mannaeyjar is a mere 30-minute ferry ride from the mainland, but feels miles away in sentiment. A boat tour of the scattered islets unveils squawk-ing seabirds, towering cliffs and postcard-worthy vistas of lonely hunting cabins perched atop rocky outcrops. The islands' 4000-plus population is focused on Heimaey (pictured; p123), a small town of windswept bungalows with a scarring curl of lava that flows straight through its centre – a poignant reminder of Iceland's volatile landscape.

Snæfellsnes Peninsula

Inspirational fjords, glaciers and a stunning ice cap

With its cache of wild beaches, bird sanctuaries, horse farms and lava fields, the Snæfellsnes Peninsula is one of Iceland's best escapes – either as a day trip from the capital or as a relaxing long weekend. Little wonder it's often called 'Iceland in miniature' – it even boasts a national park and glacier-topped stratovolcano. Jules Verne was definitely onto something when he used Snæfellsjökull's icy crown as his magical doorway to the centre of the earth.

Kirkjufellsfoss (p146)

MATTEO PROVENDOLA/SHUTTERSTOCK ©

Seyðisfjörður

Ferry into this stunning Eastfjords village

Stunning, art-fuelled Seyðisfjörður is only 27km from the Ring Road but feels worlds away, and it welcomes the weekly ferry from Europe into its mountain-lined, waterfall-studded embrace. Made up of multicoloured wooden houses and surrounded by snowcapped mountains, Seyðisfjörður is a place for hiking, biking, kayaking and communing with an eclectic international community of artists, writers and musicians.

OZZO PHOTOGRAPHY/500PX ©

Vatnajökull National Park

Explore the largest ice cap outside the poles

Europe's largest national park covers around 14% of Iceland and safeguards the mighty Vatnajökull ice cap. Scores of outlet glaciers flow down from its frosty bulk, while underneath it are active volcanoes and mountain peaks. Yes, this is ground zero for those 'fire and ice' clichés. You'll be spellbound by the diversity of landscapes, walking trails and activities inside this supersized park.

Akureyri

Go whalewatching from Iceland's second city

Nestled at the head of Eyjafjörður, Iceland's longest fjord, pretty Akureyri is Iceland's second-biggest city but would be a mere town anywhere else. Bordering the Arctic Circle, this is a base for seeking out the Northern Lights, playing a round of midnight golf, indulging in Iceland's best skiing or hitting the town in an unexpectedly cool far-northern cafe and nightlife scene. What's more, this is a fine base for Iceland's best whalewatching at nearby Húsavík.

Westfjords

Spot puffins in Iceland's most remote corner

Iceland's sweeping spectrum of superlative nature comes to a dramatic climax in the Westfjords – the island's off-the-beaten-path adventure par excellence. Broad, multihued beaches flank the southern coast, roaring bird colonies abound, fjordheads tower above and then plunge into the deep, while Hornstrandir is the final frontier of perilous sea cliffs and hiking trails that practically kiss the Arctic Circle.

JONATHAN SMITH/LONELY PLANET ©

CAROLYN BAIN/LONELY PLANET ©

CHRISTIAN SCHWEIGER/500PX ©

Clockwise from top left: Icelandic knitwear; '*Skyr* volcano' dessert at Pakkhús (p184), Höfn;
Glacier hiking in Skaftafell National Park (p170); An Icelandic sheep; Víti crater's bright blue lake (p97);
A puffin on the Dyrhólaey promontory (p119)

HENN PHOTOGRAPHY/GETTY IMAGES ©

ROXANA BASH-ROVA/SHUTTERSTOCK ©

JONATHAN GREGSON/LONELY PLANET ©

Plan Your Trip
Need to Know

When to Go

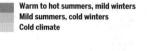

Warm to hot summers, mild winters
Mild summers, cold winters
Cold climate

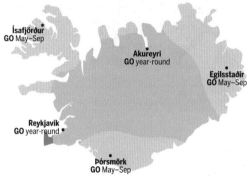

Ísafjörður
GO May–Sep

Akureyri
GO year-round

Egilsstaðir
GO May–Sep

Reykjavík
GO year-round

Þórsmörk
GO May–Sep

High Season (Jun–Aug)

o Visitors descend en masse, especially to Reykjavík and the south. Prices peak.

o Endless daylight, many festivals, busy activities.

o Highland mountain roads open to 4WDs from mid-June or later; hikers welcome.

Shoulder (May & Sep)

o Breezier weather; occasional snows in the highlands.

o Fewer crowds and lower prices.

Low Season (Oct–Apr)

o Mountain roads closed; some minor roads shut.

o Winter activities on offer include skiing, snowshoeing and visiting ice caves.

o Long nights with possible Northern Lights viewings.

Currency
Icelandic króna (plural krónur)

Languages
Icelandic, English

Visas
Generally not required for stays of up to 90 days.

Money
Iceland is an almost cashless society where credit cards reign supreme, even in the most rural reaches. PIN required for purchases. ATMs available in all towns.

Mobile Phones
Mobile (cell) coverage is widespread. Visitors with GSM phones can make roaming calls; purchase a local SIM card if you're staying a while.

Time
Iceland's time zone is the same as GMT/UTC (London); there's no daylight savings time.

Daily Costs

Budget: Less than 18,000kr

- Camping: 1500–1800kr
- Dorm bed: 4000–7000kr
- Hostel breakfast: 1800–2000kr
- Grill-bar meal or soup lunch: 1500–2200kr
- One-way bus ticket Reykjavík–Akureyri: 10,120kr

Midrange: 18,000–35,000kr

- Guesthouse double room: 18,000–28,000kr
- Cafe meal: 2000–3500kr
- Museum entry: 1000kr
- Small vehicle rental (per day): from 8000kr

Top End: More than 35,000kr

- Boutique double room: 30,000–45,000kr
- Main dish in top-end restaurant: 3500–7000kr
- 4WD rental (per day): from 15,000kr

Exchange Rates

Australia	A$1	79kr
Canada	C$1	81kr
Eurozone	€1	124kr
Japan	¥100	97kr
NZ	NZ$1	73kr
UK	UK£1	141kr
USA	US$1	107kr

For current exchange rates, see www.xe.com.

Useful Websites

Visit Iceland (www.visiticeland.com) Iceland's official tourism portal.

Visit Reykjavík (www.visitreykjavik.is) Official site for the capital.

Icelandic Met Office (http://en.vedur.is) Best resource for weather forecasts.

Icelandic Road Administration (www.road.is) Road openings and conditions.

Reykjavík Grapevine (www.grapevine.is) English-language newspaper and website.

Lonely Planet (www.lonelyplanet.com/iceland) Destination information, hotel bookings, traveller forum and more.

Arriving in Iceland

Keflavík International Airport Iceland's primary international airport is 48km southwest of Reykjavík. The most common method of transport to the capital from the airport is bus (journey time 45 to 60 minutes). Flybus and Airport Express will deliver you to their terminals (2700kr to 2950kr) or to your city accommodation (3300kr to 3950kr; a bus change at the terminal is usually required). Flybus can also deliver you to the domestic airport in Reykavík (3950kr). Taxis from Keflavík are possible, but pricey. Car rental from the airport is also popular.

Seyðisfjörður ferry port The weekly Smyril Line car ferry that connects Denmark with Iceland via the Faroe Islands arrives in the pretty town of Seyðisfjörður in East Iceland. Buses run year-round between Seyðisfjörður and Egilsstaðir, and from Egilsstaðir northwest to Akureyri and on to Reykjavík.

Getting Around

Car Vehicles can be expensive to rent but provide great freedom. A 2WD vehicle will get you almost everywhere in summer. Driving into the highlands and on F roads requires a 4WD.

Bus A decent bus network operates in July and August. Outside these months, services are less frequent (and even nonexistent). Find an invaluable online map at www.publictransport.is.

Air If you're short on time, domestic flights can help you get around efficiently.

For more on **getting around**, see p283 ➡

Plan Your Trip
Hot Spots For...

BANET/SHUTTERSTOCK ©

Hot-Pots & Pools

Hot-pots and geothermal lagoons are a highlight of Iceland for locals and visitors alike. Every town has one, but you can also find them in remote locations.

Blue Lagoon (p82)
Soak it up in Iceland's most famous geothermal pool, less than an hour from Reykjavík.

Retreat Spa
One of the most decadent spas on the planet (p85).

Mývatn (p94)
This beautiful northern lake is surrounded by geothermal activity and volcanic vents.

Mývatn Nature Baths
A gorgeous place to soak in mineral-rich waters (p96).

Laugarvatn (p87)
In the Golden Circle, Laugarvatn has a public pool and a swanky geothermal spa.

Fontana
Take a dip in this fancy public lakeside spa (p87).

PICHETW/ GETTY IMAGES ©

Volcanoes & Glaciers

Fire and ice sums up the Icelandic geological experience – get up close to Europe's most dramatic lava fields, glaciers and ice caps.

Vatnajökull National Park (p167)
Snowmobile or hike across Iceland's largest ice cap, from Skaftafell (south) or Jökulsárgljúfur (north).

Skaftafell
A breathtaking wilderness of peaks and glaciers (p170).

Jökulsárlón (p111)
This iconic glacial lagoon of drifting icebergs is a postcard symbol of Iceland.

IceGuide
Ice cave tours and kayaking among the icebergs (p116).

Snæfellsjökull National Park (p140)
This park protects the mammoth ice cap and glacier made famous in *Journey to the Centre of the Earth*.

Vatnshellir
8000-year-old lava tube with multiple caverns (p143).

Wildlife Watching

From puffin colonies to majestic breaching whales, Iceland has exciting wildlife-watching opportunities, set against dramatic sea-cliff scenery.

GIEDRIIUS/SHUTTERSTOCK ©

Whales (p194)
Whale-watching boat trips are a highlight of the Icelandic waters between June and August.

Húsavík
Iceland's whale-watching capital (p194).

Puffins & Seabirds (p216)
Puffins, Arctic terns, razorbills and guillemots abound on Iceland's sea cliffs in summer.

Látrabjarg Bird Cliffs
Dramatic cliffs and extraordinary bird numbers (p216).

Arctic Foxes (p217)
The shy Arctic fox is Iceland's only native mammal and is best spotted on Hornstrandir Peninsula.

Hornstrandir
Visitor the Arctic Fox Centre in Súðavík (p217).

History

Iceland has a rich history of Norse settlement, epic sagas, Viking feuds and modern independence. Luckily much of that history is preserved.

JONATHAN SMITH/LONELY PLANET ©

Reykjavík (p35)
The capital is a fine place to delve into Icelandic history via the National Museum.

Settlement Exhibition
Museum based on a Viking longhouse (p41).

Þingvellir National Park (p78)
This is where the Vikings established the world's first democratic parliament.

Alþingi Site
Where the parliament convened annually (p79).

Heimaey (p123)
Heimaey has had a dramatic past of settlement, pirates and volcanic eruptions.

Eldheimar
'Pompeii of the North' is a poignant museum (p131).

Plan Your Trip
Essential Iceland

BRAGI THOR JOSEFSSON/GETTY IMAGES ©

Activities

Outdoor activities define the Icelandic experience: the long days of the summer months provide perfect conditions for hiking, kayaking, horse riding and mountain biking, while winter travel is becoming increasingly popular for snowmobiling, glacier walking and skiing. Iceland's spectacular natural beauty encompasses Western Europe's largest national park and the mightiest ice cap outside the poles, plus a whale-filled ocean and the world's biggest puffin colonies. Prepare to greet soaring mountains, hidden valleys, dark canyons, roaring waterfalls, twisting rivers and fjord-riven coastlines. Getting out into it is easy and utterly exhilarating.

Less well-known activities include dry-suit scuba diving in cold but clear waters, quad biking and ice-cave tours, all with qualified local guides. Or you could just join the locals in the favourite year-round pastime of soaking and swimming in geothermal pools.

Shopping

Reykjavík is Iceland's shopping hub, but creativity and first-rate craftsmanship is on display countrywide. Even in the smallest towns, galleries and stops (plus guesthouses, cafes and museums) exhibit and sell the output of talented locals. Knitwear – especially the *lopapeysa,* the signature woollen sweater – is ubiquitous, but photography, artwork, fashion and design objects may also catch your eye. Books, foodstuffs and local booze make fine souvenirs.

Before purchasing knitwear, do look to see where it was made. A number of stores stock *lopapeysur* 'made in China from Icelandic wool' or words to that effect. Buy locally made products where you can.

Entertainment

There's an abundance of talent in Iceland. (Does everyone here play in a band?) The chances are high for stumbling across live music in unlikely places. You can track down performances easily in the capital – check

EMKA74/SHUTTERSTOCK ©

the *Reykjavík Grapevine* (www.grapevine.
is) for listings. And don't be surprised
when you pull into a tiny fjordside town and
discover a schedule for weekly summer
concerts.

   Music fans should plan their visit to
coincide with a big-name festival such as
Iceland Airwaves (p24), Secret Solstice
(p23) or Sónar Reykjavík (www.sonar
reykjavik.com).

Eating

If people know anything about Icelandic
food, it's usually to do with a plucky population tucking into boundary-pushing dishes
such as fermented shark or sheep's head.
It's a pity the spotlight doesn't shine as
brightly on Iceland's delicious, fresh-from-
the-farm ingredients, the seafood bounty
hauled from the surrounding icy waters, the
innovative dairy products (hello, *skyr* – a
yogurt-like dessert) or the clever, historical
food-preserving techniques that are finding
new favour with today's much-feted New
Nordic chefs.

★ Best for Wildlife Watching
Puffins Vestmannaeyjar (p123;
Heimaey)
Whales Húsavík (p194)
Arctic foxes Hornstrandir (p217)
Birds Mývatn (p98)
Seals Westfjords (p216)

Drinking & Nightlife

Sure, Reykjavík is small, but it's bursting
with cool coffeeshops, boho bars, crazy
clubs and the weekend *Djammið* (night
on the town). Akureyri also has a nightlife
scene but on a smaller scale. Things are
more subdued in most regional towns, but
it's possible to find quality coffee, local
microbrews and a low-key gig if you ask
around.

From left: *Lopapeysa* (woollen sweater); grey seal pup

Plan Your Trip
Month by Month

January
✖ Þorrablót

This Viking midwinter feast from late January to mid- or late February is marked nationwide with stomach-churning treats such as *hákarl* (fermented Greenland shark), *svið* (singed sheep's head) and *hrútspungar* (rams' testicles). All accompanied by shots of *brennivín* (a potent schnapps nicknamed 'black death'). Hungry?

February
✾ Winter Lights Festival

Reykjavík sparkles with this four-day winter-warmer encompassing Museum Night and Pool Night (late-opening museums and swimming pools), plus illuminated landmarks, light installations and concerts. See www.winterlightsfestival.is.

March
♟ Beer Day

It's hard to imagine, but beer was illegal in Iceland for 75 years. On 1 March, Icelanders celebrate the day in 1989 when the prohibition was overturned. Pubs, restaurants and clubs around Reykjavík are especially beer-lovin' on this night.

April
✾ Sumardagurinn Fyrsti

Rather ambitiously, Icelanders celebrate the first day of summer (the first Thursday after 18 April) with celebrations and street parades. It's a nod to the Old Norse calendar, which divided the year into just two seasons: winter and summer.

May
✾ Reykjavík Arts Festival

Culture-vultures flock to Iceland's premier cultural festival, a biennial event (even-numbered years) that showcases local and international theatre performances, film, dance, music and visual art. See www.listahatid.is for the program.

KONDRUKHOV/SHUTTERSTOCK ©

June

⚓ Seafarers' Day

Fishing is integral to Icelandic life, and Seafarers' Day (Sjómannadagurinn) is party time in fishing villages. On the first weekend in June, every ship in Iceland is in harbour and all sailors have a day off for drinking, rowing and swimming contests, tug-of-war and mock sea rescues.

⚓ Hafnarfjörður Viking Festival

The peace is shattered as Viking hordes invade this seaside town near Reykjavík for a four-day market festival in mid-June. Expect family-friendly storytelling, staged battles, archery and music. See www.visithafnarfjordur.is.

⚓ National Day

The country's biggest holiday commemorates the founding of the Republic of Iceland, on 17 June 1944, with parades and general patriotic merriment. Tradition has it that the sun isn't supposed to shine. And it usually doesn't.

★ Best Festivals

Iceland Airwaves, November
Reykjavík Culture Night, August
Þjóðhátíð, August
Bræðslan, July

☆ Secret Solstice

This excellent music festival (www.secretsolstice.is) with local and international acts coincides with the summer solstice, so there's 24-hour daylight for partying. It's held at Laugardalur in Reykjavík.

July

☆ Folk Music Festival

The small but well-regarded five-day folk music festival in Siglufjörður welcomes Icelandic and foreign musicians. Enjoy traditional tunes, courses on Icelandic music, dance and handicrafts. See www.folkmusik.is.

From left: Pedestrian street for Reykjavík Pride (p24); Drummers at Reykjavík Culture Night (p24)

☆ Eistnaflug

The end-of-the-line Eastfjords town of Neskaupstaður goes *off* in the second week of July, when the population doubles to celebrate the heavy-metal festival Eistnaflug. See www.eistnaflug.is.

☆ Bræðslan

The beloved Bræðslan pop/rock festival has earned a reputation for great music and an intimate atmosphere. Some big local names (and a few international ones) come to play in tiny, out-of-the-way Borgarfjörður Eystri in late July. Check out www.braedslan.com.

August

⚑ Verslunarmannahelgi

A public-holiday long weekend (the first weekend in August) when Icelanders flock to rural festivals, family barbecues, rock concerts and wild campground parties.

☆ Þjóðhátíð

This earth-shaking event occurs in Heimaey, Vestmannaeyjar, on the August long weekend, commemorating the day in 1874 when foul weather prevented the islanders from partying when Iceland's constitution was established. Up to 16,000 people descend to watch bands and fireworks, and drink gallons of alcohol. See www.dalurinn.is.

⚑ Reykjavík Culture Night

On Culture Night (Menningarnótt), held mid-month, Reykjavikers turn out in force for a day and night of art, music, dance and fireworks. Many galleries, ateliers, shops, cafes and churches stay open until late. See www.menningarnott.is for a full program.

⚑ Reykjavík Pride

Out and proud since 1999, this festival brings Carnival-like colour to the capital on the second weekend of August. Up to 100,000 people attend the Pride march and celebrations. See www.hinsegindagar.is/en.

⚑ Jökulsárlón Fireworks

Could there be a more beautiful location for a fireworks display than Jökulsárlón glacier lagoon? For one night in mid- to late August, an annual fundraising event is staged, with buses shuttling spectators in. See www.visitvatnajokull.is.

September

☆ Reykjavík Jazz Festival

Early in the month, Reykjavík toe-taps its way through five days dedicated to jazz, man. Local and international musicians blow their own trumpets at events across town. Check out www.reykjavikjazz.is.

⚘ Réttir

An autumn highlight, the *réttir* is the farmers' round-up of sheep that have grazed wild over summer. The round-up is often done on horseback and the animals are herded into a corral where the sorting takes place (participants and spectators welcome).

☆ Reykjavík International Film Festival

This intimate 11-day event from late September features quirky programming that highlights independent filmmaking, both home-grown and international. There are also panels and masterclasses. Check the program at www.riff.is.

November

☆ Iceland Airwaves

You'd be forgiven for thinking Iceland is just one giant music-producing machine. Since the first edition of Iceland Airwaves was held in 1998, this fab festival has become one of the world's premier annual showcases for new music (Icelandic and otherwise). Check out www.icelandairwaves.is.

Plan Your Trip
Get Inspired

JOHN A DAVIS/SHUTTERSTOCK ©

Read

The Draining Lake (Arnaldur Indriðason; 2004) One of many engrossing tales from a master of Nordic Noir.

Independent People (Halldór Laxness; 1934–35) Bleak tragicomedy from the Nobel Laureate.

The Sagas of Icelanders (Jane Smiley et al; 2005) Excellent, readable translations of Iceland's epic, often brutal, tales.

Devil's Island (Einar Kárason; 1983) American culture clashes with rural tradition in postwar Reykjavík.

The Blue Fox (Sjón; 2003) Poetic 19th-century fantasy-adventure tale.

Watch

Heima (2007) Follow band Sigur Rós as they perform throughout Iceland.

Rams (*Hrútar*; 2015) Engrossing tale of two estranged brothers and their sheep.

The Homecoming (*Blóðberg*; 2015) Sly modern comedy-drama where a 'perfect' family's life goes topsy-turvy.

Of Horses and Men (2013) A surreal portrait of the intertwining lives of men and horses.

101 Reykjavík (2000) Dark comedy exploring sex, drugs and the life of a loafer in central Reykjavík.

Listen

Takk... (Sigur Rós; 2005) Anthems to drive by from one of Iceland's most famous bands.

Floating Harmonies (Júníus Meyvant; 2016) Soul meets synths from this Vestmannaeyjar singer-songwriter.

My Head Is an Animal (Of Monsters and Men; 2011) This album was an international sensation for a good reason: it rocks.

Debut (Björk; 1993) Go back to the bedrock with Iceland's perennially boundary-pushing star.

In the Silence (Ásgeir; 2013) Grace and grandeur from a consummate songwriter and performer.

Flowers (Sin Fang; 2013) Airy, infectious harmonies with pop drive.

Above: Auroral display over Jökulsárlón (p111)

Plan Your Trip
Five-Day Itineraries

Reykjavík & the Southwest

If time is short, the best advice is to enjoy Reykjavík, with a few days exploring immediately around the capital – there's plenty to see in Iceland's southwest corner.

Golden Circle (p71) Tour the trio of top-notch attractions: Þingvellir National Park, Geysir and Gullfoss. 🚗 to Landeyjahöfn 3 hrs, then ⛴ to Heimaey ½ hrs

Reykjavík (p35) Explore Iceland's capital, including Old Reykjavík and the National Museum, and indulge in the city's legendary nightlife. 🚌 or 🚗 1 hrs to Blue Lagoon

Blue Lagoon (p82) Day trip to the iconic milky-teal water of the Blue Lagoon, fed by a geothermal power plant. 🚌 or 🚗 1½ hrs to Þingvellir

Heimaey (p123) Hike Eldfell volcano, ponder 'Pompeii of the North', and spot puffins and whales on this extraordinary volcanic island. ✈ ½ hrs to Reykjavík

Akureyri & the Diamond Circle

This short northern itinerary starts in Iceland's second city, with time for whale watching and exploring the volcanic moonscape around pretty Mývatn lake.

Akureyri (p187) Bask in midnight sun or scan the night sky for Northern Lights, ski or play golf.
🚌 or 🚗 1½ hrs to Húsavík

Húsavík (p194) Head out in search of whales at Iceland's whale-watching capital; visit the whale museum.
🚗 1 hrs to Reykjahlíð

Mývatn (p94) Explore this lovely lake and the surrounding geological wonders; detour to Dettifoss waterfall.
🚗 1½ hrs to Akureyri

Plan Your Trip
10-Day Itinerary

Best of the West

For true adventurers, the rugged and remote regions of the Snæfellsnes Peninsula and Westfjords sum up Iceland's adventurous spirit. Take a self-drive trip into the Wild West.

Hornstrandir (p220) Serious hikers and adventurers should head to this remote peninsula.

Ísafjörður (p223) The Westfjords main town is a charming hub for adventure tours, cultural museums and hikes. ⚓ 1½ hrs to Hornstrandir

Þingeyri (p229) Base for hiking, mountain biking, horse riding and boating on the Þingeyri peninsula. 🚗 1 hrs to Ísafjörður

Stykkishólmur (p148) Picturesque harbour town with good museums, dining and Helgafell mountain. ⚓ 2½ hrs to Brjánslækur, then 🚗 1½ hrs to Þingeyri

Snæfellsjökull National Park (p140) Explore the Snæfellsjökull glacier by snowmobile or hike the black-sand beach. 🚗 1½ hrs to Stykkishólmur

Grundarfjörður (p151) Northern gateway to the Snæfellsnes Peninsula; this is the base for visiting iconic Kirkjufell. 🚗 ¾ hrs to Snæfellsjökull National Park

Reykjavík (p35) Spend a couple of days enjoying the capital's museums and dining scene. 🚗 1½ hrs to Grundarfjörður

Plan Your Trip
Two-Week Itinerary

The Ring Road

The classic Iceland road trip is highway 1, better known as the Ring Road, which loops around the country, passing close to many popular sights and with easy detours to others.

Mývatn (p94) Explore wonderful Mývatn lake and the surrounding geothermal scenery and lava fields. 🚗 1½ hrs to Ásbyrgi

Akureyri (p187) Savour the midnight sun at Iceland's northern capital, day trip to Grímsey island or spot whales at Húsavík. 🚗 1½ hrs to Reykjahlíð

2

Reykjavík (p35) Rent a car in the capital and prepare for your Ring Road adventure. Depart early. 🚗 5 hrs to Akureyri

1

DENNIS VAN DE WATER/SHUTTERSTOCK ©

7

Ásbyrgi (p177) Hike the canyon and Vesturdalur before driving south to magnificent Dettifoss waterfall.
🚗 3 hrs to Seyðisfjörður

Seyðisfjörður (p153) Bask in this beautiful Eastfjords village, hiking in the hills and kayaking on the fjord.
🚗 3 hrs to Höfn

Höfn (p184) After driving through the remote and isolated east, harbourside Höfn is a good place to break the journey.
🚗 1 hr to Jökulsárlón

Jökulsárlón (p111) A Ring Road highlight, this lagoon of floating luminous icebergs is a must-see.
🚗 1 hr to Skaftafell

Skaftafell (p170) Gateway to the Vatnajökull ice cap, this is one of Iceland's most beloved wilderness areas. 🚗 4 hrs to Reykjavík

Plan Your Trip
Family Travel

Iceland may not be equipped with adventure parks or high-profile attractions for children, but the whole country is an adventure with its wide-open spaces, wildlife and science projects brought to life. It's a fairly easy place to travel with kids, and parents will find it free of most urban dangers, but do keep toddlers away from those cliffs and unfenced waterfalls!

Reykjavík is the most child-friendly place simply because it has the greatest variety of attractions and facilities. Distances can be long in the rest of the country, so you may want to limit yourselves to one or two regions.

Families might like to check out the *Íslandskort barnanna* (Children's Map of Iceland), aimed at young kids and published by Forlagið (Mál og Menning) with text in Icelandic and English.

Outdoor Activities

Dramatic scenery, an abundance of heated swimming pools and the friendliness of the locals help to keep kids happy, and they will probably love the bird colonies, waterfalls, volcanic areas and glaciers. A number of activities can keep them busy, such as short hikes, super-Jeep tours, horse riding, whale watching, boat rides and easy glacier walks (for the latter, the minimum age is around eight to 10 years).

Tips

⊙ Admission for kids to museums and swimming pools varies from half-price to free. The age at which children must pay adult fees varies (anywhere from 12 to 18 years).

⊙ On internal flights and tours with **Air Iceland Connect** (www.airicelandconnect.is), children aged two to 11 years pay half-fare and infants under two fly free.

WANDERLUSTER/GETTY IMAGES ©

- Most bus and tour companies offer a 50% reduction for children aged four to 11 years; **Reykjavík Excursions** (www.re.is) tours are free for under 11s, and half-price for those aged 12 to 15.

- International car-hire companies offer child seats for an extra cost (book in advance).

- Changeable weather and frequent cold and rain may put you off camping with kids, but children aged two to 12 are usually charged half-price for camping, hostel, farmhouse and other accommodation. Under-twos usually stay for free.

- Many places offer rooms accommodating families, including hostels, guesthouses and farmstays. Larger hotels often have cots (cribs), but you may not find these elsewhere.

- Many restaurants in Reykjavík and larger towns offer discounted children's meals, and most have high chairs.

★ Best for Kids

Blue Lagoon (p82)

Jökulsárlón (p111)

Whale watching (p194)

Reykjavík Zoo & Family Park (p57)

Golden Circle (p71)

Snowmobiling on Vatnajökull (p170)

- Toilets at museums and other public institutions may have dedicated baby-changing facilities; elsewhere, you'll have to improvise.

- Attitudes to breastfeeding in public are generally relaxed.

- Formula, nappies (diapers) and other essentials are available everywhere.

From left: Reindeer, Reykjavík Zoo & Family Park (p57); Child with Icelandic horses

REYKJAVÍK

In this Chapter

Reykjavík at a Glance...

In many ways Reykjavík is strikingly cosmopolitan for its size, loaded with excellent museums, captivating art, rich culinary choices and funky cafes and bars. When you slip behind the shiny tourist-centric veneer you'll find a mix of aesthetic-minded ingenuity and an almost quaint, know-your-neighbours sense of community. You can also get a full primer on Icelandic history right in central Reykjavík, from its Settlement Exhibition built around the unearthed Viking longhouse of the area's earliest inhabitants to the enormous National Museum, keeper of the country's most precious artefacts. Add a backdrop of snow-topped mountains and you may fall helplessly in love.

Two Days in Reykjavík

Start with a walk around the **Old Reykjavík** (p38) quarter near Tjörnin then peruse the city's best museums, such as the impressive **National Museum** (p42) or **Settlement Exhibition** (p41). In the afternoon visit **Hallgrímskirkja** (p44), taking a lift up the tower, then stroll Laugavegur, the main shopping drag. Many of the more lively restaurants turn into party hang-outs at night. On weekends, join Reykjavík's notorious pub crawl.

Four Days in Reykjavík

Enjoy brunch at **Bakarí Sandholt** (p65) or **Grái Kötturinn** (p65), then head down to the Old Harbour to wander, visit museums or go on a whale-watching tour. For hot springs, gardens and cool art, head to **Laugardalur** (p57) in the afternoon. Book ahead if you'd like a swanky evening at one of Reykjavík's top Icelandic restaurants, such as **Dill** (p67) or **Matur og Drykkur** (p66), then party late at **Paloma** (p48), **Húrra** (p48) or **Prikið** (p47).

Old Harbour
Largely a service harbour until recently, the Old Harbour and the neighbouring Grandi area have blossomed into tourist hot spots.

NORTH ATLANTIC OCEAN

TÚN

latún ark

Laugavegur
Reykjavík's main street for shopping and people-watching is bustling. The narrow, one-way lane and its side streets blossom with the capital's most interesting shops, cafes and bars.

Laugardalur

HÁALEITI SOUTH

GERÐI

Reykjavík Map (p54)
Central Reykjavík Map (p58)

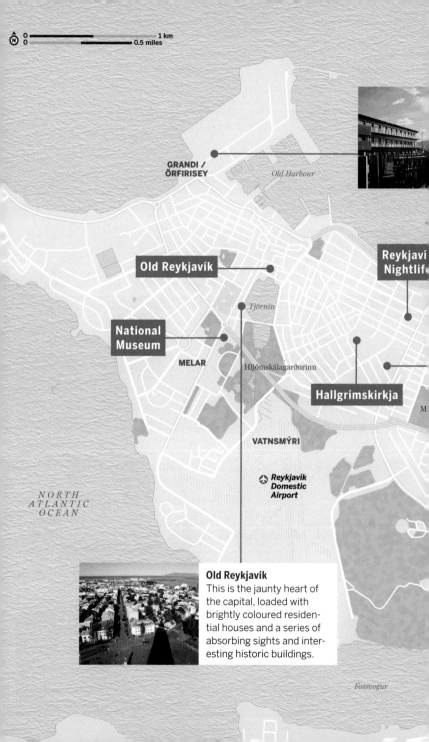

GRANDI /
ÖRFIRISEY

Old Harbour

Old Reykjavík

**Reykjaví
Nightlif**

Tjörnin

**National
Museum**

MELAR

Hljómskálagarðurinn

Hallgrímskirkja

M

VATNSMÝRI

✈ *Reykjavík
Domestic
Airport*

*NORTH
ATLANTIC
OCEAN*

Old Reykjavík
This is the jaunty heart of
the capital, loaded with
brightly coloured residential houses and a series of
absorbing sights and interesting historic buildings.

Fossvogur

Viking Age sculptures, Saga Museum (p56)

Arriving in Reykjavík

Keflavík International Airport
Iceland's primary international airport is
48km southwest of Reykjavík.

Reykjavík Domestic Airport It's a 2km
walk into town. Alternatively there's a
taxi rank or bus 15 stops near the Air
Iceland Connect terminal and goes on
to the Hlemmur bus stop.

Mjódd bus terminal Strætó operates
Reykjavík long-distance buses from
this terminal, 8km southeast of the city
centre.

BSÍ Bus Terminal Reykjavík Excursions
(and its Flybus) uses the BSÍ bus terminal, around 2km south of the city centre.

Where to Stay

Aim for a Reykjavík 101 postal code to be
centrally located. Reykjavík has loads of
accommodation choices, with hostels,
midrange guesthouses, business-class
hotels and top-end boutique hotels.
June through August accommodation
books out entirely; reservations are
essential. Enterprising locals in the capital's prized neighbourhoods rent their
apartments (or rooms) to short-stay
visitors.

Tjörnin lake (p40)

Old Reykjavík

Anchored by placid Tjörnin, the city-centre lake, Old Reykjavík is the jaunty heart of the capital, loaded with brightly coloured residential houses and a series of absorbing sights and interesting historic buildings.

Great For...

ℹ️ **Need to Know**

Main Tourist Office (p68)

★ Top Tip

Visit museums by day then return at night to sample its lively bars and clubs.

The sights in Old Reykjavík radiate out from the oldest settlements in the city's history. You can learn about them at the Settlement Exhibition, or the more expansive National Museum. It's also the area with the seats of government: city hall and parliament. Art highlights include the Reykjavík Art Museum's superb Hafnarhús and the art galley i8. It's also a satisfying area for a stroll, from scenic lake Tjörnin to the old-fashioned houses surrounding Austurvöllur and Ingólfstorg squares.

Explore

This is the heart of historic Reykjavík so plan to explore on foot, perhaps getting an early start strolling around the beautiful, small lake Tjörnin. Then take in the oldest parts of town around Austurvöllur park, where you'll find the Alþingi (p52) and

Ráðhús (p41). It's also a prime area for museums, so leave time for the Viking longhouse and high-tech displays at the Settlement Exhibition (p41), Reykjavík Art Museum's edgy Hafnarhús exhibits (p41), and the artefact-laden National Museum (p42). The area is certainly busy in tourist high season, but it also draws Reykjavikers for its great restaurants and nightlife.

Tjörnin

The placid **lake** (Map p58) at the centre of the city is sometimes locally called the Pond. It echoes with the honks and squawks of more than 40 species of visiting birds, including swans, geese and Arctic terns; feeding the ducks is a popular pastime for the under-fives. Pretty sculpture-dotted parks such as Hljómskálagarður (p52) line the southern shores, and their paths are

Sculptures by Ásmundur Sveinsson, Reykjavík Art Museum

much used by cyclists and joggers. In winter hardy souls strap on ice skates and the lake transforms into an outdoor rink.

The Settlement Exhibition

This fascinating archaeological **ruin-museum** (Landnámssýningin; Map p58; ☎411 6370; www.reykjavikmuseum.is; Aðalstræti 16; adult/child 1650kr/free; ⊘9am-6pm) is based around a 10th-century Viking longhouse and other Settlement Era finds from central Reykjavík. Fine exhibitions imaginatively combine technological wizardry and archaeology to give a glimpse into early Icelandic life. The excavations in Reykjavík have left the site's curators and archaeologists with a passion for bringing history to life.

The entire museum is constructed around a 10th-century Viking longhouse unearthed here on Aðalstræti from 2001 to 2002. Mainly a series of foundation walls now, it was thought to be inhabited for only 60 years. Exhibits to look out for are areas with animal bones deliberately built into the structure and the old spring.

> **ⓘ Did You Know?**
>
> **Aðalstræti 10** (Map p58; Aðalstræti 10; ⊘9am-4pm) `FREE`, Reykjavík's oldest timber house, dates from 1762 and is now home to changing exhibitions charting the course of the city's history.

Reykjavík Art Museum – Hafnarhús

Reykjavík Art Museum's **Hafnarhús** (Map p58; ☎411 6400; www.artmuseum.is; Tryggvagata 17; adult/child 1650kr/free; ⊘10am-5pm, to 10pm Thu; ☒1, 3, 6, 11, 12, 13, 14) is a marvellously restored warehouse converted into a soaring steel-and-concrete exhibition space. Though the well-curated exhibitions of cutting-edge contemporary Icelandic art change frequently (expect installations, videos, paintings and sculpture), you can always count on the comic-book-style paintings of Erró (Guðmundur Guðmundsson), a political artist who has donated several thousand works to the museum.

Ráðhús

Reykjavík's waterside **Ráðhús** (City Hall; Map p58; Vonarstræti; ⊘8am-4pm Mon-Fri) `FREE` is a beautifully positioned postmodern construction of concrete stilts, tinted windows and mossy walls rising from Tjörnin. Inside you'll find an interesting 3D topographical map of Iceland and the main tourist office.

IMAGE COURTESY OF REYKJAVÍK ART MUSEUM ©

> **☑ Don't Miss**
>
> The **Skúli Magnússon Statue** (Map p58) represents Skúli Magnússon, the 'Father of Reykjavík', who organised the city's early industry.

JONATHAN SMITH/LONELY PLANET ©

National Museum

Artefacts from settlement to the modern age fill the creative display spaces of Iceland's superb National Museum.

Brilliantly curated exhibits lead you through the struggle to settle and organise this forbidding island, the radical changes wrought by the advent of Christianity, the lean times of domination by foreign powers and Iceland's eventual independence.

Settlement Era Finds

The premier section of the museum describes the Settlement Era, and features swords, meticulously carved **drinking horns**, and **silver hoards**. A powerful **bronze figure of Thor** is thought to date from about 1000.

Domestic Life

Exhibits explain how the chieftains ruled and how people survived on little, lighting their dark homes and fashioning bog iron. There's everything from the remains of

Great For...

☑ Don't Miss

Bronze Thor figurine, drinking horns, *hnefatafl* game set, Viking graves.

Carved figure of a knight

JONATHAN SMITH/LONELY PLANET ©

ⓘ Need to Know

Þjóðminjasafn Íslands; Map p58; ☎530 2200; www.nationalmuseum.is; Suðurgata 41; adult/child 2000kr/free; ◷10am-5pm May–mid-Sep, closed Mon mid-Sep–Apr; 🚌1, 3, 6, 12, 14

✕ Take a Break

Café Kaffitár (Map p58; National Museum, Suðurgata 41; snacks 750-1900kr; ◷9am-5pm Mon-Fri, 10am-5pm Sat & Sun, closed Mon mid-Sep–Apr; 🛜)

★ Top Tip

The free smartphone audioguide adds loads of useful detail. The one for kids is in Icelandic or English only.

early *skyr* (Icelandic yoghurt) production to intricate pendants and brooches. Look for the Viking-era *hnefatafl* game set (a bit like chess); this artefact's discovery in a grave in Baldursheimar led to the founding of the museum.

Viking Graves

Encased in the floor you'll find Viking-era graves, with their precious burial goods: horse bones, a sword, pins, a ladle, a comb. One of the tombs containing an eight-month-old infant is the only one of its kind ever found.

Ecclesiastical Artefacts

The section of the museum that details the introduction of Christianity is chock-a-block with rare art and artefacts; for example, the priceless 13th-century **Valþjófsstaðir church door**.

The Modern Era

Upstairs, collections span from 1600 to today and give a clear sense of how Iceland struggled under foreign rule, finally gained independence and went on to modernise. Look for the papers and belongings of Jón Sigurðsson, the architect of Iceland's independence.

Visiting the Museum

● Leave a little extra time for the museum's rotating photographic exhibitions.

● Free English tours run at 11am on Wednesday, Saturday and Sunday.

GHING/SHUTTERSTOCK ©

Hallgrímskirkja

Reykjavík's soaring white-concrete church dominates the city skyline, and is visible from 20km away. The graceful church was named after poet Reverend Hallgrímur Pétursson (1614–74), who wrote Iceland's most popular hymn book, Passion Hymns.

Great For...

☑ **Don't Miss**

The church facade, tower views, organs, musical concerts, Leifur Eiríksson Statue.

The church's size and radical design caused controversy, and its architect, Guðjón Samúelsson (1887–1950), never saw its completion – it took 41 years (1945–86) to build.

Facade & Tower

The columns on either side of the church's signature 74.5m-high tower represent volcanic basalt, part of architect Guðjón Samúelsson's desire to create a national architectural style. Get a spectacular panorama of the city by taking a lift up the tower, where you'll find great photo ops from the viewing area.

Organ

In contrast to the high drama outside, the Lutheran church's interior is quite plain. The most eye-catching feature is the vast,

Pipe organ

Skólavörðustígur · Njálsgata · Bergþórugata · Lokastígur · Njarðargata · Freyjugata · Eiríksgata · Barónsstígur · **ⓘ Hallgrímskirkja**

ⓘ Need to Know

(Map p58; ☏510 1000; www.hallgrims
kirkja.is; Skólavörðustígur; tower adult/child
1000/100kr; ⊗9am-9pm May-Sep, to 5pm
Oct-Apr)

✕ Take a Break

Cross the street to **ROK** (Map p58; ☏544
4443; www.rokrestaurant.is; Frakkastígur
26a; dishes 1300-2400kr; ⊗11.30am-11pm)
for small tapas-style plates of Icelandic
fare.

★ Top Tip

Check online for the schedule of organ
and choral recitals during your visit.

gleaming 5275-pipe organ, installed in
1992. It was made in Germany by Johannes
Klais Orgelbau and individuals sponsored
each of the pipes; their names are inscribed
on them. Towards the altar, you'll find the
quaint older organ, still in use.

Concerts & Services

From mid-June to late-August, hear half-
hour **choir concerts** (www.scholacan
torum.is; 2500kr) at noon on Wednesday,
and **organ recitals** (www.listvinafelag.is) at
noon on Thursday and Saturday (2000kr),
and for one hour on Sunday at 5pm
(2500kr). Services are held on Sunday at
11am, with a small service on Wednesday at
8am. There is an English service on the last
Sunday of the month at 2pm.

Leifur Eiríksson Statue

At the front, gazing proudly into the distance, is a statue of the Viking Leifur Eiríksson, the first European to discover America.
A present from the USA on the 1000th
anniversary of the Alþingi (Parliament) in
1930, it was designed by Alexander Stirling
Calder (1870–1945), the father of the perhaps more famous, modern mobilist and
sculptor Alexander Calder (1898–1976).

Guðjón Samúelsson

Hallgrímskirkja's architect Guðjón
Samúelsson was the State Architect of
Iceland, and also designed the National
Theatre of Iceland, the main building of the
University of Iceland and the city's Roman
Catholic church.

HENN PHOTOGRAPHY/GETTY IMAGES ©

Reykjavík Nightlife

Reykjavík's nightlife and music scene is epic: excellent festivals, creative DJs and any number of home-grown bands. Djammið in the capital means going out on the town (or you could say pöbbarölt for a 'pub stroll') – either way it's a renowned weekend party scene.

Great For...

☑ Don't Miss

Kaffibarinn (p67), one of Reykjavík's coolest bars.

Much of Reykjavík's partying happens in cafes and bistros that transform into raucous beer-soaked bars on weekends, and at the many dedicated pubs and clubs. But it's not the quantity of drinking dens that makes Reykjavík's nightlife special – it's the upbeat energy that pours from them.

Thanks to the high price of alcohol, things generally don't get going until late. Icelanders brave the melee at the government liquor store **Vínbúðin** (Map p58; www. vinbudin.is; Austurstræti 10a; ⊘11am-6pm Mon-Thu & Sat, to 7pm Fri), then toddle home for a pre-pub party. Once they're merry, people hit town around midnight, party until 5am, queue for a hot dog, then topple into bed or the gutter, whichever is more convenient. Considering the quantity of booze swilling, the scene is pretty good-natured.

ℹ **Need to Know**

Check *Grapevine* (www.grapevine.is) for the latest listings.

✕ **Take a Break**

SKÁL! (p66) offers experimental Icelandic street food.

★ **Top Tip**

The best bar prices are at happy hour. Download the app *Reykjavík Appy Hour*.

Rather than settling into one venue for the evening, Icelanders like to cruise from bar to bar, getting progressively louder and less inhibited as the evening goes on. 'In' clubs may have long queues, but they tend to move quickly with the constant circulation of revellers.

Most of the action is concentrated near Laugavegur and Austurstræti. Places usually stay open until 1am Sunday to Thursday and 4am or 5am on Friday and Saturday. Expect to pay around 1200kr to 1600kr per pint of beer, and cocktails hit the 2000kr to 2800kr mark. Some venues have cover charges (around 1000kr) after midnight, and many have early-in-the-evening happy hours that cut costs by 500kr or 700kr per beer.

Best Clubs

○ **Kiki** (Map p58; www.kiki.is; Laugavegur 22; ⊙8pm-1am Wed, Thu & Sun, to 4.30am Fri & Sat) Ostensibly a queer bar, Kiki is also *the* place to get your dance on (with pop and electronica the mainstays), since much of Reyjavík's nightlife centres on the booze, not the groove.

○ **Prikið** (Map p58; 🖉551 2866; www.prikid.is; Bankastræti 12; ⊙8am-1am Mon-Thu, to 4.30am Fri, 11am-4.30am Sat, 11am-1am Sun) Being one of Reykjavík's oldest joints, Prikið feels somewhere between diner and saloon, which is great if you're up for greasy eats (mains 2000kr to 4000kr) and socialising. Things get hip-hop dance-y in the wee hours, and if you survive the night, it's popular for its next-day 'hangover killer' breakfast (3000kr).

o **Húrra** (Map p58; www.facebook.com/hurra.is; Tryggvagata 22; ☺6pm-1am Mon-Thu, to 4.30am Fri & Sat, to 11.30pm Sun; 🛜) Dark and raw, this large bar opens up its back room to create a much-loved concert venue, with a wide range of live music or DJs most nights. It's one of the best places in town to close out the evening. There's a range of beers on tap and happy hour runs till 9pm.

o **Paloma** (Map p58; http://palomaclub.is; Naustin 1; ☺8pm-1am Thu & Sun, to 4.30am Fri & Sat) At one of Reykjavík's best late-night dance clubs DJs lay down reggae, electronica and pop upstairs, and a dark deep house dance scene in the basement.

o **B5** (Map p58; www.b5.is; Bankastræti 5; ☺7pm-2am) Top 40 and bottle service pack this joint with a partying blinged-out crowd.

Best for Beer

o **Bryggjan Brugghús** (Map p54; 📞456 4040; www.bryggjanbrugghus.is; Grandagarður 8; ☺11am-midnight Sun-Thu, to 1am Fri & Sat; 🛜) Cavernous, dimly lit and dotted with vintage pub paraphernalia, harbourside Bryggjan Brugghús is a roomy microbrewery where 12 taps dispense its own fresh-tasting beers.

o **Kaldi** (Map p58; 📞581 2200; www.kaldibar. is; Laugavegur 20b; ☺noon-1am Sun-Thu, to 3am Fri & Sat) Effortlessly cool with mismatched seats and teal banquettes, plus a popular smoking courtyard, Kaldi is awesome for its range of five Kaldi microbrews, not available elsewhere. Happy hour (4pm to 7pm) gets you a beer for 750kr. Anyone can play the in-house piano.

o **Mikkeller & Friends** (Map p58; 📞437 0203; www.mikkeller.dk; Hverfisgata 12; ☺5pm-1am Sun-Thu, 2pm-1am Fri & Sat; 🛜) Climb to the top floor of the building to find a Danish craft-beer pub with 20 taps serving Mikkeller's own offerings and local Icelandic brews. Then enjoy the cool, colourful, laid-back vibe.

o **Micro Bar** (Map p58; 📞865 8389; www.facebook.com/MicroBarIceland; Vesturgata 2; ☺3pm-midnight Sun-Thu, to 1am Fri & Sat) Boutique brews are the name of the game at this low-key spot in the heart of the action. On tap you'll find 14 creations from the island's top microbreweries, and a happy hour (4pm to 7pm) of 900kr beers.

o **Skúli Craft Bar** (Map p58; 📞519 6455; www.facebook.com/skulicraft; Aðalstræti 9; ☺3-11pm Sun-Thu, to 1am Fri & Sat) The big draw here is the 14 craft beers on tap, the majority of which are normally Icelandic. Or you might want to opt for one of the bottled beers – there are around 130 brands to

★ **Live Music**

To find out who's playing, download event-listing app *Appening* (www. grapevine.is).

choose from (who's counting?). Happy hour is 4pm to 7pm.

Best Cocktail Bars

○ **Slippbarinn** (Map p58; ☏560 8080; www. slippbarinn.is; Mýrargata 2; ⊘noon-midnight Sun-Thu, to 1am Fri & Sat; 🛜) Jet setters unite at this buzzy harbourfront bar. It's bedecked with vintage record players and cool locals sipping some of the best cocktails in town. For cut-price creations drop by during happy hour (3pm to 6pm).

○ Apotek (p67) Top-flight cocktails are served in this bar that doubles as a restaurant.

○ **Pablo Diskobar** (Map p58; ☏552 7333; www.facebook.com/discobarrvk; Veltusundi 1; ⊘4pm-1am Sun-Thu, to 3am Fri & Sat) Neon-bright and nostalgic, tropical-themed

Pablo is Reykjavík's top stop for exotic drinks. Weekends bring DJ sets; Wednesday night brings deals on drinks. The bar also serves the downstairs tapas restaurant, Burro, until midnight.

○ **Marshall** (Map p54; ☏519 7766; www. marshallrestaurant.is; Grandagarður 20; ⊘11.30am-11pm Tue-Sun; 🛜; 🚌14) The perfect pit stop for art aficionados, Marshall sits in the same building as three cutting-edge galleries. It's appropriately aesthetically appealing: an industrial-chic spot with coppery colours, a beautiful back-lit bar and great city views.

> ★ **Dress Code**
>
> Dress up to fit in, although some pub-style joints are more relaxed. The legal drinking age is 20 years.

CHRIS MELLOR/GETTY IMAGES ©

Reykjavík Pub Crawl

It's Friday (or Saturday) night. You're primed to hit the town for the famous Reykjavík *Djammið* (pub crawl). Grab a bite to eat, take a deep breath and dive in...

Start Microbar, Old Reykjavík
Distance 3km
Duration Six to seven hours

1 Start at **Micro Bar** (p48) with a boutique brew during happy hour (4 to 7pm).

6 End the night near where you began at **Paloma** (p48), one of the city's best late-night dance clubs.

5 Time to start ramping the night up at **Prikið** (p47), one of Reykjavík's oldest bars and a late-night club.

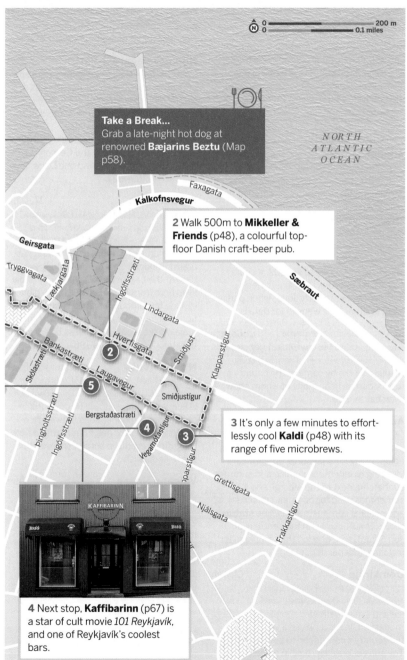

0   200 m
0   0.1 miles

Take a Break...
Grab a late-night hot dog at
renowned **Bæjarins Beztu** (Map
p58).

*NORTH
ATLANTIC
OCEAN*

Faxagata

Kalkofnsvegur

2 Walk 500m to **Mikkeller &
Friends** (p48), a colourful top-
floor Danish craft-beer pub.

Geirsgata

Tryggvagata

Lækjargata

Ingólfsstræti

Lindargata

Sæbraut

Bankastræti

Hverfisgata

Smiðjustíg

Klapparstígur

Skólastræti

2

Laugavegur

Þingholtsstræti

Ingólfsstræti

5

Smiðjustígur

Bergstaðastræti

4

Vegamótastígur

3

3 It's only a few minutes to effortlessly cool **Kaldi** (p48) with its
range of five microbrews.

Grettisgata

Njálsgata

Frakkastígur

4 Next stop, **Kaffibarinn** (p67) is
a star of cult movie *101 Reykjavík*,
and one of Reykjavík's coolest
bars.

4. ROBERTO LA ROSA/SHUTTERSTOCK © 5 WATERMELONTART/SHUTTERSTOCK ©

◎ SIGHTS

The compact city centre contains most of Reykjavík's attractions, which range from interesting walking and shopping streets to excellent museums and picturesque lakeside or seaside promenades. Around the outskirts sit the places that Reykjavikers go to relax.

◎ Old Reykjavík

Alþingi   Historic Building

(Parliament; Map p58; ☑563 0500; www.althingi.is; Kirkjustraeti) **FREE** Iceland's first parliament, the Alþingi, was created at Þingvellir in AD 930. After losing independence in the 13th century, the country gradually won back its autonomy, and the modern Alþingi moved into this current basalt building in 1881. A stylish glass-and-stone annexe was completed in 2002. Visitors can attend sessions (four times weekly mid-September to early June) when parliament is sitting; see website for details.

i8   Gallery

(Map p58; ☑551 3666; www.i8.is; Tryggvagata 16; ⊙11am-6pm Tue-Fri, 1-5pm Sat) **FREE** Displays works by some of the country's top modern artists, many of whom show overseas as well.

Austurvöllur   Park

(Map p58) Grassy Austurvöllur was once part of first-settler Ingólfur Arnarson's hay fields. Today it's a favourite spot for cafe lounging or lunchtime picnics and summer sunbathing next to the Alþingi, and is sometimes used for open-air concerts and political demonstrations. The **statue** (Map p58; Austurvöllur) in the centre is of Jón Sigurðsson, who led the campaign for Icelandic independence.

Dómkirkja   Church

(Map p58; www.domkirkjan.is; Kirkjustræti; ⊙10am-4.30pm Mon-Fri, Mass 11am Sun) Iceland's main cathedral, Dómkirkja is a modest affair, but it played a vital role in the country's conversion to Lutheranism. The current building (built in the late 18th century and enlarged in the 1840s) is small and perfectly proportioned, with a plain wooden interior animated by glints of gold.

Hljómskálagarður Park   Park

(Map p54) **FREE** Hljómskálagarður Park sits on Tjörnin's southeast corner and has a section dedicated to sculptures by five Icelandic women: Gunnfríður Jónsdóttir (1889–1968), Nína Sæmundson (1892–1962), Þorbjörg Pálsdóttir (1919–2009), Ólöf Pálsdóttir (b 1920) and Gerður Helgadóttir (1928–75); and one Dane, Tove Ólafsson (1909–92).

Gröndalshús   Museum

(Writer's Home; Map p58; ☑411 6020; www.bokmenntaborgin.is; Fischersund; ⊙1-5pm Thu-Sun mid-Jun–Aug) **FREE** The small, red former home of writer, illustrator and naturalist Benedikt Gröndal beautifully evokes turn-of-the-century Reykjavík life. Gröndal lived here from 1880 to 1907 and exhibits include his famous *Fauna of Iceland* collection of colour drawings. Look out for the majestic great auk, a flightless bird hunted to extinction by the mid-19th century.

Nordic House   Cultural Building

(Norræna Húsið; Map p54; ☑551 7030; www.nordichouse.is; Sæmundargata 11; ⊙10am-5pm, to 9pm Wed; ☐1, 3, 6, 12, 14) This cultural centre fosters connections between Iceland and its Nordic neighbours with a rich program of events, a library, an exhibition space and a bistro.

Volcano House   Museum

(Map p58; ☑555 1900; www.volcanohouse.is; Tryggvagata 11; adult/child 1990/1000kr; ⊙9am-10pm) This modern theatre with a hands-on lava exhibit in the foyer screens a 55-minute pair of films (hourly) about the Vestmannaeyjar volcanoes and Eyjafjallajökull. They show in German, French, Icelandic or Swedish once daily in summer.

◎ Old Harbour

Largely a service harbour until recently, the Old Harbour and the neighbouring Grandi area have blossomed into tourist hot spots, with key art galleries, several museums, volcano and Northern Lights films, and excellent restaurants. Whale-watching and puffin-viewing trips depart from the pier. Photo ops abound with views of fishing boats, the Harpa concert hall and snow-capped mountains beyond.

Kling & Bang
Gallery

(Map p54; ☎554 2003; http://this.is/klingand bang; Grandagarður 20, Marshall Húsið, Grandi; ⊙noon-6pm Wed & Fri-Sun, to 9pm Thu) **FREE** This perennially cutting-edge artist-run exhibition space is a favourite with locals, and now has an expanded gallery in the renovated Marshall House.

Omnom Chocolate
Factory

(Map p54; ☎519 5959; www.omnomchocolate. com; Hólmaslóð 4, Grandi; adult/child 3000/ 1500kr; ⊙11am-6pm Mon-Fri, noon-4pm Sat) Reserve ahead for a tour (2pm Monday to Friday) at this full-service chocolate factory where you'll see how cocoa beans are transformed into high-end scrumptious

delights. The shop sells its stylish bars, packaged with specially designed labels, which come in myriad sophisticated flavours.

Aurora Reykjavík
Museum

(Northern Lights Centre; Map p54; ☎780 4500; www.aurorareykjavik.is; Grandagarður 2; adult/child 1600/1000kr; ⊙9am-9pm; 🚌14) Learn about the classical tales explaining the Northern Lights, plus the scientific explanation, then watch a 35-minute surround-sound panoramic high-definition recreation of Icelandic auroras.

Nýló
Gallery

(Nýlistasafnið – The Living Art Museum; Map p54; ☎551 4350; www.nylo.is; Grandagarður 20, Mars-hall Húsið, Grandi; ⊙noon-6pm Tue, Wed & Fri-Sun, to 9pm Thu) **FREE** This dynamic centre for emerging and established contempo-rary artists, live music and other perfor-mances has a new space in the renovated Marshall House.

Icelandic Phallological Museum (p57)

CHALIE CHULAPORNSIRI/SHUTTERSTOCK ©

Reykjavík

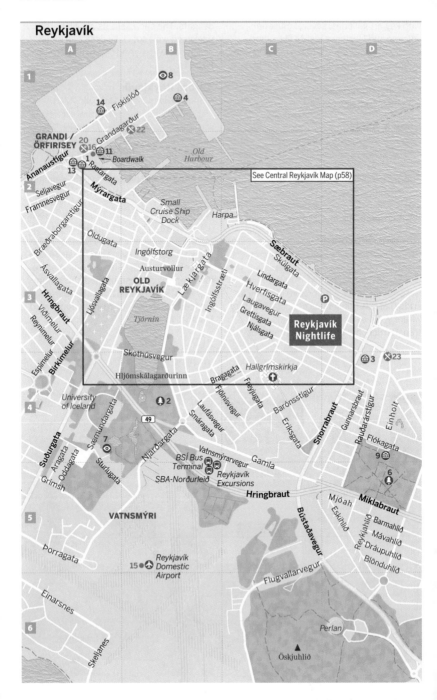

See Central Reykjavík Map (p58)

Reykjavík
Nightlife

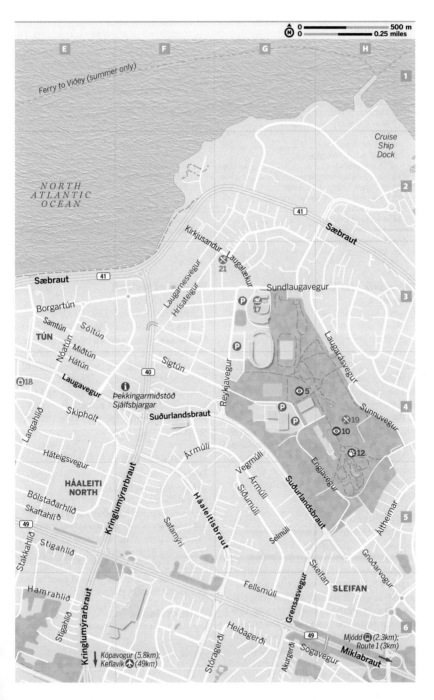

0 — 500 m
0 — 0.25 miles

Ferry to Viðey (summer only)

Cruise
Ship
Dock

*NORTH
ATLANTIC
OCEAN*

Kirkjusandur

Sæbraut

41

Sæbraut

41

Laugalækur

21

Sundlaugavegur

Borgartún

Laugarnesvegur

Hrísateigur

Samtún

Sóltún

TÚN

Nóatún

Miðtún

Hátún

Sigtún

40

17

Laugardalsvegur

18

Laugavegur

Langahlíð

Skipholt

Þekkingarmiðstöð
Sjálfsbjargar

Reykjavegur

Suðurlandsbraut

5

Sunnuvegur

Háteigsvegur

Ármúli

19

10

**HÁALEITI
NORTH**

Vegmúli

12

Bólstaðarhlíð

Ármúli

Skaftahlíð

Síðumúli

Engjavegur

49

Kringlumýrarbraut

Stígahlíð

Safamýri

Selmúli

Álfheimar

Stakkahlíð

Háaleitisbraut

Gnoðarvogur

5

Hamrahlíð

Fellsmúli

Skeifan

SLEIFAN

Stígahlíð

Heiðagerði

Grensásvegur

6

Kringlumýrarbraut

Stóragerði

Akurgerði

49

Sogavegur

Mjódd (2.3km);
Route 1 (3km)

Miklabraut

Kópavogur (5.8km);
Keflavík (49km)

Reykjavík

Reykjavík Maritime Museum
Museum

(Sjóminjasafnið í Reykjavík; Map p54; ☑411 6300; www.maritimemuseum.is; Grandagarður 8; adult/child 1650kr/free; Óðinn & museum 2600kr; ☉10am-5pm, Óðinn tours at 11am, 1pm, 2pm & 3pm; ⊕; ☐14) The crucial role fishing plays in Iceland's economy is celebrated through the imaginative displays in this former fish-freezing plant. The new exhibition **Fish & Folk** evokes 150 years of the industry, using artefacts, sepia photos and interactive games to chart a course from the row boats of the late 1800s to the trawlers of the 21st century. Make time for one of the daily guided tours of the former coastguard ship *Óðinn* (1300kr).

Saga Museum
Museum

(Map p54; ☑511 1517; www.sagamuseum.is; Grandagarður 2; adult/child 2200/800kr; ☉10am-6pm; ☐14) The endearingly bloodthirsty Saga Museum is where Icelandic history is brought to life by eerie silicon models and a multi-language soundtrack featuring the thud of axes and hair-raising screams. Don't be surprised if you see some of the characters wandering around town, as moulds were taken from Reykjavík residents (the owner's daughters are the Irish princess and the little slave gnawing a fish).

Whales of Iceland
Museum

(Map p54; ☑571 0077; www.whalesoficeland. is; Fiskislóð 23; adult/child 2900/1500kr; ☉10am-5pm; ☐14) Ever strolled beneath a blue whale? This museum houses full-sized models of the 23 species of whale found off Iceland's coast. The largest museum of this type in Europe, it also displays models of whale skeletons, and has good audio guides and multimedia screens to explain what you're seeing. There's a cafe and gift shop, too.

◉ Laugavegur & Around

Reykjavík's main street for shopping and people-watching is bustling, often-pedestrianised Laugavegur. The narrow, one-way lane and its side streets blossom with the capital's most interesting shops, cafes and bars. At its western end, its name changes to Bankastræti, then Austurstræti. Running uphill off Bankastræti, artists' street Skólavörðustígur ends at spectacular modernist church, Hallgrímskirkja (p44).

Culture House
Gallery

(Þjóðmenningarhúsið; Map p58; ☑530 2210; www.culturehouse.is; Hverfisgata 15; adult/child incl National Museum 2000kr/free; ☉10am-5pm May–mid-Sep, closed Mon mid-Sep–Apr)

This fantastic collaboration between the National Museum, National Gallery and four other organisations creates a superbly curated exhibition covering the artistic and cultural heritage of Iceland from settlement to today. Priceless artefacts are arranged by theme, and highlights include 14th-century manuscripts, contemporary art and the skeleton of a great auk (now extinct). Check the website for guided tours.

Harpa   Arts Centre

(Map p58; ☑ box office 528 5050; www.harpa. is; Austurbakki 2; ☺ 8am-midnight, box office noon-6pm) With its ever-changing facets glistening on the water's edge, Reykjavík's sparkling Harpa concert hall and cultural centre is a beauty to behold. In addition to a season of top-notch shows (some free), the shimmering interior with harbour vistas is worth stopping in for, or take a highly recommended 30-minute guided tour (1500kr); these run two to three times daily year-round, with up to eight daily tours between mid-June and mid-August.

Icelandic Phallological Museum   Museum

(Hið Íslenzka Reðasafn; Map p54; ☑ 561 6663; www.phallus.is; Laugavegur 116; adult/child 1500kr/free; ☺ 10am-6pm, from 9am Jun-Aug) Oh, the jokes are endless here, but although this unique museum houses a huge collection of penises, it's actually very well done. From pickled pickles to petrified wood, there are 286 different members on display, representing all Icelandic mammals and beyond. Featured items include contributions from sperm whales and a polar bear, minuscule mouse bits, silver castings of each member of the Icelandic handball team and a single human sample – from deceased mountaineer Páll Arason.

National Gallery of Iceland   Museum

(Listasafn Íslands; Map p58; ☑ 515 9600; www.listasafn.is; Fríkirkjuvegur 7; adult/child 1800kr/free; ☺ 10am-5pm daily mid-May–mid-Sep, 11am-5pm Tue-Sun mid-Sep–mid-May)

This pretty stack of marble atriums and spacious galleries overlooking Tjörnin offers ever-changing exhibits drawn from a 10,000-piece collection. The museum can only exhibit a small sample at any one time; shows range from 19th- and 20th-century paintings by Iceland's favourite artists (including Jóhannes Kjarval and Nína Sæmundsson) to sculptures by Sigurjón Ólafsson and others.

Reykjavík Art Museum – Kjarvalsstaðir   Gallery

(Map p54; ☑ 411 6420; www.artmuseum.is; Flókagata 24, Miklatún Park; adult/child 1650kr/free; ☺ 10am-5pm) The angular glass-and-wood Kjarvalsstaðir, which looks out onto **Miklatún Park** (Map p54), is named for Jóhannes Kjarval (1885–1972), one of Iceland's most popular classical artists. He was a fisherman until his crew paid for him to study at the Academy of Fine Arts in Copenhagen, and his wonderfully evocative landscapes share space alongside changing installations of mostly Icelandic 20th-century paintings.

◉ Laugardalur

Laugardalur encompasses a verdant stretch of land 4km east of the city centre. It was once the main source of Reykjavík's hot-water supply and is a favourite with locals for its huge swimming complex, fed by the geothermal spring.

Reykjavík Zoo & Family Park   Zoo

(Fjölskyldu og Húsdýragarðurinn; Map p54; ☑ 411 5900; www.mu.is; Laugardalur; adult/child 880/660kr, 1-/10-ride ticket 330/2520kr; ☺ 10am-6pm Jun–mid-Aug, to 5pm mid-Aug–May; ☻; ☒ 2, 5, 15, 17) Sunny days see happy local families flocking to this children's park in Laugardalur. Don't expect lions and tigers; think seals, foxes and farm animals in simple enclosures, and tanks of cold-water fish. The family park section is jolly, with a mini-racetrack, child-size bulldozers, a giant trampoline, boats and fairground rides for kids.

Central Reykjavík

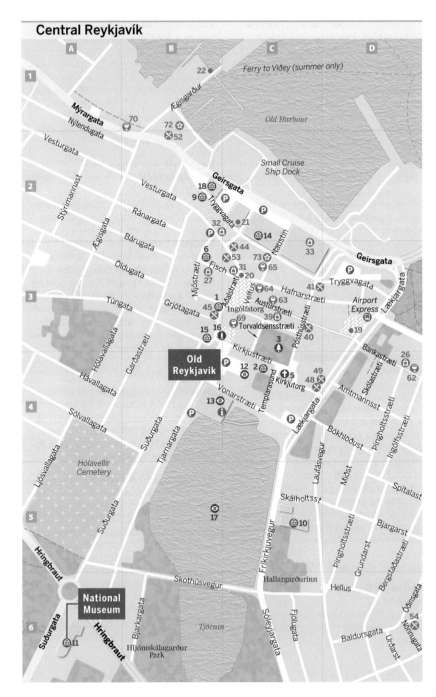

Ferry to Viðey (summer only)

Old Harbour

Small Cruise
Ship Dock

Myrargata
Nýlendugata
Vesturgata
Geirsgata
Tryggvagata
Naustin
Geirsgata
Tryggvagata
Styrimannast
Ránargata
Ægisgata
Bárugata
Öldugata
Vesturgata
Mjóstræti
Fisch
Aðalstræti
Veltus
Hafnarstræti
Austurstræti
Airport
Express
Lækjargata
Túngata
Grjótagata
Ingólfstorg
Torvaldsenssstræti
Pósthússtræti
Hólavallagata
Garðastræti
Kirkjustræti
Bankastræti
Hávallagata
Old
Reykjavík
Templarasund
Kirkjutorg
Amtmannsst
Skólastræti
Vonarstræti
Lækjargata
Þingholtsstræti
Ingólfsstræti
Sólvallagata
Suðurgata
Tjarnargata
Bókhlöðust
Miðst
Spítalast
Ljósvallagata
Hólavellir
Cemetery
Skálholtsst
Bjargarst
Friðkirkjuvegur
Suðurgata
Þingholtsstræti
Grundarst
Bergstaðastræti
Hringbraut
Skothúsvegur
Hallargarðurinn
Hellus
Óðinsgata
National
Museum
Bjarkargata
Tjörnin
Sóleyjargata
Fjólugata
Baldursgata
Urðarst
Nönnugata
Suðurgata
Hringbraut
Hljómskálagarður
Park

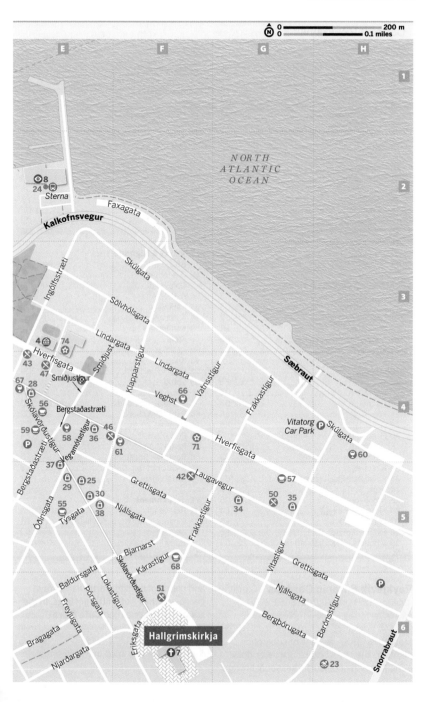

Central Reykjavík

Reykjavík Botanic Gardens Gardens
(Grasagarður; Map p54; ☏411 8650; www.
grasagardur.is; Laugardalur; ⏰10am-10pm
May-Sep, to 3pm Oct-Apr; ₪2, 5, 14, 15, 17) **FREE**
More than 5000 varieties of subarctic
plants fill the city's botanic gardens, deliv-
ering a wealth of colourful seasonal flowers
and plenty of birdlife, particularly grey
geese and their fluffy little goslings. In the
summer the acclaimed **Café Flóra** (Flóran;
Map p54; ☏553 8872; www.floran.is; cakes from
950kr, mains 1550-3150kr; ⏰8am-10pm May-
Sep; 🅿) ✿ sets up shop in the greenhouse.

ACTIVITIES

Creative Iceland   Art
(☑615 3500; www.creativeiceland.is) Get involved with knitting (19,500kr), cooking (24,900kr), graphic design, arts, crafts, music...you name it. This service hooks you up with local creative people offering workshops in their specialities.

Bryggjan Brugghús   Brewery
(Map p54; ☑456 4040; www.bryggjan brugghus.is; Grandagarði 8; tours 3500-5000kr; ⊙noon-10pm) The 30-minute tours of the gleaming vats at this waterfront microbrewery come with either a three- or six-beer tasting flight. Tours leave on the hour; there's no need to book.

Sundhöllin   Geothermal Pool
(Sundhöll Reykjavíkur; Map p58; ☑411 5350; www.reykjavik.is/stadir/sundholl-reykjavikur; Barónsstígur 16; adult/child 950/150kr; ⊙6.30am-10pm Mon-Fri, from 8am Sat & Sun; ⊛) Our top pick for a Reykjavík city centre swim, Sundhöll reopened in 2017 after a year-long revamp that added an entire outdoor area with hot tubs, sauna and a swimming pool. The original indoor pool remains open, as well as the secret upstairs hot tub with excellent city views.

Laugardalslaug   Geothermal Pool
(Map p54; ☑411 5100; www.reykjavik.is/stadir/laugardalslaug; Sundlaugavegur 30a, Laugardalur; adult/child 950/150kr, suit/towel rental 850/570kr; ⊙6.30am-10pm Mon-Fri, 8am-10pm Sat & Sun; ⊛; ☐12, 14) One of the largest pools in Iceland, with the best facilities: an Olympic-sized indoor pool and several outdoor pools, a string of hot-pots, a saltwater tub, a steam bath and a curling 86m water slide.

Bláfjöll   Skiing
(☑561 8400; www.skidasvaedi.is; Blafjallavegur 1; day pass adult/child 3650/920kr) The ski slopes at 84-sq-km Bláfjöll have 16 lifts and downhill, cross-country and snowboarding facilities. You can hire gear at decent rates. The slopes often have enough snow from around late December through to March.

TOURS

All sorts of tours originate in Reykjavík, from dog sledding and horse riding to ice climbing and lava-tube caving. The tourist office (p68) has lists of local operators.

Literary Reykjavík   Walking
(Map p58; www.bokmenntaborgin.is; Tryggvagata 15; ⊙3pm Thu Jun-Aug) FREE The Dark Deeds city centre walking tour focuses on crime fiction and starts at the main library. There's also a downloadable Culture Walks app with themes including Settlement, Crime Fiction and Queer Literature.

Haunted Walk   Walking
(Map p58; www.hauntedwalk.is; adult/child 2500kr/free; ⊙8pm Sat-Thu early Jun-Aug) A 90-minute tour, including folklore and ghost spotting, departing from the junction of Aðalstræti and Vesturgata. Bookings not required.

Free Walking Tour Reykjavik   Walking
(Map p58; www.freewalkingtour.is; ⊙noon & 2pm Jun-Aug, 1pm Sep-May) FREE A 90-minute, 1.5km walking tour of the city centre, starting at the little clock tower on Lækjartorg Sq.

Reykjavík Bike Tours   Cycling
(Map p58; ☑694 8956; www.icelandbike.com; Ægisgarður 7; bike rental per 4hr from 3500kr, tours from 7500kr; ⊙9am-5pm Jun-Aug, shorter hours Sep-May; ☐14) This outfitter rents bikes and offers tours such as Classic Reykjavík (2½ hours, 7km), Coast of Reykjavík (2½ hours, 18km), and Golden Circle & Bike (eight hours, 25km of cycling in 1½ hours). This is the most convenient place to rent a bike before catching the ferry to Viðey island.

TukTuk Tours   Tours
(Map p58; ☑788 5500; www.facebook.com/tuktukiceland; Harpa concert hall, Austurbakki 2; from 30min adult/child 4700/2700kr) Zip around town on a *tuk tuk* tour, including one that does a pub hop. Tours depart from Harpa.

🔒 SHOPPING

Handknitting Association of Iceland
Clothing

(Handprjónasamband Íslands; Map p58; ☑552 1890; www.handknit.is; Skólavörðustígur 19; ⊘9am-10pm Mon-Fri, to 6pm Sat, 10am-6pm Sun) Traditional handmade hats, socks and sweaters are sold at this knitting collective. You can also buy yarn, needles and knitting patterns and do it yourself. The association's smaller branch sells made-up items only.

66° North
Clothing

(Map p58; ☑535 6680; www.66north.is; Bankastræti 5; ⊘9am-8pm Mon-Sat, 10am-8pm Sun) Iceland's premier outdoor-clothing company began by making all-weather wear for Arctic fishermen. This metamorphosed into costly, fashionable streetwear: jackets, fleeces, hats and gloves. Friendly staff can explain the different materials and their uses to help you make an educated choice. It has another city-centre store at Laugavegur 17.

KronKron
Clothing

(Map p58; ☑561 9388; www.kronkron.com; Laugavegur 63b; ⊘10am-6pm Mon-Fri, to 5pm Sat) This is where Reykjavík goes high fashion, with labels such as Marc Jacobs and Vivienne Westwood. But we really enjoy its Scandinavian designers (including Kron by KronKron) and the offering of silk dresses, knit capes, scarves and even woollen underwear. The handmade shoes are off the charts; they are also sold down the street at Kron.

Kron
Shoes

(Map p58; ☑551 8388; www.kron.is; Laugavegur 48; ⊘10am-6pm Mon-Fri, to 5pm Sat) Kron sells its own outlandishly wonderful handmade shoes with all the flair you'd expect of an Icelandic label. Colours are bright; textures are cool; and they're even wearable (those practical Icelanders!).

Skúmaskot
Arts & Crafts

(Map p58; ☑663 1013; www.facebook.com/skumaskot.art.design; Skólavörðustígur 21a; ⊘10am-6pm Mon-Fri, to 5pm Sat, noon-4pm Sun) Local designers create unique handmade

Whales of Iceland (p56)

porcelain items, women's and kids' clothing, paintings and cards. It's in a large renovated gallery that beautifully showcases the creative Icelandic crafts.

Kirsuberjatréð   Arts & Crafts

(Cherry Tree; Map p58; ☑562 8990; www.kirs.is; Vesturgata 4; ⊙10am-7pm Mon-Fri, to 5pm Sat & Sun) Talented designers show their works at this long-running women's art-and-design collective. Highlights include bracelets and purses made from soft, supple, brightly coloured fish skin leather, music boxes made from string, and, our favourite, beautiful coloured bowls made from radish slices.

Kolaportið Flea Market   Market

(Map p58; www.kolaportid.is; Tryggvagata 19; ⊙11am-5pm Sat & Sun) Kolaportið is a Reykjavík institution. Weekends see a huge industrial building by the harbour filled with a vast tumble of secondhand clothes, old toys and cheap imports. A food section sells traditional eats like *rúgbrauð* (geothermally baked rye bread) and *brauðterta* ('sandwich cake'; a layering of bread with mayonnaise-based fillings).

Fischer   Concept Store

(Map p58; www.fischersund.com; Fischersund 3; ⊙noon-6pm Mon-Sat) Formally the recording studio of Icelandic musician Jónsi, best known as the Sigur Rós frontman, this concept store feels like walking through an immersive exhibition. Perfumes, Icelandic herbs, hand-crafted soap bars and candles, ethereal music and visual artwork all play with the senses.

12 Tónar   Music

(Map p58; ☑511 5656; www.12tonar.is; Skólavörðustígur 15; ⊙10am-6pm Mon-Sat, from noon Sun) A very cool place to hang out, in two-storey 12 Tónar you can listen to CDs, drink coffee, and on summer Fridays sometimes catch a live performance. 12 Tónar is responsible for launching some of Iceland's favourite bands.

¶◎¶ Frú Lauga

Reykjavík's trailblazing **farmers market** (Map p54; ☑534 7165; www.frulauga.is; Laugalækur 6; ⊙10am-6pm Mon-Fri, to 4pm Sat; ☑) ✔ sources its ingredients from all over the countryside, featuring treats such as *skyr* (Icelandic yoghurt) from Erpsstaðir, organic vegetables, rhubarb conserves, honey and meat. It also stocks a range of carefully curated international pastas, chocolates and wine.

Skyr topped with blueberries
ROSEMARY CALVERT/GETTY IMAGES

Fóa   Arts & Crafts

(Map p58; ☑571 1433; www.facebook.com/foaiceland; Laugavegur 2; ⊙10am-6pm Mon-Fri, 11am-7pm Sat, noon-6pm Sun) A great place to stock up on witty souvenirs and cool handmade stationery, jewellery and ceramics.

Geysir   Clothing

(Map p58; ☑519 6000; www.geysir.com; Skólavörðustígur 16; ⊙10am-7pm Mon-Sat, 11am-6pm Sun) One of the city's best bets for traditional Icelandic clothing and modern designs. Geysir's menswear store boasts an elegant selection of sweaters, blankets, clothes, shoes and bags.

Mál og Menning   Books

(Map p58; ☑580 5000; www.bmm.is; Laugavegur 18; ⊙9am-10pm Mon-Fri, 10am-10pm Sat; ☑) A friendly, well-stocked independent bookshop with a strong selection of English-language books offering insights to Iceland. It also sells maps, CDs, games and newspapers, and has a good cafe (soup and bread 1000kr).

Rammagerðin
Gifts & Souvenirs

(Iceland Gift Store; Map p58; ☑535 6690; www.icelandgiftstore.com; Skólavörðustígur 12; ⏰10am-9pm) One of the city's better souvenir shops, Rammagerðin offers loads of woollens, crafts and collectibles. It also has branches at Skólavörðustígur 20, Bankastræti 9 and Keflavík International Airport.

⭐ ENTERTAINMENT

Gaukurinn
Live Music

(Map p58; www.gaukurinn.is; Tryggvagata 22; ⏰2pm-1am Sun-Thu, to 3am Fri & Sat) Grungy and glorious, Gaukurinn is a solid stop for live music, comedy, karaoke and open mikes. Happy hour is 7pm to 9pm.

Bíó Paradís
Cinema

(Map p58; ☑412 7711; www.bioparadis.is; Hverfisgata 54; adult 1600-1800kr; 📶) This totally cool cinema, decked out in movie posters and vintage officeware, screens specially curated Icelandic films with English subtitles and international flicks. It's a chance to see movies that you may not find elsewhere.

Cinema at Old Harbour Village No 2
Cinema

(Map p58; ☑898 6628; www.thecinema.is; Geirsgata 7b; adult/child 1800/900kr; 📶14) A tiny theatre perches in the top of one of the rehabbed Old Harbour warehouses. Nature films cover volcanoes (Eyjafjallajökull, Westmann Islands), the creation of Iceland, and the Northern Lights, and are mostly shown in English with occasional German screenings. See schedule online.

National Theatre
Theatre

(Þjóðleikhúsið; Map p58; ☑551 1200; www.leikhusid.is; Hverfisgata 19; ⏰closed Jul) The National Theatre puts on everything from modern Icelandic works to musicals, opera and Shakespeare. The five separate performance areas include the main stage and studio, children's and puppet spaces.

✖ EATING

Grandi Mathöll
Street Food €

(Map p54; ☑577 6200; www.grandimatholl.is; Grandagarður 16; mains from 1200kr; ⏰11am-9pm Mon-Thu, to 10pm Fri-Sun) There's no

National Theatre

GNAGEL/GETTY IMAGES ©

neater encapsulation of Grandi's rejuvenation than the transformation of this old fish factory into a pioneering street food hall. Long trestle tables sit beside stalls selling a diverse range of lamb, fish and veggie delights – look out for the Gastro Truck, whose succulent signature chicken burger has quite a jalapeño kick.

Sægreifinn
Seafood €

(Seabaron; Map p58; ☑553 1500; www. saegreifinn.is; Geirsgata 8; mains from 1500kr; ⏱11.30am-10pm) Sidle into this green harbourside shack for the most famous lobster soup in the capital, or choose from a fridge full of fresh fish skewers to be grilled on the spot. Though the original sea baron sold the restaurant some years ago, the place retains its unfussy, down-to-earth charm.

Flatey Pizza
Pizza €

(Map p54; ☑588 2666; www.flatey.pizza; Grandagarður 11; pizza 1750-2650kr; ⏱11am-10pm) Flatey raises pizza making to something akin to an art form. Their sourdough circles are made from organic wheat and are baked for just one minute at 500°C to keep the toppings tasty. It's very hip and very classy. As you can't book, be prepared to queue.

Bakarí Sandholt
Bakery €

(Map p58; ☑551 3524; www.sandholt.is; Laugavegur 36; snacks 700-2700kr; ⏱7am-7pm Sun-Thu, 6.30am-9pm Fri & Sat; 🛜) Reykjavík's favourite bakery is usually crammed with folks hoovering up the generous assortment of fresh baguettes, croissants, pastries and sandwiches. The soup of the day (1850kr) comes with delicious sourdough bread.

Gló
Organic, Vegetarian €

(Map p58; ☑553 1111; www.glo.is; Laugavegur 20b; mains 1000-2400kr; ⏱11.30am-10pm; 🛜🍽) Join the cool cats in this airy upstairs restaurant serving fresh daily specials loaded with Asian-influenced herbs and spices. Though not exclusively vegetarian, it's a wonderland of raw and organic foods, with a broad bar of elaborate salads, from root veggies to Greek.

Discount Cards

Reykjavík City Card (www.citycard.is; per 24/48/72hr 3800/5400/6500kr) offers admission to 10 of Reykjavík's municipal swimming/thermal pools and to most of the main galleries and museums, plus discounts on some tours, shops and entertainment. It also gives free travel on the city's Strætó buses and on the ferry to Viðey.

Geothermal pool
ALLA LAURENT/SHUTTERSTOCK ©

Grái Kötturinn
Cafe €

(Map p58; ☑551 1544; www.facebook.com/ graikotturinn; Hverfisgata 16a; mains 1100-2500kr; ⏱7.15am-2pm Mon-Fri, 8am-2pm Sat & Sun) Blink and you'll miss this tiny six-table cafe (a favourite of Björk's). It looks like a cross between an eccentric bookshop and an underground art gallery, and dishes up delicious breakfasts of toast, bagels, pancakes, or bacon and eggs served on thick, buttery slabs of freshly baked bread.

Icelandic Street Food
Street Food €

(Map p58; ☑691 3350; www.icelandicstreet food.com; Laekjargata 8; mains from 1300kr; ⏱8am-11pm) For a budget taste of old Iceland, squeeze into this tiny canteen that just loves showcasing home-cooked food. Owner Unnar has drafted in his grandmother to cook some of the dishes that range from fish stew and lamb soup to rolled-up pancakes dusted with sugar. Her principle that no one leaves her house hungry means free food refills.

☕ Coffee Culture

Reykjavikers take their coffee seriously, and there are many spots to dwell and sip your brew, or grab it on the go.

Reykjavík Roasters (Map p58; ☑517 5535; www.reykjavikroasters.is; Kárastígur 1; ⊙7am-6pm Mon-Fri, 8am-5pm Sat & Sun) This hipster joint is easily spotted on warm days with its smattering of wooden tables. Swig a perfect latte with a flaky croissant.

Kaffi Mokka (Map p58; ☑552 1174; www. mokka.is; Skólavörðustígur 3a; ⊙9am-6.30pm, to 9pm Jun-Aug) The decor at Reykjavík's oldest coffeeshop has changed little since the 1950s, giving it a retro charm.

Kaffi Vínyl (Map p58; ☑537 1332; www. facebook.com/kaffivinyl; Hverfisgata 76; ⊙8am-11pm Sun-Thu, to 1am Fri & Sat; 🛜) This hip fixture of the Reykjavík coffee, restaurant and music scene has a chill vibe, great music and delicious vegan and vegetarian food.

Stofan Kaffihús (Map p58; ☑546 1842; www.facebook.com/stofan.cafe; Vesturgata 3; dishes 1650-1900kr; ⊙10am-10pm Sun-Wed, to midnight Thu-Sat; 🛜) This spacious and welcoming cafe fills a character-laden historic building in the city centre.

Café Haiti (Map p58; ☑588 8484; www. cafehaiti.is; Geirsgata 7c, Marshall Húsið, Grandi; ⊙8am-10pm Sun-Thu, to midnight Fri & Sat) Owner Elda roasts and grinds beans on-site, producing what regulars swear is Iceland's best coffee.

C is for Cookie (Map p58; www.facebook. com/cookie.reykjavik; Týsgata 8; ⊙7.30am-5pm Mon-Sat, 10am-6pm Sun) A cheerful spot with super coffee, plus great home-made cakes, salad, soup and grilled sandwiches.

Kaffifélagið (Map p58; www.kaffifelagid.is; Skólavörðustígur 10; ⊙7.30am-6pm Mon-Fri, 10am-4pm Sat) A popular hole-in-the-wall for a quick cuppa on the run; has a couple of outdoor tables, too.

Hverfisgata 12   Pizza €€
(Map p58; ☑437 0203; www.hverfisgata12. is; Hverfisgata 12; pizza 2450-3450kr; ⊙5-10.30pm Mon-Fri, 11.30am-10.30pm Sat & Sun; 🍴) There's no sign, but those in the know come to this cream-coloured converted corner house for some of the city's best gourmet pizza and fabulous cocktails. Cheerful staff pull pints of craft beer from behind the copper bar, and the weekend brunches (11.30am to 3pm) are a big draw.

SKÁL!   Street Food €€
(Map p54; ☑775 2299; www.skalrvk.com; Laugavegur 107; mains 1000-2500kr; ⊙noon-10pm Sun-Wed, to 11pm Thu-Sat; 🍴) SKÁL! demands your attention – with its capital lettering and punctuation but most emphatically with its food. Experimental offerings combine unusual flavours (fermented garlic, birch sugar, Arctic thyme salt) with Icelandic ingredients to impressive effect, best sampled at a stool beside its neon-topped bar. There's an impressive list of vegan creations and the cocktails feature foraged herbs.

Hlemmur Mathöll   Food Hall €€
(Map p54; www.hlemmurmatholl.is; Laugavegur 107; mains from 800kr; ⊙8am-11pm) If only all bus terminals had a food court like this. Some 10 vendors rustle up multicultural foods including Danish *smørrebrød* (rye bread), Mexican tacos and Vietnamese street food. The pick is innovative SKÁL!. Most stalls kick into action by lunchtime.

Matur og Drykkur   Icelandic €€
(Map p54; ☑571 8877; www.maturogdrykkur. is; Grandagarður 2; lunch/dinner mains from 1900/3400kr; tasting menu 10,000kr; ⊙11.30am-3pm & 6-10pm, closed Sun lunch; 🍴; 🚌14) One of Reykjavík's top high-concept restaurants, Matur Og Drykkur means 'Food and Drink', and you'll surely be plied with the best of both. The brainchild of brilliant chef Gísli Matthías Auðunsson, who also owns the excellent Slippurinn (p134), it creates inventive versions of traditional Icelandic fare. Book ahead in high season and for dinner.

Messinn   Seafood €€

(Map p58; ☑546 0095; www.messinn.com;
Lækjargata 6b; lunch mains 1850-2200kr, dinner
mains 2700-4200kr; ☺11.30am-3pm & 5-10pm;
🐾) Make a beeline to Messinn for the best
seafood that Reykjavík has to offer. The
speciality here is the amazing pan-fried
dishes: your pick of fish is served up in a
sizzling cast-iron skillet, accompanied by
buttery potatoes and salad.

Dill   Icelandic €€€

(Map p58; ☑552 1522; www.dillrestaurant.is;
Hverfisgata 12; 5/7 courses 11,900/13,900kr;
☺6-10pm Wed-Sat) Exquisite New Nordic
cuisine is the major draw at Reykjavík's
elegant Michelin-starred bistro. Skilled
chefs use a small number of ingredients to
create highly complex dishes in a parade
of courses. The owners are friends with
Copenhagen's famous Noma clan and take
Icelandic cuisine to similarly heady heights.
It's hugely popular; book well in advance.

Nostra   New Nordic €€€

(Map p58; ☑519 3535; www.nostrarestaurant.
is; Laugavegur 59; 4/6/8 courses 8900/11,900/
13,900kr; ☺5.30-10pm Tue-Sat; 🍴) Fine-dining
Nostra is where fresh, local ingredients —
à la New Nordic cuisine — are turned into
French-inspired multicourse tasting menus,
including those for vegans, vegetarians and
pescatarians. Nostra refers to its menus
as 'experiences' and with their intense
flavours and picture-perfect presentation,
they're not wrong.

Þrír Frakkar   Icelandic, Seafood €€€

(Map p58; ☑552 3939; www.facebook.com/
3frakkar.is; Baldursgata 14; mains 4200-6250kr;
☺11.30am-2.30pm & 6-10pm Mon-Fri, 6-11pm
Sat & Sun) Owner-chef Úlfar Eysteinsson has
built up a consistently excellent reputation
at this snug little restaurant. Specialities
range throughout the aquatic world from
salt cod and halibut to *plokkfiskur* (fish
stew) with black bread. Non-fish items run
towards guillemot, horse, lamb and whale.

Apotek   Fusion €€€

(Map p58; ☑551 0011; www.apotekrestaurant.
is; Austurstræti 16; mains 2800-6000kr;

☺noon-11pm Sun-Thu, to midnight Fri & Sat) This
beautiful restaurant and bar with shining
glass fixtures and a cool ambience is equally known for its delicious menu of small
plates that are perfect for sharing and its
top-flight cocktails.

Fiskfélagið   Seafood €€€

(Map p58; ☑552 5300; www.fishcompany.
is; Vesturgata 2a; mains lunch 2700-4600kr,
dinner 4800-6600kr; ☺11.30am-2.30pm &
5.30-10.30pm, closed Sat & Sun lunch) The
'Fish Company' takes Icelandic seafood
recipes and spins them through a variety
of far-flung inspirations from Fiji coconut
to Spanish chorizo. Dine out on the terrace
or in an intimate-feeling stone-and-timber
room with copper light fittings.

Fiskmarkaðurinn   Seafood €€€

(Fishmarket; Map p58; ☑578 8877; www.
fiskmarkadurinn.is; Aðalstræti 12; mains 4800-
9900kr, tasting menu 11,900kr; ☺5-10.30pm)
Dramatic presentations of elaborate dishes
fill the tables of this intimate, artistically lit
restaurant, where chefs excel at infusing
Icelandic seafood with Asian flavours
such as lotus root. The tasting menu is
acclaimed, and the place is renowned for
its excellent sushi bar (3600kr to 4100kr).

🍸 DRINKING & NIGHTLIFE

Laugavegur is the epicentre of Reykjavík's
nightlife and you could begin (and end) a
night here. Bar hop until the clubs light up
for dancing (late), then wander home under
the early-morning sun.

See p46 and p48 for more on Reykjavík's
nightlife.

Kaffibarinn   Bar

(Map p58; ☑551 1588; www.kaffibarinn.is;
Bergstaðastræti 1; ☺3pm-1am Sun-Thu, to 4.30am
Fri & Sat; 🐾) This old house with the London
Underground symbol over the door contains
one of Reykjavík's coolest bars; it even had a
starring role in the cult movie *101 Reykjavík*
(2000). At weekends you'll feel like you need
either a famous face or a battering ram to
get in. At other times it's a place for artistic
types to chill with their Macs.

# #

KEX Bar Bar

(Sæmundur í Sparifötunum; Map p58; www.
kexhostel.is; Skúlagata 28; ⏱11.30am-11pm; 🛜)
Locals love this hostel bar-restaurant in an
old cookie factory (*kex* means 'biscuit') for
its broad sea-view windows, inner courtyard and own-brew beer. Happy hipsters
soak up the 1920s Vegas vibe: saloon
doors, an old-school barber station, happy
chatter and scuffed floors. Look out for
regular, free, live jazz sessions.

Port 9 Wine Bar

(Map p58; 📞832 2929; www.facebook.com/
portniu; Veghúsastígur 7; ⏱4-11pm Tue-Sat,
to 9pm Sun & Mon) Port 9 sauntered onto
Reykjavík's drinking scene supremely
confident in the quality of its wines and
the knowledge of its staff – offerings here
range from affordable tipples by the glass
to vintages to break the bank. Low lighting,
an arty clientele and a secret hang-out
vibe (it's tucked down a tiny street) make it
worth tracking down.

Loft Hostel Bar Bar

(Map p58; www.lofthostel.is; Bankastræti 7;
⏱noon-11pm) On sunny days locals pack the
roof terrace at this lively patio bar at the
hostel of the same name.

Loftið Cocktail Bar

(Jacobsen Loftið; Map p58; 📞551 9400; www.
facebook.com/loftidbar; 2nd fl, Austurstræti 9;
⏱4pm-1am Wed-Sat) Loftið is all about high-
end cocktails and good living. Dress up to
join the fray at this airy upstairs lounge,
which features a zinc bar, retro tailor-
shop-inspired decor, vintage tiles and a
swanky, older crowd. The basic booze here
is top-shelf liquor elsewhere, and jazzy
bands play from time to time.

ℹ INFORMATION

Main Tourist Office (Upplýsingamiðstöð
Ferðamanna; Map p58; 📞411 6040; www.visit
reykjavik.is; Ráðhús, Tjarnargata 11; ⏱8am-8pm;
🛜) Friendly staff and mountains of free brochures, plus maps, Reykjavík City Card (p65) and
Strætó city bus tickets. Books accommodation,
tours and activities.

ℹ GETTING THERE & AWAY

AIR

Iceland's primary international airport, **Keflavík
International Airport** (p282), is 48km west of
Reykjavík, on the Reykjanes Peninsula.

Reykjavík Domestic Airport (p282) is in
central Reykjavík, just 2km south of Tjörnin.

BUS

Bus services are ever-changing in Iceland, so it
pays to get up-to-date information on schedules
and fares from bus company websites or tourist
offices. The free Public Transport in Iceland map
(www.publictransport.is) has a good overview
of routes.

BSÍ Bus Terminal (Map p54; 📞580 5400; www.
bsi.is; Vatnsmýrarvegur 10; 🛜) Reykjavík Excursions (and its Flybus) uses the BSÍ bus terminal,
around 2km south of the city centre.

Strætó (www.bus.is) Operates Reykjavík
long-distance buses from **Mjódd bus terminal**
(📞540 2700; www.bus.is; ⏱ticket office 7am-
6pm Mon-Fri, 10am-6pm Sat, 12.30-6pm Sun),
8km southeast of the city centre.

ℹ GETTING AROUND

Foot The best way to see central Reykjavík.

Bus There's excellent coverage in the city centre
and environs; they run from 7am until 11pm or
midnight daily (from 11am on Sunday). A limited
night-bus service runs until 4.30am on Friday
and Saturday.

TO/FROM THE AIRPORT

The journey from Keflavík International Airport
to Reykjavík takes about 50 minutes. Three easy
bus services connect Reykjavík and the airport
and are the best transport option; kids get
discounted fares.

Flybus (📞580 5400; www.re.is; one-way ticket
2950kr; 🛜)

Airport Express (Map p58; 📞540 1313; www.
airportexpress.is; 🛜)

Airport Direct (📞497 5000; www.reykjaviksight
seeing.is/airport-direct; one way/return from
5500/10,000kr; 🛜)

Taxis from Keflavík airport to Reykjavík cost
around 16,100kr.

Where to Stay

There is no shortage of accommodation options in Reykjavík, with hostels, guesthouses and business hotels galore, while new top-end boutique hotels and apartments seem to open daily. From June through August accommodation books out; reservations are essential.

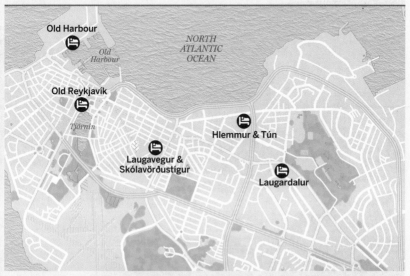

Neighbourhood	Atmosphere
Old Reykjavík	Central, easy with higher-end options. Can be crowded, busier and more expensive.
Old Harbour	Less busy once back from the harbour. Guesthouses and hostels are more affordable, though are slightly less central.
Laugavegur & Skólavörðustígur	Perfect for shopping and partying. A good range of options with certain quiet pockets; touristy on the main streets.
Hlemmur & Tún	Loads of high-rise hotels are popping up here. The areas are on the bland side and a bit far from the city centre.
Laugardalur	Near large park and swimming complex. New high-rise hotels. Further from the city centre.

THE
GOLDEN CIRCLE

The Golden Circle at a Glance...

Diving in glacial waters, walking the Mid-Atlantic Ridge canyon, absorbing the grandeur of the first-ever parliamentary site and watching the earth belch boiling water 40m high – and all within an easy couple of hours' drive from the capital.

The route spans roughly 300km and takes in three main sights: Þingvellir, where tectonic plates meet; Geysir, where water erupts more than 100 times a day; and Gullfoss, where the voluminous waterfall roars. It can get crowded here in summer, but the Golden Circle remains one of the most memorable routes on the planet.

Two Days in the Golden Circle

With two days you can easily fit in the three main attractions at a leisurely pace, overnighting at whichever place takes your fancy. Most people (and tours from Reykjavík) start at **Þingvellir National Park** (p78) before heading east to **Geysir** (p74) via Laugarvatn and then on to **Gullfoss** (p76) before returning to the Ring Road at Selfoss.

Four Days in the Golden Circle

With four days you can really explore the Golden Circle beyond the main sights and add a side trip to the Reykjanes Peninsula. Take in the geothermal fields at Hveragerði, go river rafting on the Hvítá river from Reykholt, or explore the explosion crater at **Kerið** (p88) north of Selfoss. On your final day, head west for a soak in the famous **Blue Lagoon** (p82).

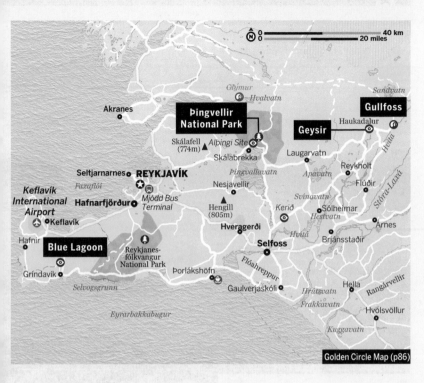

Golden Circle Map (p86)

Arriving in the Golden Circle

Car Having your own vehicle will give you the most flexibility. It's just over 40km from Reykjavík to Þingvellir on Rte 36 and it takes about four hours to drive the loop.

Bus There are currently no buses to Þingvellir, aside from full tours ticking off all the major sights – bookable with **Reykjavík Excursions** (p89), plus Bus Travel Iceland (www.bustravel.is), Arctic Adventures (www.adventures.is) and more) – from 6750kr.

Where to Stay

There are accommodation options, including camping, at Þingvellir and Geysir as well as a hotel at Gullfoss. A popular alternative base between Þingvellir and Geysir is the village of Laugarvatn, which has a small range of guesthouses and restaurants.

ROC CANALS PHOTOGRAPHY/GETTY IMAGES ©

Geysir

One of Iceland's most famous tourist attractions, Geysir (gay-zeer; literally 'gusher') is the original hot-water spout after which all other geysers are named.

Geysir sits in the Haukadalur geothermal area – a valley of hot springs with trans-lucent blue pools, mud pots and colourful mineral details. Watch your step as some natural water features hover around the 100°C mark.

Great Geysir

The most famous of them all, the Great Geysir has dramatically ejected water for around 800 years. In the year 2000 (after an earthquake), the Geysir erupted more than 120m into the sky. But the geyser goes through dormant periods and at the time of writing it was considered inactive. No matter, the very active Strokkur geyser nearby still performs every five to 10 min-utes, typically shooting a sizeable 15m to 40m in height before crashing back into the cavern below.

Great For...

☑ **Don't Miss**

The reliably erupting Strokkur geyser.

Strokkur

Follow the path to where a circle of people is usually waiting in anticipation. They are here to see this magnificent geyser erupt every five to 10 minutes, so make sure you are on the right side of it unless you want to get wet. It sits near the famous Great Geysir. Strokkur, like all hot geysers, is caused by water meeting magma-heated rock, then boiling and erupting under pressure.

Geysir Activities

Geysir Hestar   Horse Riding

(Map p86; 📞847 1046; www.geysirhestar. com; Kjóastaðir 2; ⏱1/2/3hr rides 10,000/15,000/18,000kr) Four kilometres east of Geysir at Kjóastaðir horse farm, this outfit offers horse riding in the area as well as along Hvítá river canyon to Gullfoss,

with trips for all skill levels. It also has great lodging: guesthouse rooms (from 8600kr without bathroom) or a cottage (sleeping up to six guests from 38,000kr).

Iceland Safari   Driving

(📞896 4019; www.icelandsafari.com; Golden Circle bus tours per person from 9900kr, super-Jeep tours per person from 38,000kr) Super-Jeep tours and minibus tours around the southwest.

Geysir Golf Course   Golf

(Haukadalsvöllur; Map p86; 📞893 8733; www. geysirgolf.is; Haukadalur 3; 9 holes Mon-Fri 2000kr, Sat & Sun 2500kr, 18 holes Mon-Fri 2500kr, Sat & Sun 3200kr, club rental 1500kr) Eighteen well-groomed holes look out on Geysir.

Gullfoss

It's one of the Golden Circle's most impressive and popular sights: the mesmerising and voluminous Gullfoss tumbles down a two-tiered drop into a rugged canyon.

Great For...

☑ Don't Miss
The magnificent views.

The Falls

Dropping into the canyon of the Hvítá river, Gullfoss (Golden Falls) is a key stop on Golden Circle tours. It's made up of two cascades: the first drop is 11m and the second is 21m, through which around 38 million tonnes of water charge on a daily basis. The sheer volume of water here is a sight to behold.

Each day, thousands of gallons (around 80 cubic metres per second) of water plummet 32m, before charging along a narrow chasm. On sunny days, when the waterfall's mist hits the rays, it's possible to spy rainbows. In winter the water often twinkles as the light hits ice particles.

Views & Photo Ops

A tarmac path leads from the main car park and visitor centre to a grand **lookout** over

the falls. Stairs then continue down to the level of the falls. Alternatively, drive in on the spur below the tourist centre at falls-level for disabled-accessible parking. A path then continues down the valley towards the thundering falls for the most captivating video shots.

History

Visited since 1875, the falls came within a hair's breadth of destruction during the 1920s, when a team of foreign investors wanted to dam the Hvítá river for a hydro-electric project. The landowner, Tómas Tómasson, refused to sell to them, but the developers went behind his back and obtained permission directly from the government. Tómasson's daughter, Sigríður, walked (barefoot!) to Reykjavík to protest, even threatening to throw herself into the waterfall if the development went ahead.

Thankfully, the investors failed to pay the lease, the agreement was nullified, and the falls escaped destruction.

Gullfoss was donated to the nation, and since 1979 it's been a nature reserve. Look for the memorial to Sigríður near the foot of the stairs from the visitor centre.

The Kjölur Route

Gullfoss is the final stop on traditional Golden Circle tours. You can continue along magnificent Rte F35 beyond the falls (the Kjölur route) for 14.8km while it's paved, after which you need to have a 4WD.

Transport

Reykjavík Excursions (p89) runs the 'Iceland On Your Own' service between Reykjavík and Geysir, which continues on to Gullfoss and then Akureyri. There's one daily from mid-June to early September, departing at 8am from Reykjavík's BSÍ bus terminal. A one-way fare to Gullfoss from Reykjavik costs 5000kr; the journey takes roughly 2½ hours.

Þingvellir National Park

Site of the world's first democratic parliament, Þingvellir National Park is Iceland's most important historical site and a place of vivid beauty.

Great For...

☑ **Don't Miss**

The site of the Alþingi, the Vikings' parliament.

At Þingvellir National Park, 40km northeast of central Reykjavík, the Vikings established the world's first democratic parliament, the Alþingi (pronounced ál-thingk-ee, also called Alþing), in AD 930. The meetings were conducted outdoors and, as with many Saga sites, there are only the stone foundations of ancient encampments left. The site has a superb natural setting, in an immense, fissured rift valley, caused by the meeting of the North American and Eurasian tectonic plates, with rivers and waterfalls. The country's first national park, Þingvellir was made a Unesco World Heritage Site in 2004.

History

Many of Iceland's first settlers had run-ins with royalty back in mainland Scandinavia. These chancers and outlaws decided

ℹ Need to Know

(Map p86; www.thingvellir.is; Rte 36/
Þingvallavegur; parking 300-500kr)

✗ Take a Break

There is a small **cafe** (Map p86; Rte 36,
Þingvellir Information Centre; grilled sandwiches from 400kr; ☺9am-10pm Apr-Oct,
shorter hours Nov-Mar) with a mini-mart
at the Þingvellir Information Centre;
otherwise bring your own food.

★ Top Tip

Free one-hour guided tours run most
days from June to August at 10am and
3pm; check schedules at the visitor
centre.

that they could live happily without kings
in the new country, and instead created
district *þings* (assemblies) where justice
could be served by and among local *goðar*
(chieftains).

Eventually a nationwide *þing* became
necessary. Bláskógur – now Þingvellir
(Parliament Fields) – lay at a crossroads
by a huge fish-filled lake. It had plenty of
firewood and a setting that would make
even the most tedious orator dramatic, so
it fitted the bill perfectly. Every important
decision affecting Iceland was argued out
on this plain – new laws were passed, marriage contracts were made, and even the
country's religion was decided here. The
annual parliament was also a great social
occasion, thronging with traders
and entertainers.

Over the following centuries, escalating
violence between Iceland's most powerful
groups led to the breakdown of law and
order. Governance was surrendered to
the Norwegian crown and the Alþingi was
stripped of its legislative powers in 1271. It
functioned solely as a courtroom until 1798,
before being dissolved entirely. When it regained its powers in 1843, members voted
to move the meeting place to Reykjavík.

Alþingi Site

Near the dramatic Almannagjá fault and
fronted by a boardwalk is the **Alþingi Site**
(Map p86; accessible via Rte 36 & Rte 362).
Lögberg (Law Rock) is where the Alþingi
(Parliament) convened annually. This was
where the *lögsögumaður* (law speaker)
recited the existing laws to the assembled
parliament (one-third each year). After
Iceland's conversion to Christianity, the site

shifted to the very foot of the Almannagjá cliffs, which acted as a natural amplifier, broadcasting the voices of the speakers across the assembled crowds. That site is marked by the Icelandic flag.

Decisions were reached by the Lögrétta (Law Council), made up of 146 men (48 voting members, 96 advisers and two bishops), who are thought to have assembled at Neðrivellir (Low Fields), the flat area in front of the cliffs.

Other Sites

The little farmhouse in the bottom of the rift, **Þingvallabær** (Map p86; accessible via Rte 363; parking 300kr) was built for the 1000th anniversary of the Alþing in 1930 by state architect Guðjón Samúelsson. It's now used as the park warden's office and prime minister's summer house.

Behind the farmhouse, **Þingvallakirkja** (Map p86; ✆482 2660; www.thingvellir.is; parking 300kr; ⊙9am-5pm Jun-Aug) is one of Iceland's first churches. The original was consecrated in the 11th century, but the current wooden building dates from 1859. Inside are several bells from earlier churches, a 17th-century wooden pulpit and a painted altarpiece from 1834. Independence-era poets Jónas Hallgrímsson and Einar Benediktsson are buried in the cemetery behind the church. Use the car park at the end of Rte 363, cross the Óxará river bridge and follow the footpath on the left.

Tectonic Plates

The Þingvellir plain is situated on a tectonic-plate boundary where North America and Europe are tearing away from each other at a rate of 1mm to 18mm per year. As a result, the plain is scarred by dramatic fissures, ponds and rivers, including the great rift Almannagjá. An atmospheric path runs through the dramatic crevice and along the fault between the clifftop visitor centre and the Alþingi site.

The river Öxará cuts the western plate, tumbling off its edge in a series of pretty cascades. The most impressive of these cascades is Öxarárfoss, on the northern

edge of the Alþingi site. The pool Drekkingarhylur was used to drown women found guilty of infanticide, adultery or other serious crimes.

There are other smaller fissures on the eastern edge of the site. During the 17th century, nine men accused of witchcraft were burned at the stake in Brennugjá (Burning Chasm). Nearby are the fissures of Flosagjá (named after a slave who jumped his way to freedom) and Nikulásargjá (named after a drunken sheriff discovered dead in the water). The southern end of Nikulásargjá is known as Peningagjá (Chasm of Coins) for the thousands of coins tossed into it by visitors (an act forbidden these days). There are a few different car parks around the sights; a parking fee may be payable at some of them.

Snorkelling Silfra fissure

Dive Silfra

One of the most otherworldly activities in Iceland is donning a scuba mask (or snorkel) and dry suit and exploring the crystalline **Silfra fissure**, one of the cracks in the rift valley. There's also a rift, **Davíðsgjá**, out in Þingvallavatn lake, which is harder to reach. You must book ahead with **Dive Silfra** (Map p86; accessible via Rte 363; snorkelling/diving from 13,900/34,900kr; ⏱9am-6pm) in Reykjavík. People with their own equipment must have licences, dive in groups of at least two, and buy the permit (1000kr) from the visitor centre or www.thingvellir.is.

Þingvallavatn

Filling much of the rift plain, **Þingvallavatn** (Map p86; accessible via Rte 361; parking 300kr) is Iceland's largest lake (84 sq km). Pure glacial water from Langjökull filters through bedrock for 40km before emerging here.

It's joined by the hot spring **Vellankatla**, which spouts from beneath the lava field on the northeastern shore. Þingvallavatn is an important refuelling stop for migrating birds (including the great northern diver, barrow's golden-eye and harlequin duck).

Weirdly, the waters here are full of *bleikja* (Arctic char) that have been isolated for so long that they've evolved into four subspecies. It's possible to submerge into the depths of the the lake with Dive Silfra and potentially see them up close.

🛏 Accommodation

There is **camping** (www.thingvellir.is; Rte 361; sites per adult/tent/child 1300/300kr/free; ⏱Jun-Sep) in Þingvellir National Park, and hotels, guesthouses and cabin accommodation around the southern part of Þingvallavatn lake.

VICPHOTORIA/SHUTTERSTOCK ©

The Blue Lagoon

Paris has the Eiffel Tower, Iceland has the Blue Lagoon... It might get crowded but you'll be missing something iconic if you don't go. While not part of the Golden Circle, the Blue Lagoon is an easy day trip from Reykjavík.

Great For...

❶ Need to Know

(Bláa Lónið; ☎420 8800; www.bluelagoon. com; Norðurljosavegur 9; adult/child from 7000kr/free, premium entry from 9600kr/ free; ⊗7am-midnight Jul–mid-Aug, to 11pm late May-Jun, 8am-10pm Jan-late May & mid-Aug–Sep, to 9pm Oct-Dec)

★ **Top Tip**
Prebooking is essential and there is an hourly cap on admissions; get e-tickets from the website or vouchers from tour companies (such as Reykjavík Excursions).

Surrounded by jagged, moss-dusted black-lava scenes, the milky-teal spa is delivered water via the Svartsengi geothermal plant. Look out for the billowing wafts of steam emerging from the plant's silver towers, while spa-goers prance around covered in white silica mud – it's a bizarre scene.

With a combination of superheated 70% sea water and 30% fresh water, the Blue Lagoon is a perfect 38°C. Spa lovers travel the world to soak in this combination of natural mineral salts, rich blue-green algae and silica mud. These super properties leave skin unbelievably soft and silky – some even believe they can heal certain skin conditions.

Visiting the Blue Lagoon

o Look online for ticket packages, special promotions and winter rates.

o It can get packed in summer (especially between 10am and 2pm). Aim to go first thing or after 7pm.

o Lagoon water can corrode silver and gold; leave watches and jewellery in your locker.

o You must practise standard Iceland pool etiquette: thorough naked pre-pool showering.

o Entry to the lagoon includes shampoo and conditioner (you'll need lots of conditioner afterwards as briny water plays havoc with hair).

o Your entry wristband is used to scan entry to lockers and to pay for drinks in the in-lagoon bar.

o You can stay in the complex for a half-hour after closing.

● Going to the lagoon on a tour or in transit to the airport can sometimes save time and money. By bus, Reykjavík Excursions (p281) connects Keflavík International Airport, the Blue Lagoon and Reykjavík.

● At the car park you'll find a luggage check (550kr per bag per day); perfect if you're going to the lagoon on your way to/from the airport.

> ### ✕ Take a Break
>
> The **Blue Cafe** (☏ 420 8800; snacks 850kr, sandwiches 1200kr, cold meal trays 2200kr; ⊙7am–midnight Jun–mid-Aug, shorter hours mid-Aug–May; ☏) and the high-priced **LAVA Restaurant** (☏420 8800; www.bluelagoon.com; mains lunch/dinner 4500/5900kr, tasting menu 10,300kr; ⊙11.30am-9.30pm Jun-Aug, to 8.30pm Sep-May; ☏) are located at the lagoon.

● You don't need to know how to swim to visit the lagoon.

● Rental towels are free with your ticket, but you are welcome to bring your own if preferred.

Accommodation

The Blue Lagoon has three modern, top-end hotels in close proximity, all with earthy aesthetics to complement the natural features around them. Alternatively, staying in Reykjavík or towns along the Reykjanes Peninsula is more affordable and very accessible.

Guided Tours

In addition to the spa opportunities at the Blue Lagoon, you can combine your visit with package tours, or hook up with nearby **ATV Adventures** (4x4 Adventures Iceland; ☏857 3001; www.4x4adventuresiceland.is; Tangasund; 1hr ATV tour 13,000kr, 2-3hr bike tour 10,900kr, bike rental per 4/24hr 4900/6900kr) for quad-bike or cycling tours (from 10,900kr) or bicycle rental. The company can pick you up and drop you off at the lagoon.

Retreat Spa

One of the most decadent spas on the planet, the **Retreat Spa** (☏420 8703; www.bluelagoon.com; The Retreat Hotel; 4hr entry for minimum 2 people from 29,000kr, treatments 5300-31,200kr; ⊙8am-noon, treatments 9am-7pm) is home to the two-hour in-water massage, during which you float on a mattress in a lava-surrounded sulfur pool while being kneaded from top to bottom. The entry fee gets you a private changing room, and access to the Retreat Hotel's private lagoon, the Blue Lagoon. Treatments cost extra.

Other therapies on offer include foot and leg silica wraps (with a geothermal sea salt rub and massage), hot-stone massages and facials.

> ### ☑ Don't Miss
>
> A soak in the mineral-rich waters.

Golden Circle

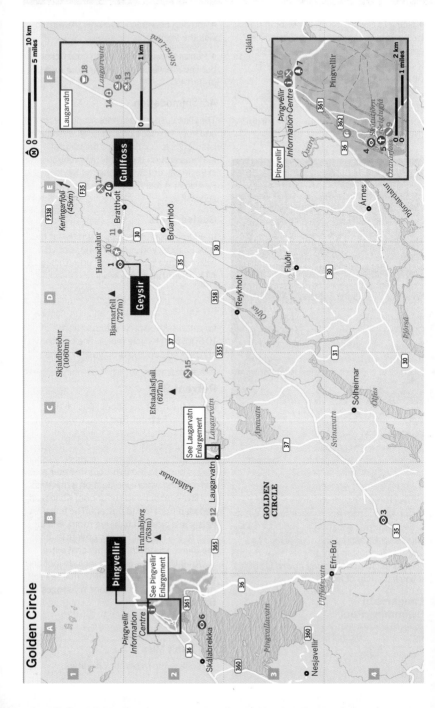

Golden Circle

Laugarvatn

Laugarvatn (Hot Springs Lake) is fed not only by streams running from the misty fells behind it, but also by the hot spring **Vígðalaug**, famous since medieval times. A village, also called Laugarvatn, sits on the lake's western shore in the lap of the foothills. It is one of the more popular bases in the Golden Circle area.

⊕ ACTIVITIES

Fontana   Geothermal Pool
(Map p86; ☎486 1400; www.fontana.is; Hverabraut 1; adult/child 3800/2000kr; ☺10am-11pm early Jun-late Aug, 11am-10pm late Aug-early Jun) This swanky lakeside soaking spot boasts three modern wading pools, and a cedar-lined steam room that's fed by a naturally occurring vent below. The cool cafe (buffet lunch/dinner 2900/3900kr) has lake views. You can rent towels or swimsuits (800kr each) and dressing gowns (1500kr) if you left yours at home.

**Laugarvatn
Swimming Pool**   Geothermal Pool
(Map p86; ☎480 3041; Hverabraut 2; adult/child 1000/550kr; ☺10am-9pm Mon-Fri, to 6pm Sat & Sun Jun–mid-Aug, shorter hours mid-Aug–May) If

you want skip the Fontana hot-pot hoopla, there's a regular geothermal swimming pool, hot-pots and sauna next door that costs a third of the price, with none of the glitz.

ⓖ TOURS

**Laugarvatn
Adventures**   Rock Climbing, Caving
(Map p86; ☎862 5614; www.caving.is; Laugarvatnshellir; caving trips from 9900kr; ☺10am-6pm) Runs two- to three-hour caving and rock-climbing trips in the hills around town. Tours often start from Laugarvatnshellir – a house built into the rock and cave within, where two families have lived the past 100 years.

ⓐ SHOPPING

Gallerí Laugarvatn   Arts & Crafts
(Map p86; ☎486 1016; www.gallerilaugarvatn.is; Háholt 1; ☺8am-6pm Thu-Tue) Local handicrafts, from Icelandic sweets and ironwork to ceramics and woollens.

Samkaup Strax   Food & Drinks
(Map p86; www.samkaup.is; Dalbraut 8; ☺9am-9pm Mon-Fri, 10am-9pm Sat & Sun) Groceries, camping supplies and a fast-food counter serving hot dogs and burgers. ATM outside.

★ **Top Five Sights**

Geysir (p74)

Gullfoss (p76)

Þingvellir National Park (p78)

The Blue Lagoon (p82)

Kerið (p88)

From left: Kerið crater; Fontana (p87); Þingvellir National Park (p78)

🍴 EATING

Good Burger   Burgers €
(Map p86; ☎666 1234; Dalbraut 6; burgers from 1100kr; ☺11am-9pm) Serving the best burgers for miles, this simple joint has only four types of flavoursome beef patties. Choose them small, medium or large (like really large!). The Aruba burger (with an onion ring on top of the patty) is our choice. Veggies, bacon, cheese, Bearnaise sauce and fries can be ordered as extras.

 Kerið

Around 15.5km north of Selfoss on Rte 35, **Kerið** (Map p86; Biskupstungnabraut; adult/child 400kr/free; ☺8.30am-9pm Jun-Aug, daylight hours Sep-May) is a 6500-year-old explosion crater with vivid red and sienna earth and containing an ethereal green lake. Björk once performed a concert from a floating raft in the middle. Visitors can walk around the entire rim (it takes between 10 and 20 minutes), and go down to the lake in the crater.

Efstidalur II   Icelandic €€
(Map p86; ☎486 1186; www.efstidalur.is; Efstidalur 2; ice cream per scoop 500kr, mains 2250-5800kr; ☺ice cream bar 10am-10pm, restaurant 11.30am-10pm; 🅿🛜) Located 12km northeast of Laugarvatn on a working dairy farm with brilliant views of hulking Hekla, Efstidalur offers tasty farm-fresh meals and amazing ice cream. The restaurant serves beef (ribeye steak) from the fields and trout (fillet served with baked veggies) from the lake. The fun ice-cream bar has windows looking into the dairy barn.

Lindin   Icelandic €€
(Map p86; ☎486 1262; www.laugarvatn.is; Lindarbraut 2; mains 2200-5600kr; ☺noon-10pm May-Sep, shorter hours Oct-Apr; 🅿🛜) Owned by Baldur, an affable, celebrated chef, Lindin could be the best restaurant for miles. In a sweet little silver house, with simple decor and wooden tables, the restaurant faces the lake and is purely gourmet, with high-concept Icelandic fare featuring local or wild-caught ingredients. Order everything from soup to an amazing reindeer burger. Book ahead for dinner in high season.

GARY LATHAM/LONELY PLANET ©

DRINKING & NIGHTLIFE

Galleri Laugarvatn Cafe   Cafe
(Map p86; www.gallerilaugarvatn.is; Háholt 1;
menu items from 950kr; ⊗8am-6pm Thu-Tue)
Simple cafe with a nice outdoor terrace,
serving good coffee plus hot-spring-baked
rye bread with smoked trout or brie. Soup,
waffles, cookies and muffins also available.

GETTING THERE & AWAY

Strætó (p281) bus 75 from Selfoss (adult/
child 1840/880kr, 1¼ hours, two to three daily
Monday to Friday, one Saturday and Sunday)
stops in Laugarvatn.

Reykjavík Excursions (⌕580 5400; www.
ioyo.is) runs the 'Iceland On Your Own'
service between Reykjavík and Akureyri,
stopping at Laugarvatn en route. There's
one daily mid-June to early September,
leaving at 8am from Reykjavík's BSÍ bus
terminal. Fares cost 17,900kr all the way to
Akureyri, or a one-way fare to Laugarvatn
costs 3500kr.

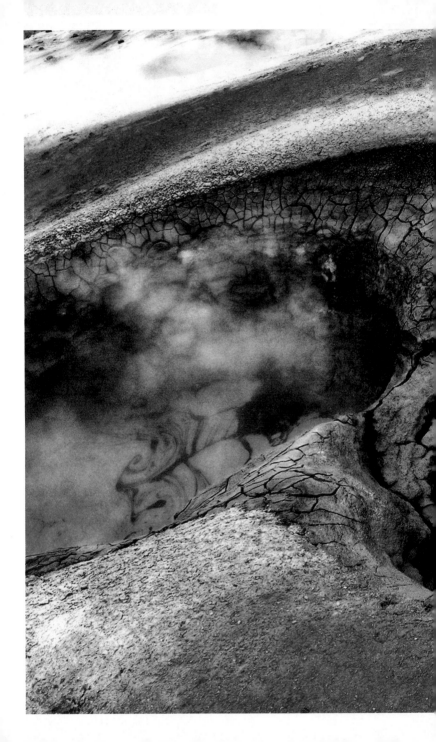

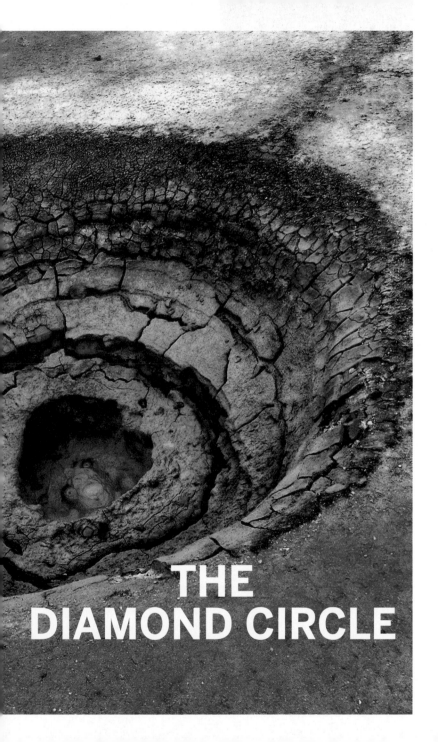

THE
DIAMOND CIRCLE

The Diamond Circle at a Glance...

Iceland's northeast has some real gems, but the 'Diamond Circle' is a relatively new tourist-brochure term to describe the route encompassing the Mývatn lake region, the lava fields of Krafla, and the raging Dettifoss waterfall. Whatever you call it, this is a captivating expanse of geothermal activity, rich birdlife and natural beauty, so tantalisingly close to the Arctic Circle that winter nights bring a strong chance of witnessing the coveted Northern Lights.

Two Days in the Diamond Circle

From a base in **Reykjahlíð** (p108), start exploring Mývatn's lakeshore, taking in the lava fields at **Dimmuborgir** (p100) and **Hverfjall** (p100), the lava cave at **Lofthellir** (p100), the pseudocraters at **Skútustaðagígar** (p101) and the excellent opportunities for birdwatching. Finish the day with a soak in **Mývatn Nature Baths** (p96), the north's answer to the Blue Lagoon.

Four Days in the Diamond Circle

Heading east from Reykjahlíð it's time to immerse yourself in the geothermal landscape of **Bjarnarflag** (p97) and the lunar-like mudpots and hot springs at **Hverir** (p96). Next stop is Krafla, where you can trek to the intimidating **Leirhnjúkur crater** (p97) and hike around the rim of **Víti volcano** (p97). Finally, don't miss the trip east to **Dettifoss** (p104), one of Iceland's most spectacular waterfalls.

Previous page: Volcanic landscape at Hverir (p96)

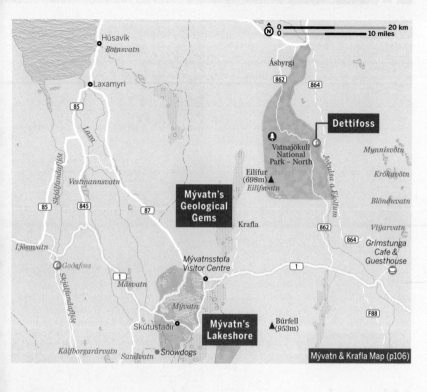

Myvatn & Krafla Map (p106)

Arriving in the Diamond Circle

Air The nearest airports are at Húsavík and Akureyri, with regular flights from Reykjavík.

Bus All buses pick up/drop off passengers at the visitor centre in Reykjahlíð; buses also stop in Skútustaðir, by the Sel-Hótel.

Car Mývatn is just under 500km from Reykjavík via the Ring Road.

Where to Stay

Accommodation everywhere in the Mývatn area is in strong demand, and prices reflect this. Book ahead in summer. Although there are guesthouses and hotels dotted around the lake, Reykjahlíð is the main village with camping and guesthouses. Alternative places for accommodation options in the region include Akureyri and Húsavík.

Námafjall (p97)

Mývatn's Geological Gems

Steaming vents and craters await at Krafla, an active volcanic region 7km north of the Ring Road, while more geological gems lie in the northern Mývatn regions and east of Reykjahlíð.

Great For...

❶ Need to Know

Mývatnsstofa Visitor Centre (p109) in Reykjahlíð has displays on the local geology.

☑ **Don't Miss**

The Leirhnjúkur crater and its solfataras (volcanic vents emitting hot gases).

Northern Mývatn's collection of geological gems lie along the Ring Road (Rte 1) as it weaves through the harsh terrain between the north end of the lake and the turn-off to **Krafla**. There are plenty of paths for exploring the area on foot.

Hverir

The magical, ochre-toned world of **Hverir** (Map p106; Rte 1), also called Hverarönd, is a lunar-like landscape of mud cauldrons, steaming vents, radiant mineral deposits and piping fumaroles. Belching mudpots and the powerful stench of sulphur may not sound enticing, but Hverir's ethereal allure grips every passer-by.

Safe trails through the features have been delineated by ropes; to avoid risk of serious injury and damage to the natural features, avoid any lighter-coloured soil and respect the ropes. A walking trail loops from Hverir up Námafjall ridge. This 30-minute climb provides a grand vista over the steamy surroundings.

Mývatn Nature Baths

Northern Iceland's answer to the Blue Lagoon, **Mývatn Nature Baths** (Map p106; Jarðböðin; ☑464 4411; www.myvatnnaturebaths. is; off Rte 1; adult/child 4700kr/free; ☺9am-midnight May-Sep, noon-10pm Oct-Apr), 3km east of Reykjahlíð, is blessedly smaller and more low-key than its southern counterpart. It's also less hyped and a gorgeous place to soak in powder-blue, mineral-rich waters while enjoying the panorama. Also try one of two natural steam baths or grab a bite at the simple cafeteria (soup 1700kr). Arrive early or late to avoid tour groups.

Hverir's geothermal landscape

Námafjall

Vaporous vents cover the pinky-orange **Námafjall ridge** (Map p106; Rte 1), which lies 3km east of Bjarnarflag (on the south side of the Ring Road). Produced by a fissure eruption, the ridge sits squarely on the spreading zone of the Mid-Atlantic Ridge.

Víti

The ochre crater of **Víti** (Map p106; Rte 863) reveals a secret when you reach its rim – a cerulean pool of floodwater at its heart. The 300m-wide explosion crater was created in 1724 at the beginning of the destructive Mývatn Fires, when many of the fissure vents

✕ Take a Break

There is no food available here, but Rey-kjahlíð's restaurants and supermarkets are only 15km away.

MIKHAIL VARENTSOV/SHUTTERSTOCK ©

opened up. There is a circular path from the car park around the rim.

Bjarnarflag

Bjarnarflag (Map p106; Rte 1), 3km east of Reykjahlíð, is an active geothermal area where the earth hisses and bubbles, and steaming vents line the valley. Historically the area has been home to a number of economic ventures attempting to harness the earth's powers. (Early on, farmers tried growing potatoes here, but these often emerged from the ground already boiled.)

In the 1960s, 25 test holes were bored at Bjarnarflag to ascertain the feasibility of a proposed geothermal power station. One is 2300m deep and the steam still roars out of the pipe at a whopping 200°C.

Leirhnjúkur

Krafla's most impressive, and potentially most dangerous, attraction is the **Leirhnjúkur crater** (Map p106) and its solfataras, which originally appeared in 1727, starting out as a lava fountain and spouting molten material for two years before subsiding.

A well-defined track leads northwest to Leirhnjúkur from the Krafla parking area (which has toilets); with all the volcanic activity, high temperatures, bubbling mudpots and steaming vents, it's best not to stray from the marked paths.

In 1975 the Krafla Fires began with a small lava eruption by Leirhnjúkur, and after nine years of on-and-off action Leirhnjúkur became the ominous-looking, sulphur-encrusted mudhole that tourists love today. The Earth's crust here is extremely thin and in places the ground is ferociously hot.

Krafla Power Station

The idea of constructing a geothermal power-er station at Krafla was conceived in 1973, and preliminary work commenced with the drilling of holes to determine project feasibility. In 1975, after a long rest period, the Krafla fissure burst into activity. The project went ahead and has been expanded since. The power plant's visitor centre explains how it all works.

Mývatn's Lakeshore

Mývatn's eastern lakeshore is a highlight with linked hiking trails, lava fields and caves, but continue on to explore the pseudocraters of the southern region and the fabulous birdwatching in the west.

Great For...

❶ Need to Know

The Mývatnsstofa Visitor Centre (p109) has a useful Mývatn map, which gives a decent overview of hiking trails in the area.

★ **Top Tip**

Mývatn's name (pronounced *mee*-vaht) translates as 'Lake of Midges' – pack insect spray and perhaps a head net.

Dimmuborgir

The giant jagged lava field at **Dimmuborgir** (Map p106; Rte 884), which translates literally as 'Dark Castles', is one of the most fascinating flows in the country. A series of nontaxing, colour-coded walking trails runs through the landscape. The most popular path is the easy **Church Circle** (2.3km). Check with the visitor centre in Reykjahlíð or at the cafe at Dimmuborgir about free guided ranger walks in summer.

It's commonly believed that Dimmuborgir's strange pillars and crags were created about 2000 years ago when a lake of lava from the Þrengslaborgir and Lúdentarborgir crater rows formed here, over marshland or a small lake. The water of the marsh started to boil, and steam jets rose through the molten lava and cooled it, creating the pillars. As the lava continued flowing towards lower ground, the hollow pillars of solidified lava remained.

Hverfjall

Dominating the lava fields on the eastern edge of Mývatn is the classic tephra ring **Hverfjall** (Map p106; off Rte 848), also called Hverfell. This near-symmetrical crater appeared 2700 years ago in a cataclysmic eruption. Rising 452m from the ground and stretching 1040m across, it is a massive and awe-inspiring landmark in Mývatn.

The crater is composed of loose gravel, but an easy track leads from the north-western end (where there's toilets) to the summit and offers stunning views of the crater itself and the surrounding landscape. A path runs along the western rim of the crater to a lookout at the southern end before descending steeply towards Dimmuborgir.

Access the walking track via a signed gravel road – it's about 2.5km from the main road to the car park.

Lofthellir

The dramatic lava cave at Lofthellir is a stunning destination, with magnificent natural ice sculptures dominating the interior. Although it's one of Mývatn's highlights, the cave is on private property and can only be accessed on a half-day tour with Geo Travel (p102). The tour

Dimmuborgir

involves a one-hour 4WD journey and a 25-minute walk across gorgeous lava fields to reach the cave, and then special equipment (headlamps, studded boots etc) and intensely physical wriggling through tight spaces. Wear warm, waterproof gear.

Skútustaðagígar

The **Skútustaðagígar pseudocraters** (Map p106) of southern Mývatn were formed when molten lava flowed into Mývatn lake, triggering a series of gas explosions. These dramatic green dimples then came into being when trapped subsurface water boiled and popped, forming small scoria cones and craters.

The most accessible pseudocrater swarm is located along a short path just across from Skútustaðir, which also takes in the nearby pond, Stakhólstjörn, a haven for nesting waterfowl.

Sigurgeir's Bird Museum

For superb birdwatching background, visit **Sigurgeir's Bird Museum** (Map p106; Fuglasafn Sigurgeirs; ☎464 4477; www.fuglasafn.is; off Rte 1, Ytri-Neslönd farm; adult/child 1500/800kr; ☺noon-5pm mid-May–Oct, shorter hours rest of

★ Grjótagjá

Game of Thrones fans may recognise this as the place where Jon Snow is, ahem, deflowered by Ygritte. **Grjótagjá** (Map p106; Rte 860) is a gaping fissure with a 45°C water-filled cave. It's on private property – it's prohibited to bathe here, but the owners allow the public to visit and photograph. This is a beautiful spot, particularly when the sun filters through the cracks in the roof and illuminates the interior. There is easy road access.

year), housed in a beautiful lakeside building that fuses modern design with traditional turf house. Inside you'll find an impressive collection of taxidermied avians (more than 180 types from around the world), including every species of bird that calls Iceland home (except one – the grey phalarope). Detailed captions, designer lighting and a small cafe further enhance the experience.

The menagerie of stuffed squawkers started as the private collection of a local named Sigurgeir Stefansson. Tragically, Sigurgeir drowned in the lake at the age of 37 – the museum was erected in his honour. The museum also lends out high-tech telescopes to ornithological enthusiasts, plus it has hides for rent.

Guided Tours

Geo Travel Adventure Tour
(☑464 4442; www.geotravel.is) A small company owned by two well-connected local guys who plant trees to carbon offset their tours. They offer excellent year-round small-group trips, from tours of lava and ice cave Lofthellir (17,500kr) to super-Jeep excursions to Askja and Holuhraun (34,900kr), Northern Lights tours (17,500kr) and half-hour snowmobile trips (14,900kr). They're also birdwatching specialists.

Snowdogs Dog Sledding
(☑847 7199; www.snowdogs.is; off Rte 849; sled tour adult/child 30,000/10,000kr) Sæmi and his family run winter dog-sledding tours across snow-white wilderness on remote farm Heiði, about 8km off Rte 848 in southern Mývatn (take Rte 849 west of Skútustaðir). Tours vary depending on the dogs, people, weather and trail conditions, but guests are generally on the snow for 45 to 60 minutes and cover around 8km. Dog cart rides in summer (19,000kr).

Mývatn Activity – Hike&Bike Adventure Tour
(Map p106; ☑899 4845; www.hikeandbike. is) Hike&Bike has a booth by the Gamli Bærinn (p108) tavern in Reykjahlíð that offers tour bookings and mountain-bike rental (adult/child per day 5000/4000kr).

A vast program of cycling and hiking tours includes a fat-bike ride to Lofthellir lava and ice cave (24,900kr), a one-hour ATV-ride (22,500kr) and an evening sightseeing cycle that ends with a soak at the Nature Baths (p96; including baths admission 13,500kr).

Mýflug Air Scenic Flight
(Map p106; ☑464 4400; www.myflug.is; Reykjahlíð Airport) Mýflug Air operates daily flightseeing excursions (weather permitting) including a 20-minute trip over Mývatn and Krafla (19,000kr). A two-hour 'super tour' (57,000kr) also includes Dettifoss, Ásbyrgi, Kverkfjöll, Herðubreið and Askja. Or fly north for a one-hour stop in Grímsey (48,000kr).

Hverfjall (p100)

Saltvík   Horse Riding

(Map p106; ☏847 6515; www.saltvik.is; Rte 848; 2hr tour 9900kr) Just south of Reykjahlíð, Saltvík operates horseback sightseeing tours around Mývatn (suitable for all skill levels, including beginners), from June to August. They also have a larger operation in Húsavík (p196).

Safarí Hestar   Horse Riding

(Map p106; ☏464 4203; www.safarihorserental. com; Rte 848, Álftagerði III; 1/2hr tour 7000/ 11,000kr) Scenic horse tours operate from Álftagerði III farm on the south side of the lake (400m west of **Sel-Hótel** (☏464 4164; www.myvatn.is; Rte 848, Skútustaðir), and take in the lakeshore and pseudocraters.

SBA-Norðurleið   Bus Tour

(☏550 0700; www.sba.is) SBA has one tour from Reykjahlíð (15,300kr; late June to August) to Dettifoss and Ásbyrgi, ending in Akureyri. Plus other sightseeing trips in the northeast.

✕ Take a Break

There's a small cafe inside Sigurgeir's Bird Museum (p101).

❶ Did You Know?

Marimo balls are bizarre little spheres of green algae that are thought to grow naturally in colonies in only a handful of places in the world (including Mývatn and Lake Akan in Japan). The name *marimo* is the Japanese word for 'algae ball' – around Mývatn, the locals call 'em *kúluskítur*, which literally means 'ball of shit'. Swing by Sigurgeir's Bird Museum to check them out.

LEONOV-O/SHUTTERSTOCK ©

Dettifoss

The power of nature can be seen in all its glory at mighty Dettifoss, one of Iceland's most impressive waterfalls.

Although Dettifoss is 'only' 45m high and 100m wide, a massive 400 cu metres of water thunders over its edge every second in summer, creating a plume of spray that can be seen 1km away. With the greatest volume of any waterfall in Europe, this truly is nature at its most spectacular. On sunny days, brilliant double rainbows form above the churning milky-grey glacial waters, and you'll have to jostle with other visitors for the best views.

Viewing Dettifoss

The falls can be seen from either side of the canyon, but there is no link (ie no bridge) between the sides at the site itself. Both viewpoints are grand and have pros and cons, and both require a walk from the respective car park of around 15 to 20 minutes to reach the falls. Many photographers

Great For...

☑ Don't Miss

You can't miss Dettifoss!

🛈 Need to Know

Gljúfrastofa Visitor Centre (📞470 7100; www.vjp.is; Rte 85, Ásbyrgi; ⏱9am-6pm late May-Aug, 10am-4pm Sep-Oct, shorter hours rest of year; 🛜)

✕ Take a Break

Grímstunga Cafe & Guesthouse (📞464 4294; www.grimstunga.is; Rte 864, Grímstunga 1 at Grímsstaðir a Fjöllum; d with/without bathroom from 24,500/17,500kr; 🛜), to the south, has a simple coffee-and-cake cafe.

★ Top Tip

Visit late in the day to avoid the tour groups.

---

rate the east side as their preferred side, especially in winter; road access is easier on the west side (making it busier with tour buses). Consider visiting either side under the summertime midnight sun for smaller crowds. Take care on the paths, made wet and slippery from the spray.

A sealed road, Rte 862, links the Ring Road with the **western bank of Dettifoss**, ending in a large car park and toilet facilities. From the car park, it's 1km to the falls, or a 2.5km loop walk takes in the dramatic, canyon-edge viewpoint of Dettifoss plus views of a smaller cataract, **Selfoss**. Bring waterproof gear to keep the spray at bay.

If you visit the **eastern side of the falls** via unsealed Rte 864, be sure, also, to drive 2km north of the Dettifoss car park and look for the sign to **Hafragilsfoss** – smaller, photogenic falls downriver from Dettifoss with a brilliant viewpoint over the canyon.

Where to Stay

There is nowhere to overnight here, but there are a couple of guesthouses on the east side (Rte 864) near the Ring Road. Visitors drop in to view Dettifoss from various points, but the closest major settlement is at Reykjahlíð (Mývatn), 52km away. There is a tiny, basic campground north of Dettifoss on Rte 862, strictly reserved for hikers.

Transport

Loads of tours visit the falls, but in summer 2018, public buses were cut completely. Check the park website, local tourist offices or www.publictransport.is for the latest news. Things will almost certainly change when Rte 862 is fully sealed.

Mývatn & Krafla

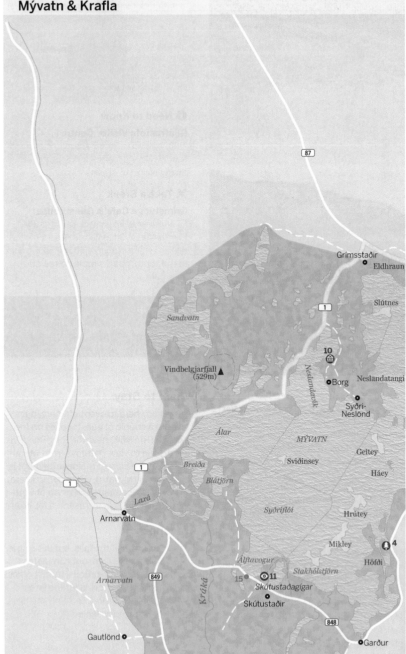

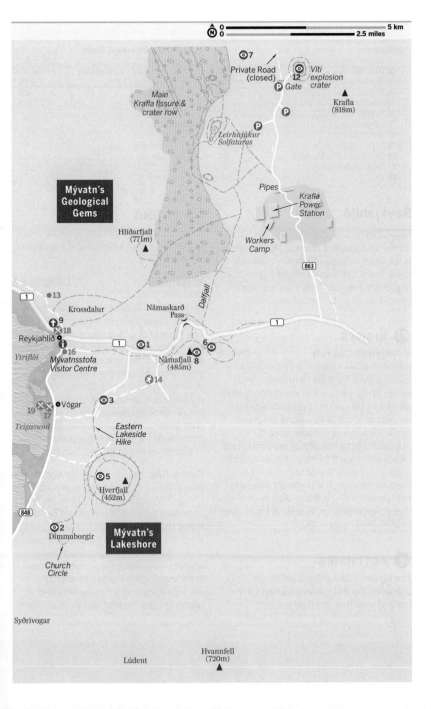

0 5 km
0 2.5 miles

⊙**7**
Private Road
(closed)

⊚**12** *Víti
explosion
crater*

ⓟ *Gate*

▲
*Krafla
(818m)*

*Main
Krafla fissure &
crater row*

ⓟ

*Leirhnjúkur
Sólfataras*

**Mývatn's
Geological
Gems**

ⓟ

Pipes

*Krafla
Power
Station*

*Hlíðarfjall
(771m)*
▲

*Workers
Camp*

863

●**13**

1

Krossdalur

*Námaskarð
Pass*

Dalfjall

1

ⓕ**9**
✕**18**
Reykjahlíð ●
ⓘ
●**16**
*Mývatnsstofa
Visitor Centre*

1

⊙**1**

6⊙

Ytriflói

▲
Námafjall
8
(485m)

ⓕ**14**

✕ ✕
19 17
●*Vógar*

⊙**3**

Teigasund

*Eastern
Lakeside
Hike*

⊙**5**
▲
*Hverfjall
(452m)*

848

⊚**2**
Dimmuborgir

**Mývatn's
Lakeshore**

*Church
Circle*

Syðrivogar

Lúdent

*Hvannfell
(720m)*
▲

Mývatn & Krafla

Reykjahlíð

Reykjahlíð (pronounced rey-kya-leeth), on the northeastern shore of Mývatn lake, is the main village and Mývatn's obvious base. There's little to it beyond a collection of guesthouses and hotels, a supermarket, petrol station and information centre.

⊙ SIGHTS

Reykjahlíð Church   Church
(Map p106; Reykjahlíðarkirkja) During the Krafla eruption of 1727, the Leirhnjúkur (p97) crater, 11km northeast of Reykjahlíð, kicked off a two-year period of volcanic activity, sending streams of lava along old glacial moraines towards the lakeshore. On 27 August 1729 the flow ploughed through the village, destroying farms and buildings, but amazingly (some would say miraculously) the wooden church was spared when the flow parted, missing the church by only metres. It was rebuilt on its original foundation in 1876, then again in 1962.

🏃 ACTIVITIES

The Mývatn Nature Baths (p96) are a smaller and less crowded option for a mineral soak than the Blue Lagoon.

🍽 EATING

There's not a huge amount of dining choices, and they're all in demand at the peak of summer.

Vogafjós   Icelandic €€
(Map p106; 🖂464 3800; www.vogafjos.net; Rte 848; dishes 2000-5900kr; ⊙10am-11pm Jun-Aug, shorter hours rest of year; 🛜🖂👪) The 'Cowshed', 2.5km south of Reykjahlíð, is a memorable restaurant where you can enjoy views of the lush surrounds, or of the dairy shed of this working farm (cows are milked at 7.30am and 5.30pm). The menu is an ode to local produce: smoked lamb, house-made mozzarella, dill-cured Arctic char, geysir bread, home-baked cakes, homemade ice cream. It's all delicious.

Kitchen closes at 10pm in summer.

Gamli Bærinn   Icelandic €€
(Map p106; 🖂464 4270; www.myvatnhotel.is; Rte 1; mains 2100-4000kr; ⊙10am-11pm; 🛜) The cheerfully busy 'Old Farm' tavern beside **Hótel Reynihlíð** (🖂444 4000; www.icelandairhotels.com) serves up good-quality pub-style meals all day, ranging from lamb soup, burgers and grilled trout to pizzas. In the evening it becomes a local hangout – opening hours may be extended at weekends, but the kitchen closes at 10pm.

Mývatn Nature Baths (p96)

Daddi's Pizza   Pizzeria €€

(Map p106; ☑773 6060; www.vogahraun.
is; Rte 848, Vógar; small pizza 1720-2900kr;
☺noon-11pm; ☑) At **Vogár** (☑464 4399; www.
vogahraun.is; Rte 1) campground, this small
space cranks out tasty pizzas to eat in or
take away. Try the house speciality: smoked
trout, nuts and cream cheese (tastier than
it sounds).

ℹ INFORMATION

Mývatnsstofa Visitor Centre (☑464 4390;
www.visitmyvatn.is; Hraunvegur 8; ☺8.30am-
6pm Jun-Aug, shorter hours rest of year) This
well-informed centre has good displays on local
geology, and park rangers to advise on local

sights. Pick up a copy of the useful Mývatn map,
which gives a decent overview of hiking trails in
the area (though it's not to scale).

All tours and buses leave from the car park
here.

ℹ GETTING THERE & AWAY

Reykjahlíð is the transport hub of the Mývatn
region. All buses stop here (by the visitor
centre; p109), and tours and activities generally depart from here.

If you visit without your own wheels, you can
hire a bike from Mývatn Activity – Hike&Bike
(p102).

JÖKULSÁRLÓN

Jökulsárlón at a Glance...

A host of spectacular, luminous-blue icebergs drift through Jökulsárlón (pronounced yokul-sar-lon) glacier lagoon, right beside the Ring Road between Höfn and Skaftafell. It's worth spending a couple of hours here, admiring the wondrous ice sculptures, scouting for seals or taking a boat trip.

The icebergs calve from Breiðamerkurjökull, an offshoot of Vatnajökull, crashing down into the water and drifting towards the Atlantic Ocean. They can spend up to five years floating in the lagoon, melting, refreezing and occasionally toppling over.

One Day in Jökulsárlón

Jökulsárlón itself can easily be visited in a single day, though it's too far to be a realistic day trip from Reykjavík – plan to stay overnight in the area. Spend the morning (or evening) walking around the lagoon shoreline, enjoying good light for photography. In the afternoon take an amphibious boat tour of the lagoon and check out **Diamond Beach** (p116).

Two Days in Jökulsárlón

On day two book a tour to the ice caves (winter), a guided glacier walk or a snowmobiling excursion on the Vatna-jökull glacier, or a kayaking trip among the icebergs (summer). If the weather is good and you're fit, consider hiking the **Breiðármörk Trail** (p117). Finish the day with the drive to Höfn, passing more glaciers and a chance for a dip in a hot-pot.

Θ 0 _____ 20 km
(N) 0 _____ 10 miles

Þórisvatn

Litlisjör   *Langisjór*   Skaftárjökull   *Grænalón*   Vatnajökull

Vetbraun   ▲Fögrufjöll   Síðujökull   Vatnajökull   Breiðamerkurjökull
(1090m)   National   *Breiðárlón*
Park

Fjallabak   Núpsstaðarskógar   Skaftafell   ▲
Nature   Skaftafell   Hvannadalshnúkur   Diamond
Reserve   Kalfafell   (2110m)   Beach
Sandfell   ○Hof

Fagrifoss   Öræfi
Ⓦ   *Foss á Síðu*
Ⓦ

Skeiðarársandur

Kirkjubæjarklaustur ○

Mýrdalsjökull
Katla   209   Eldhraun
(1250m)
▲   Mýrdalssandur   *Kúðafljót*
NORTH
ATLANTIC
OCEAN

○   Álftaver

○
Vík

**Glaciers &
Black Beaches**

South Coast – Jökulsárlón Map (p118)

Arriving in Jökulsárlón

Jökulsárlón is on the Ring Road (Rte 1),
so any passing bus can drop you here.
By car it's 375km (about 4½ hours)
from Reykjavík. **Sterna** (p284) has
a daily summer bus from Reykjavík,
returning to Vík.

Where to Stay

The closest accommodation is at the
hamlet of Hali, 13km east (there is no
camping at Hali; the next campground
east of Jökulsárlón is in Höfn). The
nearest towns of any size are Vík to the
west and Höfn to the east.

Auroral display, Jökulsárlón

Glaciers & Black Beaches

The lagoon boat trips are excellent, but you can get almost as close to those cool-blue masterpieces by walking along the shore, and you can taste ancient ice by hauling it out of the shallows. On the Ring Road (Rte 1) west of the car park, there are designated parking areas where you can walk over the mounds to visit the lake at less-touristed stretches of shoreline.

Great For...

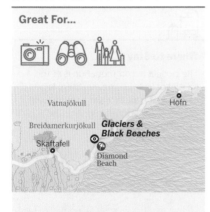

Vatnajökull
Höfn
Breiðamerkurjökull **Glaciers & Black Beaches**
Skaftafell
Diamond Beach

❶ Need to Know

Jökulsárlón is within the boundaries of the vast **Vatnajökull National Park** (www.vjp.is).

★ **Top Tip**

In winter Jökulsárlón is the base and starting point for many ice cave tours: book ahead!

Diamond Beach

At the Jökulsá river mouth you'll see ice boulders and bergs resting photogenically on the black-sand beach as part of their final journey out to sea. Tourists have dubbed the site Diamond Beach, and the name has stuck.

There are car parks on the ocean side of the Ring Road, on both sides of the bridge over the river.

Guided Tours

This is a true Iceland highlight, so countless day tours take in Jökulsárlón. Trying to do a trip from Reykjavík to the lagoon and back to the capital in one day is not recommended (it's 375km, or about a 4½-hour drive each way).

In summer, the lagoon is a hub for boat tours and some kayaking. In winter, the car park swells with super-Jeeps ready to cart travellers to ice caves. This is generally the location with easiest access to some of the most-visited caves, so tour operators meet participants here. The tours are run by companies that have summer bases elsewhere along the stretch between Skaftafell and Höfn, including **Arctic Adventures** (p174), **IceGuide** (✆661 0900; www.iceguide. is; double kayak adult/child 10,900/5900kr), **Glacier Journey** (✆478 1517; www.glacierjourney.is) and **Ice Explorers** (✆866 3490; www.explorers.is).

Reynisdrangur (p119)

Glacier Lagoon Amphibious Boat Tours

Take a memorable 40-minute trip in an **amphibious boat** (☑478 2222; www.ice lagoon.is; adult/child 5700/2000kr; ⊘9am-7pm Jun-Sep, 10am-5pm May & Oct), which trundles along the shore like a bus before driving into the water. On-board guides regale you with factoids about the lagoon, and you can taste 1000-year-old ice. See the website for timetables, and to prebook tickets. Trips run from the eastern car park (by the cafe) frequently – up to 40 a day in summer.

Note that the last boat tour departs about one hour before closing time. Tours may be available in April and November, depending on demand and weather conditions – contact the operators.

The same company also offers a handful of hour-long lagoon tours in Zodiacs (adult/child 9800/5000kr; not recommended for kids under 10). These run on a set schedule, and it's worth booking ahead online.

Breiðármörk Trail

A **walking trail** has been marked from the western car park at Jökulsárlón, leading to the lagoons Breiðárlón (10km one way) and Fjallsárlón (15.3km). It's classified as challenging. There is a plan to build out this walking route from Skaftafell in the west to Lónsöræfi in the east. The visitor centre at Höfn sells a trail map (250kr).

ANDREY BAYDA/SHUTTERSTOCK ©

★ Jökulsárlón Film Credits

Jökulsárlón is a natural film set, and a popular backdrop for commercials. It starred briefly in *Lara Croft: Tomb Raider* (2001), pretending to be Siberia – the amphibious tourist-carrying boats were even painted grey and used as Russian ships. You might also have seen it in *Batman Begins* (2005), or the James Bond film *Die Another Day* (2002), for which the lagoon was specially frozen and six Aston Martins were destroyed on the ice.

ⓘ Did You Know?

In June and July, the area close to the car park at Jökulsárlón is a popular nesting site for Arctic terns – and these are territorial birds! They may give you some grief; but as the sign from the national park says, 'The Arctic tern flew 19,000km to nest and lay its eggs here. It took over one and a half months. Be considerate and give the birds space.'

South Coast – Jökulsárlón

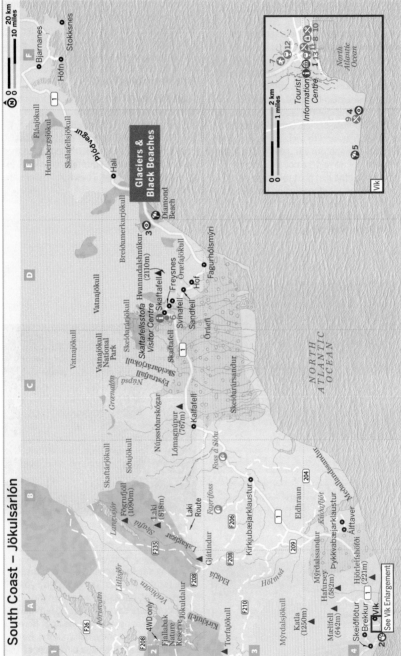

Glaciers & Black Beaches

See Vík Enlargement

South Coast - Jökulsárlón

Vík

The welcoming little community of Vík (aka Vík í Mýrdal) has become a booming hub for a very beautiful portion of the South Coast. Iceland's southernmost town, it's also the rainiest, but that doesn't stop the madhouse atmosphere in summer, when every room within 100km seems to be booked solid. With loads of services, Vík is a convenient base for the beautiful basalt beach Reynisfjara just to the west and its puffin cliffs. There's also the rocky plateau Dyrhólaey and the volcanoes running from Skógar to Jökulsárlón glacier lagoon and beyond. Along the coast, white-capped waves wash up on black sands and the cliffs glow green from all that rain. Put simply, it's pretty special.

◎ SIGHTS

Dyrhólaey   Wildlife Reserve
(Map p118; Rte 218) One of the South Coast's most recognisable natural formations is the rocky plateau and huge stone sea arch at Dyrhólaey (deer-lay), which rises dramatically from the surrounding plain 10km west of Vík, at the end of Rte 218. Visit its crashing black-sand beaches and get awesome views from atop the promontory. The islet is a nature reserve that's rich in bird life, including puffins; some or all of it can be closed during nesting season (15 May to 25 June).

There are two parking areas: one on the top of the cliff near the Dyrhólaey Lighthouse and one at the base. Those without 4WD are better off using the bottom car park as the road up is filled with deep potholes and can be tricky in rain. The best view of the archway is from Reynisfjara along the coast.

According to *Njál's Saga*, Kári – the only survivor of the fire that wiped out Njál's clan – had his farm here. Another Viking Age connection is the cave **Loftsalahellir**, reached by a track just before the causeway to Dyrhólaey, which was used for council meetings in Saga times.

Reynisdrangur   Landmark
(Map p118; Rte 215) Vík's most iconic cluster of sea stacks is known as Reynisdrangur, and rises from the ocean like ebony towers at the western end of Vík's black-sand beach. Tradition says they're masts of a ship that trolls were stealing when they got caught in the sun. The nearby cliffs are good for puffin watching. A bracing walk up from Vík's western end takes you to the top of **Reynisfjall ridge** (340m), which offers superb views.

Reynisfjara   Beach
(Map p118; Rte 215) On the western side of Reynisfjall, the high ridge above Vík, Rte 215 leads 5km down to the black-sand beach Reynisfjara. It's backed by an incredible stack of **basalt columns** that look like a magical church organ, and there

Seljalandsfoss & Gljúfurárbui

From the Ring Road you'll see the beautiful high falls at Seljalandsfoss, which tumble over a rocky scarp into a deep, green pool. A (slippery) path runs around the back of the waterfall. A few hundred metres further down the Þórsmörk road, Gljúfurárbui gushes into a hidden canyon.

are outstanding views west to Dyrhólaey. Surrounding cliffs are pocked with caves formed from twisted basalt, and puffins belly-flop into the crashing sea during summer. Immediately offshore are the towering Reynisdrangur (p119) sea stacks. At all times watch for rogue waves: people are regularly swept away.

You may recognise the scene from Bon Iver's 2011 music video *Holocene,* which is practically an ode to Iceland. The beach can get busy in high season, so try to come early in the day or late in the evening.

Brydebúð Museum

(Map p118; ☑487 1395; Víkurbraut 28; adult/child 500kr/free; ☺10am-6pm Mon-Fri, noon-7pm Sat & Sun Jun-Aug) In town, the tin-clad house Brydebúð was built in Vestmannaeyjar in 1831 and moved to Vík in 1895. Today it houses the Tourist Information Centre, the Halldórskaffi restaurant and a small museum with displays on the Katla Geopark.

🟢 ACTIVITIES

True Adventure   Paragliding

(Map p118; ☑698 8890; www.trueadventure.is; Suðurvíkurvegur 5; paragliding from 35,000kr; ☺May-Oct) Based at the Vík HI Hostel, this adventure outfit takes groups on thrilling one- to two-hour tandem tours, during which you soar over Vík and Iceland's southern landscape like a puffin.

🟢 TOURS

Katla Track   Driving

(☑849 4404; www.katlatrack.is; ice cave & volcano tours from 19,900kr) Katla Track runs tours of the area taking in local landmarks and the Mýrdalsjökull glacier.

🔒 SHOPPING

Icewear   Gifts & Souvenirs

(Map p118; ☑487 1250; www.icewear.is; Austurvegur 20; ☺8am-10pm) The big Icewear souvenir and knitwear shop next to the N1 petrol station on the edge of Vík is a coach-tour hit. You can peek inside the factory portion to see woollen wear being made and there are Icelandic souvenirs by the bucketload, plus the Ice Cave Restaurant.

🔵 EATING

Ice Cave Restaurant   International €

(Map p118; ☑788 5070; Austurvegur, Rte 1; mains from 1450kr; ☺11am-9pm) In the same complex as the Icewear shop, this modern canteen-style dining room has futuristic lighting (with electric tree-like centre-pieces) and serves surprisingly satisfying deli-style food from trays. Pick from sandwiches, salads, noodles, marinated chicken legs, lamb chops, chicken curry and burgers.

Víkurskáli   International €

(Map p118; ☑487 1230; Austurvegur 18; mains 1250-1900kr; ☺11am-8.30pm) Grab a booth and a burger at the old-school grill inside the N1 petrol station with a view of Reynisdrangur. Daily specials range from casseroles to traditional Icelandic lamb stew.

Suður-Vík   Icelandic, Asian €€

(Map p118; ☑487 1515; www.facebook.com/Sudurvik; Suðurvíkurvegur 1; mains 1300-5350kr; ☺noon-10pm, shorter hours in winter) The friendly ambience, in a warmly lit building with hardwood floors, exposed beams and interesting artwork, help to elevate this restaurant beyond its competition. Food is Icelandic hearty, ranging from farm plates and quinoa salad with chicken to pizzas and Asian dishes (think spicy Panang curry with rice). Book ahead in summer. For an nightcap head to the Man Cave downstairs.

Halldórskaffi
International €€

(Map p118; ☑487 1202; www.halldorskaffi.com; Víkurbraut 28; mains 2000-5000kr; ☺noon-10pm Jun-Aug, to 9pm Sep-May) Inside Brydebúð museum, this lively timber-lined all-rounder is very popular in high season for its crowd-pleasing menu ranging from burgers and pizza to lamb fillet. Be prepared to wait in summer since it doesn't take reservations. The cakes are too tempting to resist – the Icelandic meringue cake is particularly good.

Black Beach Restaurant
Cafe €€

(Map p118; Svarta Fjaran; ☑571 2718; www. svartafjaran.com; Reynisfjara, Rte 215; snacks 990kr, dinner mains 2200-4000kr; ☺11am-9pm; 🛜) Black volcanic cubes, meant to mimic the nearby black-sand beach Reynisfjara with its famous basalt columns, house this contemporary cafe that serves homemade cakes and snacks during the day, plus fish and chips, soups and chicken salads. Plate-glass windows give views to the ocean and Dyrhólaey beyond.

Ströndin Bistro
International €€

(Map p118; ☑487 1230; www.strondin.is; Austurvegur 18; mains 2000-5000kr; ☺6-10pm; 🛜) Behind the N1 petrol station is this semi-smart wood-panelled option enjoying sea-stack vistas. Go local with lamb soup or fish stew, or global with pizzas and burgers.

🍷 DRINKING & NIGHTLIFE

Smiðjan Brugghús
Microbrewery

(Map p118; http://smidjanbrugghus.is; Sunnu-braut 15; ☺11.30am-midnight Sun-Thu, to 1am Fri & Sat) Vík's hippest hang-out is warehouse-style place with grey walls, windows looking onto the brewing room and blackboards displaying 10 craft beers on tap. Hop aficionados can try Icelandic IPA, pale ale, porter and farmhouse ale with a handful of different burgers (including a vegan patty).

Man Cave
Bar

(Map p118; ☑487 1515; Suðurvíkurvegur 1; beers from 1000kr; ☺6pm-late) In the basement of the Suður-Vík Restaurant, this cosy watering hole pours local beers on tap and limited wines.

ℹ️ INFORMATION

Tourist Information Centre (☑487 1395; www. kotlusetur.i; Víkurbraut 28; ☺10am-8pm May-Sep, noon-6pm Oct-Apr; 🛜) Inside the Brydebúð museum. Has friendly advice about the local area, plus maps, books and a small gift shop.

ℹ️ GETTING THERE & AWAY

Vík is a major stop for all Reykjavík–Höfn bus routes; buses stop at the N1 petrol station in the centre of town on Austurvegur/Rte 1.

Strætó (p281) bus 51 from Reykjavík (1840kr, 2¾ hours, two daily) stops in Vík on the way to Höfn. If you take the early bus you can stop in Vík then continue on to Höfn on the later bus; how-ever, from September to May service is reduced and you can't count on that connection.

Sterna (p284) bus 12/12a from Reykjavík to Höfn stops in Selfoss and Vík en route. There's one daily service between Selfoss (3800kr, 3¼ hours) and Vík from June to mid-September.

Reykjavík Excursions (p281) bus 20/20a from Reykjavík (7800kr, four to five hours, one daily June to early September) to Skaftafell stops in Vík.

Vík is an easy self-drive destination. The Ring Road (Rte 1) runs right through the centre; it's 2¼ hours from Reykjavík by car.

HEIMAEY

Heimaey at a Glance...

Jagged and black, the Vestmannaeyjar (sometimes called the Westman Islands) form 15 eye-catching silhouettes off Iceland's southern shore.

Heimaey is the only inhabited island. Its little town and sheltered harbour lie between dramatic klettur (escarpments) and two ominous volcanoes – blood-red Eldfell and conical Helgafell. These days Heimaey is famous for its puffins (around 10 million birds come here to breed); Þjóðhátíð, Iceland's biggest outdoor festival, held in August; and a state-of-the-art volcano museum.

Two Days in Heimaey

Spend day one getting acquainted with the village, visiting the excellent **Eldheimar** (p131) and **Skansinn** (p130) historical sites and the local museums, finishing with dinner at **Slippurinn** (p134). Day two should be spent on one of the boat tours through the Vestmannaeyjar archipelago. Finish the day with dinner and drinks at **Gott** (p134).

Four Days in Heimaey

Days three and four can be set aside for hiking and puffin viewing, starting with the rocky peninsula **Stórhöfði** (p129). Hike the 221m-high volcanic cone **Eldfell** (p128) or take the easy scramble up **Helgafell** (p128; 226m). Finish with a pampering massage at **Heilsueyjan Spa** (p133) and a seafood dinner at **Einsi Kaldi** (p135).

The following labels appear on the map:

N 0 2 km / 0 1 miles

Skellir
Faxasker
Faxi
Ystiklettur
Stóri Örn
Stóraklif
Miðklettur
Heimaklettur
Klettsnef
Grasleysa Hrauney
West Coast
Herjólfur Ferry Terminal
Stafnsnes
Blátindur (273m)
Há
HEIMAEY
Viðlagafjara
Hani
Smæyjar
Hæna
Eldfellshraun
Vestmannaeyjar
Eldfell (221m)
Prestafjara

Historic Heimaey

Helgafell
Helgafell (226m)
Eldfellshraun (New land created by 1973 Eruption)

Vestmannaeyjar Airport

Heimaey's Great Outdoors

Lyngfell
Sæfjall
Litlistakkur
Stóristakkur
Landstakkur
Litlihöfði
NORTH ATLANTIC OCEAN

Brimurð
Fjósin
Stórhöfði
Höfðahellir
Ketilssker

Heimaey Map (p132)

Arriving in Heimaey

Vestmannaeyjar Airport About 3km south of central Heimaey. Atlantsflug (www.flightseeing.is) runs scheduled flights from Bakki (near the ferry port at Landeyjahöfn; one way adult/child 8500/6900kr). There are two daily flights between Reykjavík's domestic airport and Vestmannaeyjar (from around 17,000kr one way) on Eagle Air (www.eagleair.is)

Ferry Take Eimskip's Herjólfur (www.eimskip.is) from Landeyjahöfn (about 12km off the Ring Road (Rte 1) between Hvolsvöllur and Skógar) to Heimaey year-round.

Where to Stay

Although many people visit Heimaey as a day trip, spending the night here is highly recommended. Out of festival season it's usually not hard to find lodging, from camping and hostels to a more upmarket hotel. Visit www.vestmannaeyjar.is for a full list of accommodation options.

Heimaey's Great Outdoors

The island's sights are clustered in and around the main village, but walks through the volcanic lava fields, along puffin-nesting areas and on the island's western shores, are particularly ethereal.

Great For...

ⓘ Need to Know

The **Tourist Information Centre** (☎482 3683; www.vestmannaeyjar.is; Strandvegur; ⊙9am-6pm Mon-Fri, 10am-4pm Sat, 1-4pm Sun; 🛜) has a walking and cycling map.

★ **Top Tip**
Most boat tours coincide with ferry departures, making them convenient for day trippers.

Volcanic Landscapes

The 221m-high volcanic cone **Eldfell** (off Fellavegur) appeared from nowhere in the early hours of 23 January 1973. Once the fireworks finished, heat from the volcano provided Heimaey with geothermal energy from 1976 to 1985. Today the ground is still hot enough in places to bake bread or char wood. Eldfell is an easy climb from town, up the collapsed northern wall of the crater; stick to the path, as the islanders are trying to save their latest volcano from erosion. Known as **Eldfellshraun** (accessible via Eldfellsvegur), the Mars-like land created by the 1973 lava flow is now criss-crossed with a maze of otherworldly hiking tracks that run down to the Skansinn fort (p130) and the area where the lava meets the town's houses, and all around the bulge of the raw, red eastern coast. Here you'll find small black-stone beaches, the Gaujulundur lava garden and a lighthouse.

Helgafell (Helgafell Rd; 226m) erupted 5000 years ago. Its cinders are grassed over today, and you can scramble up here without much difficulty from the football pitch on the road to the airport.

Surtsey

In November 1963 the crew on the fishing boat *Ísleifi II* noticed something odd – the sea south of Heimaey appeared to be on fire. Rather than flee, the boat drew up for a closer look – and its crew were the first to set eyes on the world's newest island.

The incredible subsea eruption lasted for 4½ years, throwing up cinders and ash to form a 2.7 sq km piece of real estate (since eroded to 1.4 sq km). What else could it be called but Surtsey (Surtur's Island), after the Norse fire giant who will burn the world to ashes at Ragnarök.

It was decided that the sterile island would make a perfect laboratory, giving a unique insight into how plants and animals colonise new territory. Surtsey (www.surtsey.is) is therefore totally off limits to visitors (unless you're a scientist specialising in biocolonisation). Just so you know: in the race for the new land, the blue-green algae *Anabaena variabilis* got there first.

Wildlife Watching

Ribsafari   Boating
(Map p132; ☏661 1810; www.ribsafari.is; Básaskersbryggja 8, Harbour; 1hr tour adult/child 11,900/6500kr, 2hr 17,950/9500kr; ⊗mid-Apr–Oct) High-adrenaline tours run daily in a souped-up Zodiac that jets through the archipelago. The small boat allows the captain to navigate through little caves and between rocky outcrops for up-close views of bird colonies. If you're very lucky you might even get to see whales and seals.

View of Heimaey from Eldfell

★ **Top Tip**

A good way to get around Heimaey is by bicycle. Rent A Bike (p135) operates near the ferry landing. Book ahead.

Stórhöfði
Hiking, Birdwatching

(Rte 240) A windy **meteorological station** has been built on Stórhöfði (122m), the rocky peninsula at Heimaey's southern end. It's linked to the main island by a narrow isthmus (created by lava from Helgafell's eruption 5000 years ago), and there are good views from the summit. There's also a small **birdwatching hut** for puffin viewing about halfway up the hill; go from the first turnout on the right to the end of a trail across sheep pasture, marked with a hiking sign.

Viking Tours
Boat Tour, Bus Tour

(Map p132; ☎488 4884; www.vikingtours. is; Strandvegur 65; adult/child boat trips from 7400/6400kr, bus trips from 6400/5400kr; ⏰10am-6pm May–mid-Sep) Boat trips take in the big bird-nesting sites on the South Coast and sail into the sea cave Klettshellir. Bus trips tour the island.

West Coast
Hiking, Birdwatching

(Dalvegur) Several perilous tracks climb the steep slopes around Herjólfsdalur, running along the top of Norðklettur to **Stafnsnes**, one of the prime puffin-breeding areas. The ascent is exhilarating, but there are some sheer drops. A gentler walk runs south along the western coast of the island, passing above numerous lava caves where local people hid from pirates (p130) in 1627. At **Ofanleitishamar**, hundreds of puffins nest in the cliffs.

❶ Boat Trips

Both Ribsafari and Viking Tours run boat trips around Surtsey (no entry on the island). You can get a vicarious view of Surtsey's thunderous birth by visiting the display at the museum Eldheimar (p131).

BILDAGENTUR ZOONAR GMBH/SHUTTERSTOCK ©

Skansinn fort

CHLAUS LOTSCHER/GETTY IMAGES ©

Historic Heimaey

Marauding pirates, English fortifications and violent volcanic eruptions have contributed to the spectacular history of this little island, much of it explained in local museums.

Over the centuries, the island of Heimaey was a marauders' favourite. The English raided the island throughout the 15th century, building the stone fort Skansinn as their HQ. In 1627 Heimaey suffered its most violent attack at the hands of Algerian pirates, who went on a killing spree, murdering 34 islanders and kidnapping more than 230 (almost three-quarters of the population). The rest managed to escape by abseiling down cliffs or hiding in caves along the west coast. Those who were kidnapped were taken as slaves to north Africa; years later, 27 islanders had their freedom bought for them...and had a long journey home.

Skansinn

The oldest structure on the island, **Skansinn** (Map p132; Skansinn, off Skansvegur)

Great For...

☑ Don't Miss

Eldheimar, the poignant museum known as the 'Pompeii of the North'.

was a 15th-century fort built to defend the harbour (not too successfully, however – when Algerian pirates arrived they simply landed on the other side of the island). Its walls were swallowed up by the 1973 lava, but some have been rebuilt. Above them, you can see the remains of the town's old water tanks, which were also crushed by molten rock.

Eldheimar

More than 400 buildings lie buried under lava from the 1973 eruption, and on the edge of the flow 'Pompeii of the North' is a **museum** (Map p132; Pompeii of the North; 📞488 2700; www.eldheimar.is; Gerðisbraut 10; adult/child 2300/1200kr; ⊘11am-6pm) revolving around one house excavated from 50m of pumice. It was once home to Gerður Sigurðardóttir and Guðni Ólafsson, and their two children and baby. During the eruption the family was forced to leave in the middle of the night with only time to grab one item, a baby bottle.

The modern volcanic-stone building allows a glimpse into the home with its crumbling walls and intact but toppled knick-knacks and is filled with multimedia exhibits on the eruption and its aftermath, from compelling footage and eyewitness accounts to the story of the home owners. An audio guide leads you through it all; upstairs there's a catwalk over the wreckage, a space dedicated to all things Surtsey, and a cafe with broad views across town.

Sagnheimar Byggðasafn

Housed in the city library, this interactive folk **museum** (Map p132; Folk Museum; 📞488 2045; www.sagnheimar.is; Raðhústræti; adult/child 1000kr/free; ⊘11am-5pm mid-May–mid-Sep, 1-4pm Sat mid-Sep–mid-May) tells the story of Heimaey from the era of marauding pirates up to the 1973 eruption and beyond. Displays also shed light on local sports heroes, religion, volcanic activity and native bird life.

Heimaey

◎ SIGHTS

Sæheimar   Aquarium

(Map p132; ☑481 1997; www.saeheimar.is; Heiðarvegur 12; adult/child aged 10-17yr/child to 9yr 1200/500kr/free; ◷10am-5pm May-Sep, 1-4pm Sat Oct-Apr; ♿) The Aquarium & Natural History Museum has an interesting collection of stuffed birds and animals, videos on puffins and catfish, and fish tanks of Icelandic fish. It's great fun for the family, and there's often a puffin wobbling about. The museum is an informal bird hospital as well.

Landlyst   Museum

(Map p132; off Strandvegur; ◷11am-5pm mid-May–mid-Sep) **FREE** Shockingly, three out of four of Heimaey's babies once died of tetanus, due to water deficiency and contaminated soil. In the 1840s an island woman,

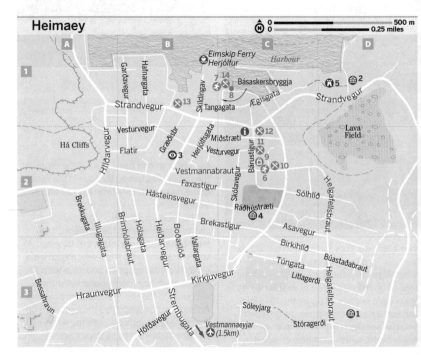

Heimaey

Sólveig, was sent abroad to be trained as a midwife. The tiny wooden house Landlyst was Sólveig's maternity hospital (and is the second-oldest building on the island). Today it contains a retro medicine cabinet, a small display of her blood-letting equipment and other 19th-century paraphernalia.

🛫 ACTIVITIES

Heilsueyjan Spa Massage

(Map p132; 📞481 1513; www.facebook.com/heilsueyjanspa; Vestmannabraut; 30/60min massage from 4500/8000kr, infrared sauna 1500kr; ⊙10am-6pm Mon-Fri, 1pm-6pm Sat & Sun) Offer various treatments from healing massages to manicures and an infrared sauna experience.

🎫 TOURS

Lyngfell Horse Riding

(📞898 1809; www.lyngfell.123.is; off Rte 240; 1hr hour from 7000k; ⊙Jun-Aug) Lyngfell, on the road to Stórhöfði, offers horse rides along black-sand beaches and along the cliffs when the wind is low. Find it on the left when heading along Rte 240 towards Stórhöfði.

Eyja Tours Bus

(Map p132; 📞852 6939; www.eyjatours.com; Básaskersbryggja; puffin & volcano tours adult/child 7000/3500kr) Bus tours covering the island's highlights, such as the puffin colonies and volcanoes.

🛍 SHOPPING

Útgerðin Clothing, Arts & Crafts

(Map p132; 📞891 9060; www.facebook.com/utgerdin; Vestmannabraut 30; ⊙11am-6pm Mon-Sat) A good bet for Icelandic crafts and design.

🍴 EATING

Heimaey has a surprisingly robust food scene for such a remote location, including one of Iceland's best restaurants. There is a nice selection of cafes and eateries on and around Bárustigur. Petrol-station snack bars serve fast food, and there are plenty of grocery stores.

📖 The 1973 Eruption

Without warning, at 1.45am on 23 January 1973 a mighty explosion blasted through the winter's night as a 1.5km-long volcanic fissure split the eastern side of the island. The eruption area gradually became concentrated into a growing crater cone, which fountained lava and ash into the sky.

Normally the island's fishing boats would have been out at sea, but a force-12 gale had prevented them from sailing the previous afternoon. Now calm weather and a harbourful of boats allowed all but two to three hundred of the island's 5273 inhabitants to be evacuated to the mainland. Incredibly, there was just a single fatality (from toxic gases).

Over the next five months more than 30 million tonnes of lava poured over Heimaey, destroying 360 houses and creating a brand-new mountain, the red cinder cone Eldfell. One-third of the town was buried beneath the lava flow, and the island increased in size by 2.5 sq km.

As the eruption continued, advancing lava threatened to close the harbour and make the evacuation permanent – without a fishing industry, there would have been little way to survive on the island. In an attempt to slow down the inexorable flow of molten rock, firefighters hosed the lava with more than six million tonnes of cold sea water. The lava halted just 175m short of the harbour mouth – actually improving the harbour by creating extra shelter!

The islanders were billeted with friends and family on the mainland, watching the fireworks and waiting to see if they could ever go home. Two-thirds of the islanders eventually returned. Weird lava formations can still be seen close to some houses around town.

From left: Heimaey's harbour; Kittiwake colonies; Surtsey island (p128)

Slippurinn   Icelandic €€

(Map p132; ☑481 1515; www.slippurinn.com; Strandvegur 76; lunch 2400-7200kr, dinner mains 3700-4900kr, set menu 6400-9900kr; ⊙noon-2.30pm & 5-10pm early May–mid-Sep; 🛜) Lively Slippurinn fills the upper storey of a beautifully remodelled old machine workshop that once serviced the ships in the harbour and now has great views. The food is delicious Icelandic fare with a level of creativity that sets it above most restaurants in the country. Ingredients are exquisite, and combinations of fish, local produce and locally sourced meats divine.

Gott   Fusion €€

(Map p132; ☑481 3060; www.gott.is; Bárustigur 11; mains 1390-4800kr; ⊙11am-1pm Mon, to 9pm Tue & Sun, 11.30am-9pm Wed-Sat; 🌠) Fresh fusion food is done with care, using organic, healthy ingredients in this jolly wood-floored dining room with coloured chairs. Menu items range from goat's cheese and beetroot salad or avocado, hummus and pesto toast to spelt-wrapped grilled chicken. Plus vegan options.

Pítsugerðin   Pizza €€

(Map p132; ☑551 0055; Bárustígur 1; pizzas 1700-3200kr; ⊙11.30am-10pm) Top spot for a pizza. All pies are cooked in a wood-burning oven. Classic styles include margarita and calzone, plus some more bonkers flavours such as 'deluxe' lobster pizza and the 'pizza dessert' with Nutella, bananas and strawberries. Takeaway available.

Outdoor Festival

Three-day **Þjóðhátíð** (National Festival Þjóðhátíð Vestmannaeyjar; www.dalurinn. is; Dalvegur; ticket/ferry 23,900/1380kr) is the country's biggest outdoor festival. Held at Herjólfsdalur festival ground over the last weekend in July or the first weekend in August, it involves music, dancing, fireworks, a big bonfire, gallons of alcohol and a light display with an eruption of red torches, a nod to the island's volcanoes. Upwards of 17,000 people attend.

Tanginn   Icelandic €€

(Map p132; 414 4420; www.facebook.com/
tanginn.is; Básaskersbryggja 8; mains 2200-
3000kr; 11.30am-9.30pm Sun-Wed, to 1pm Thu,
to 2pm Fri & Sat;) With giant windows
looking onto the harbour and comfortable,
modern decor in slate and wood, Tanginn
makes for a fun stop for fresh fish, burgers,
crêpes, creative salads and the like. Dishes
are well presented and there's Icelandic
beer on tap.

Einsi Kaldi   Seafood €€€

(Map p132; 481 1415; www.einsikaldi.is; Vestmannabraut 28; mains 2900-7000kr; 5-10pm
Jun–mid-Sep, shorter hours mid-Sep–May;)
On the ground floor of Hótel Vestmannaeyjar, Einsi Kaldi is Heimaey's highest-end
dining experience, with well-crafted
seafood recipes and modern mood lighting.
The Vestmannaeyjar-born chef creates
dishes like monk fish or lobster or beef
tenderloin (all usually locally sourced), and
skyr (Icelandic yoghurt) panna cotta or lava
flow chocolate cake to finish.

ℹ INFORMATION

Tourist Information Centre (482 3683;
www.vestmannaeyjar.is; Strandvegur; 9am-
6pm Mon-Fri, 10am-4pm Sat, 1-4pm Sun;)
The summer tourist office is staffed by a local
cafe-bookshop.

ℹ GETTING AROUND

Heimaey is a small island. At roughly 8km long,
it's easily walkable, taking about 1½ hours to
walk from one end to the other. You can bring
your own wheels (bikes are allowed on the
ferry, and cars can drive onto the ferry with
pre-booking) or hire a **bike** (Map p132; 896
3340; https://visitwestmanislands.com/tours/
rent-a-bike/; Básaskersbryggja 8; 5/24hr bike
rental 3900/5900kr; hours vary) **at the ferry
landing at Heimaey.**

SNÆFELLSNES PENINSULA

Snæfellsnes Peninsula at a Glance...

Sparkling fjords, dramatic volcanic peaks, sheer sea cliffs, sweeping golden beaches and crunchy lava flows make up the diverse and fascinating landscape of the 100km-long Snæfellsnes Peninsula. The area is crowned by the glistening ice cap Snæfellsjökull, immortalised in Jules Verne's Journey to the Centre of the Earth. Good roads and regular buses mean that it's an easy trip from Reykjavík, offering a cross-section of the best Iceland has to offer in a very compact region.

Two Days in Snæfellsnes Peninsula

Grundarfjörður (p151) is the ideal gateway to the peninsula. Visit the **Saga Centre** (p151), take a selfie with **Kirkjufell** (p146) in the background and savour a seafood dinner at **Bjargarsteinn Mathús** (p151). Arrange a day trip to **Snæfellsjökull National Park** (p140), taking in a glacier tour and a walk on black-sand **Djúpalón Beach** (p142) to Malarrif Lighthouse.

Four Days in Snæfellsnes Peninsula

With four days you can delve deeper into **Snæfellsjökull National Park** with a tour of Vatnshellir lava tubes before exploring the scenic coastal route between between Grundarfjörður and **Stykkishólmur** (p148). Along the way make the short climbs up **Saxhöll Crater** (p146) and the holy mountain of **Helgafell** (p146).

Stykkishólmur Map (p149)
Snæfellsnes Peninsula Map (p150)

Arriving in Snæfellsnes Peninsula

Bus You can get between the Snæfellsnes Peninsula and Reykjavík (2½ hours) by changing in Borgarnes. Strætó buses then continue on to Stykkishólmur and Grundarfjörður. All services are greatly reduced in winter.

Ferry The reliable Baldur Ferry (p151) runs between Stykkishólmur and Brjánslækur in the Westfjords (2½ hours) via Flatey (1½ hours).

Where to Stay

You'll find high-quality guesthouse lodging around the coast of the entire peninsula, and there are a few campgrounds and larger hotels as well. Stykkishólmur has the full range of sleeping options: from a campground to guesthouses and a boutique hotel, while Grundarfjörður has a broad collection of guesthouses, excellent rental apartments and a basic campground.

Djúpalón Beach (p142)

Snæfellsjökull National Park

Indulge in your Jules Verne fantasies at Snæfellsjökull National Park, where the mammoth ice cap fills an ancient volcanic caldera.

Great For...

❶ Need to Know

(Map p150; ☎436 6860; www.snaefellsjokull. is)

★ Top Tip

Join a tour: you're not permitted to ascend the glacier without a local guide.

Snæfellsjökull National Park encompasses much of the western tip of Snæfellsnes Peninsula and wraps around the rugged slopes of the glacier Snæfellsjökull (pronounced sneye-fells-yo-kutl), the icy fist at the end of the long Snæfellsnes arm. Around its flanks lie lava tubes, protected lava fields, which are home to native Icelandic fauna, and prime hiking and coastal birdwatching and whale-spotting locations.

Snæfellsjökull

It's easy to see why Jules Verne selected Snæfell for his adventure *Journey to the Centre of the Earth*. The peak was torn apart when the volcano beneath it exploded and then collapsed back into its own magma chamber, forming a huge caldera. Among certain New Age groups, Snæfellsjökull is considered one of the world's great 'power centres'. Today the crater is filled with the ice cap (highest point 1446m) and is a popular summer destination.

Djúpalón Beach

On the southwest coast, Rte 572 leads off Rte 574 to wild black-sand beach **Djúpalónssandur** (Map p150). It's a dramatic place to walk, with rock formations (an elf church and a *kerling* – a troll woman), two brackish pools (for which the beach was named) and the rock-arch **Gatklettur**. Some of the black sands are covered in pieces of rusted metal from the English trawler *Eding*, which was shipwrecked here in 1948. An asphalt car park and public toilets allow tour-bus access, and crowds.

Down on the beach you can still see four lifting stones where fishing-boat crews would test the strength of aspiring fishermen. The smallest stone is Amlóði (Bungler) at 23kg, followed by Hálfdrættingur (Weak) at 54kg, Hálfsterkur (Half-Strong) at 100kg, and the largest, Fullsterker (Fully Strong), at 154kg. Hálfdrættingur marked the frontier of wimphood, and any man who couldn't heft it was deemed unsuitable for a life at sea.

A series of rocky sea stacks, some of which are thought to be a troll church, emerge from the ocean up the coast as you tramp north over the craggy headland to reach the black-sand beach at Dritvík. From the 16th to the 19th century Dritvík was the largest fishing station in Iceland, with up to 60 fishing boats, but now there are only ruins near the edge of the lava field.

Malarrif lighthouse

ⓘ Information

The **Visitor Centre** (Snæfellsjökull National Park Visitor Centre; ☏436 6888, 591 2000; www.snaefellsjokull.is; ☺10am-5pm late Apr-Oct, 11am-4pm Mon-Fri rest of year; ☏) FREE in Malarrif has maps and brochures, as well as displays on local geology, history, flora, fauna and customs.

Adventure Tours

The best way to reach the glacial summit is to take a tour.

Snæfellsjökull Glacier Tours
Snowmobile Tour

(Map p150; 865 0061; www.theglacier.is; Litli-Kambur; snowcat tour adult/child 7900/5000kr, snowmobile tour 18,000kr; May-Aug) Two-hour snowcat (truck with chain wheels) and snowmobile tours ascend the glacier to about 1410m.

Summit Adventure Guides
Adventure

(787 0001; www.summitguides.is) Offers much-loved 45-minute tours of the **Vatnshellir lava tube** (adult/child 3750kr/free). Guides shed light on the fascinating geological phenomenon and region's troll-filled lore. Helmet and torch included.

Dress warmly and wear hiking boots, and preferably gloves too. The outfit also runs myriad Snæfellsjökull glacier tours (13,900kr to 22,900kr) with a skiing option. They also have challenging fat-biking tours up **Rauðhóll volcano** (25,900kr).

☑ Don't Miss

About 2km south of Djúpalónssandur, a paved road leads down to the rocket-shaped lighthouse at **Malarrif**, from where you can walk 1km east along the cliffs to the rock pillars at Lóndrangar (an eroded crater; it also has its own parking off Rte 574), which surge up into the air in surprising pinnacles. Locals say that elves use the lava formations as a church. A bit further to the east lie the Þúfubjarg bird cliffs, also accessible from Rte 574.

Kirkjufell (p146)

Mountains & Sagas

Snæfellsjökull National Park is not the only stunning part of this peninsula. The scenic stretch between Stykkishólmur and Grundarfjörður is filled with myth and mystique, from spiritual mountains to saga-storied lava fields.

Great For...

❶ Need to Know

Visit the Saga Centre (p151) for information and maps.

★ **Top Tip**

Read up on the Icelandic sagas in advance.

Kirkjufell

Kirkjufell (Map p150; 463m), guardian of Grundarfjörður's northwestern vista, is said to be one of the most photographed spots in Iceland, appearing in *Game of Thrones* and on everyone's Instagram. Ask staff at the Saga Centre if you want to climb it; they may be able to find you a guide. Two spots involving a rope climb make it dangerous to scale when wet or without local knowledge.

Kirkjufell is backed by the roaring waterfalls, Kirkjufellsfoss; more camera fodder.

Saxhöll Crater

Southeast of the Öndverðarnes area, on Rte 574, follow the marked turn-off to the roadside scoria crater **Saxhöll** (Map p150), which was responsible for some of the lava in the area. There's a drivable track leading to the base, from where it's an uneven 300m climb for magnificent views over the enormous Neshraun lava flows.

Helgafell

About 5km south of Stykkishólmur, the holy mountain **Helgafell** (Map p150; 73m) was once venerated by worshippers of the god Þór. Although quite small, the mountain was so sacred in Saga times that elderly Icelanders would seek it out near the time of their death.

In the late 10th century, Snorri Goði, a prominent Þor worshipper, converted to Christianity and built a church at the top of the hill; its ruins remain. The nearby farm of the same name was where the conniving Guðrun Ósvífursdóttir of *Laxdæla Saga* lived out her later years in isolation. Her grave marks the base of the mount.

Rauðfeldsgjá

Just north of Arnarstapi and Stapafell, on Rte 574, a small track branches off to the stunning **Rauðfeldsgjá** (Map p150) – pronounced roith-felds-gyow – a steep, narrow cleft that mysteriously disappears into the cliff wall. Birds wheel overhead, a stream runs along the bottom of the gorge, and you can slink between the sheer walls for quite a distance. The gorge figures in a dramatic part of the local saga of Bárður, described on a sign at the parking area.

Hellnar

Bárður, the subject of *Bárðar saga Snæfellsáss,* was part giant, part troll and part human. He chose an area near Hellnar, a picturesque spot overlooking a rocky bay, as his home (called Laugarbrekka). Towards the end of his intense saga, he became the guardian spirit of Snæfell. Today Hellnar is a tiny fishing village (once huge)

Helgafell volcano

where the shriek of seabirds fills the air and whales are regularly sighted.

Berserkjahraun

According to *Eyrbyggja Saga,* long ago a farmer from Hraun grew weary of having to walk around the jagged lava flows to visit his brother at the farm in Bjarnarhöfn. Returning from a voyage to Norway, he brought back two berserkers – insanely violent fighters who were employed as hired thugs in Viking times – to work on his farm, but to his dismay one of the berserkers took a liking to his daughter. He turned to the local chieftain, Snorri Goði, for advice, but Snorri had his eye on the farmer's daughter as well and he recommended setting the berserker an impossible task. The farmer decided to promise the amorous berserker his daughter's hand in marriage if he was able to clear a passage through the troublesome lava field – surely impossible.

To the shock and horror of both Snorri and the farmer, the two berserkers quickly set to work and managed to rip a passage straight through the treacherous moonscape. Rather than honouring his promise, the farmer trapped the berserkers in a sauna and murdered them, allowing Snorri to marry his daughter.

Today a path through the **Berserkjahraun** (Map p150) can still be seen, and a grave was discovered containing the remains of two large men.

❶ Further Reading

The Complete Sagas of Icelanders, edited by Viðar Hreinsson, is a must for saga fiends. It's a summary translation of saga tales, featuring all the main yarns, along with a few shorter fantasy tales.

LOUIELEA/SHUTTERSTOCK ©

Stykkishólmur

The charming town of Stykkishólmur, the largest on the Snæfellsnes Peninsula, is built up around a natural harbour tipped by a basalt islet. It's a picturesque place with a laid-back attitude and brightly coloured buildings from the late 19th century.

◉ SIGHTS

Norska Húsið   Museum
(Map p149; Norwegian House; ☑433 8114; www.norskahusid.is; Hafnargata 5; adult/child 1000kr/free; ☺11am-6pm May-Aug, 2-5pm Tue-Thu Sep-Apr) Stykkishólmur's quaint maritime charm comes from the cluster of wooden warehouses, shops and homes around the town's harbour. Most date back about 150 years. One of the most interesting (and oldest) is the Norska Húsið, now the regional museum. Built by trader and amateur astronomer Árni Thorlacius in 1832, the house has been skilfully restored and displays a wonderfully eclectic selection of local antiquities.

Súgandisey   Island
The basalt island Súgandisey features a scenic **lighthouse** (Map p149) and grand views across Breiðafjörður. Reach it via the causeway at Stykkishólmur harbour.

Volcano Museum   Museum
(Map p149; Eldfjallasafn; ☑433 8154; www.eldfjallasafn.is; Aðalgata 8; adult/child 1000kr/free; ☺10am-5pm Jun-Aug, 11am-5pm Tue-Sat Sep-May) The Volcano Museum, housed in the town's old cinema, is the brainchild of vulcanologist Haraldur Sigurðsson, and features art depicting volcanoes, plus a small collection of interesting lava ('magma bombs') and artefacts from eruptions.

❸ ACTIVITIES

Stykkishólmur
Swimming Pool   Geothermal Pool
(Map p149; Sundlaug Stykkishólms; ☑433 8150; Borgarbraut 4; adult/child 900/300kr; ☺7am-10pm Mon-Thu, to 7pm Fri, 10am-6pm Sat & Sun Jun-Aug, shorter hours rest of year) Water slides and hot-pots are the highlights at the town's geothermal swimming pool in the municipal sports complex.

⊕ TOURS

Ocean Adventures   Wildlife Tour
(Map p149; ☑898 2028; www.oceanadventures.is; Sæbraut; ☺9am-6pm) Try your hand at angling (adult/child 11,000/9000kr) or go on a puffin-viewing tour (adult/child 7000/4500kr) with this popular outfit with a kiosk on the harbour.

Seatours   Boating
(Map p149; Sæferðir; ☑433 2254; www.seatours.is; Smiðjustígur 3; ☺8am-8pm mid-May–mid-Sep, 9am-5pm rest of year) Various boat tours, including the much-touted 'Viking Sushi': a one-/two-hour boat ride (6220/7700kr) taking in islands, bird colonies (puffins until August) and basalt formations. A net brings up shellfish to devour raw. Also offers dinner cruises and runs the Baldur Ferry (p151) to Flatey. Kids under 15 travel free.

⊜ SHOPPING

Gallerí Lundi   Arts & Crafts
(Map p149; ☑893 5588; Aðalgata 4a; ☺12.30-6pm May-Sep) Local handicrafts sold by friendly villagers. Also offers coffee.

Leir 7   Arts & Crafts
(Map p149; ☑894 0425; www.leir7.is; Aðalgata 20; ☺2-5pm Mon-Fri, to 4pm Sat) Artist Sigriður Erla produces beautiful ceramics from the fjord's dark clay at this pottery studio in the heart of town. There's also woodcraft by Lára Gunnarsdóttir.

✖ EATING

Nesbrauð   Bakery €
(Map p149; ☑438 1830; www.facebook.com/nesbraudehf; Nesvegur 1; snacks 400-1200kr; ☺7.30am-5pm, from 8am Sat & Sun) On the road into town, this bakery is a good choice for a quick breakfast or lunch. Stock up on sugary confections such as *kleinur* (traditional twisty doughnuts) or *ástar pungur* (literally 'love balls'; fried balls of dough and raisins).

Stykkishólmur

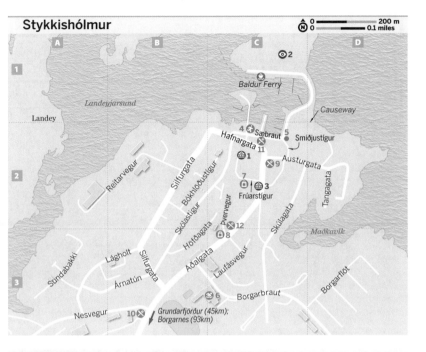

Narfeyrarstofa Icelandic €€

(Map p149; ☑533 1119; www.narfeyrarstofa.is; Aðalgata 3; mains 2000-5000kr; ⊙11.30am-10pm May-Sep, shorter hours Oct-Apr; ✍) This charming restaurant is the Snæfellsnes' darling fine-dining destination. Book a table on the 2nd floor for the romantic lighting of antique lamps and harbour views. Ask your waiter about the portraits on the wall – the building has an interesting history.

Sjávarpakkhúsið Icelandic €€

(Map p149; ☑438 1800; www.sjavarpakkhusid.is; Hafnargata 2; mains 2800-3500kr; ⊙noon-10pm;

🛜) This old fish-packing house has been transformed into a wood-lined cafe-bar with harbour-front outdoor seating. The speciality is blue-shell mussels straight from the bay. It's a great daytime hang-out too, and on weekend evenings it turns into a popular bar where locals come to jam.

Skúrinn International €€

(Map p149; ☑544 4004; Þvervegur 2; mains 1900-3200kr; ⊙noon-2pm & 6-9pm; 🛜) A casual spot for grabbing a pizza, burger, nachos, fish and chips, and beer, with a nice deck for sunny days.

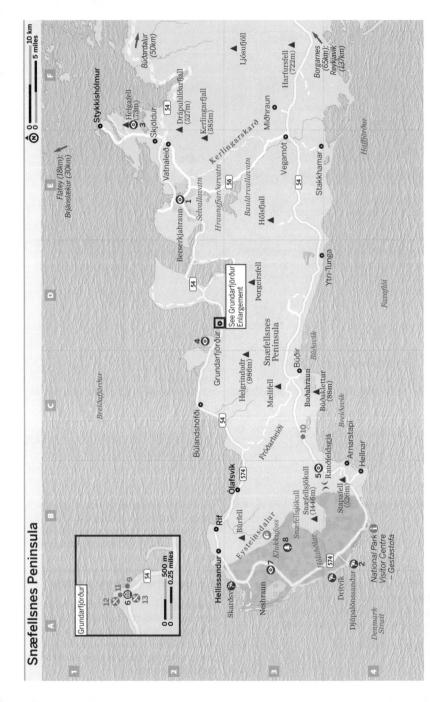

Snæfellsnes Peninsula

Flatey (18km);
Brjánslækur (30km)

Búðardalur
(50km)

Borgarnes
(65km);
Reykjavík
(137km)

Ljósufjöll

Harðursfell
(722m)

Stykkishólmur

Helgafell
(73m)
3
Skjöldur
Drápuhlíðarfjall
(527m)
Kerlingarfjall
(585m)
Miðhraun

Vatnaleið

54

Vegamót

Kerlingarskarð

Berserkjahraun

Selvallavatn

1

Hraunsfjarðarvatn

Bauðrvallavatn

Hólsfjall

56

Stakkhamar

54

Þorgeirsfell

See Grundarfjörður
Enlargement

Grundarfjörður

Ytri-Tunga

54

4

Snæfellsnes
Peninsula

Helgrindudr
(986m)

Búðir

Búðavik

Breiðabólstaðafjörður

Bárðavik

Búlandshöfði

Mælifell

Búðahraun

Búðaklettur
(88m)

54

Arnarstapi

10

Rauðfeldsgjá

Hellnar

Ólafsvík

574

Fróðárheiði

Breiðvík

Stapafell
(526m)

Rif

Bárðfell

Snæfellsjökull

5

Hellissandur

Eysteinsdalur

Klukkufoss

Snæfellsjökull
(1446m)

Hólahólar

574

Skarðsv

8

7

Neshraun

574

Dritvík

National Park
Visitor Centre
– Gestastofa

2

Djúpalónssandur

Denmark
Strait

Grundarfjörður

12
6
11
9
13

54

0   500 m
0   0.25 miles

0   10 km
0   5 miles

Snæfellsnes Peninsula

ⓘ GETTING THERE & AWAY

Baldur Ferry (☏433 2254; www.seatours.is) Car ferry between Stykkishólmur and Brjánslækur in the Westfjords (2½ hours) via Flatey (1½ hours). From June to August there are daily departures from Stykkishólmur at 9am and 3.45pm, returning from Brjánslækur at 12.15pm and 7pm. During the rest of the year there is only one ferry per day, leaving Stykkishólmur at 3pm (no boats on Fridays and Saturdays), returning at 6pm.

Grundarfjörður

Spectacularly set on a dramatic bay, little Grundarfjörður is backed by waterfalls and surrounded by ice-capped peaks often shrouded in cottony fog. More prefab than wooden, the town feels like a typical Icelandic fishing community, but the tourist facilities are good and the surrounding landscape can't be beaten, with its iconic Kirkjufell.

◉ SIGHTS

Saga Centre   Museum
(Map p150; Eyrbyggja Heritage Centre; ☏438 1881; www.grundarfjordur.is; Grundargata 35; ☺9am-5pm) FREE The Saga Centre is a tourist information centre, cafe, library, internet point and small museum rolled into one.

☺ TOURS

Láki Tours   Whale Watching, Wildlife
(Map p150; ☏546 6808; www.lakitours.com; Nesvegur 5) Láki Tours has excellent fishing, puffin-spotting and whale-watching trips from Grundarfjörður or Ólafsvík. Puffin tours from Grundarfjörður go to wonderful basalt island, **Melrakkaey**. Whale-watching

tours cover the area's best whale habitat; orca, fin, sperm, blue, minke and humpbacks are all possibilities.

Snæfellsnes Excursions   Bus Tour
(Map p150; ☏616 9090; www.sfn.is; Sólvellir 5; tours from 10,000kr) Private day trips around the major sites of Snæfellsnes Peninsula, from Stykkishólmur, Grundarfjörður and Ólafsvík. Also offers a Snæfellsjökull glacier tour (7900kr) departing from Arnarstapi.

✪ EATING

Café Emil   Cafe €
(Map p150; Kaffi Emil; ☏897 0124; www.facebook.com/pg/KaffiEmil; Grundargata 35, Saga Centre; mains 1200-2000kr; ☺9am-6pm; ☎) This cheery cafe is tops for cappuccinos, hot soup and sandwiches.

Bjargarsteinn Mathús   Seafood €€
(Map p150; ☏438 6770; www.facebook.com/Bjargarsteinnrestaurant; Sólvellir 15; mains 2800-4900kr; ☺4-10pm Jun-Aug, 5-9pm Sep–mid-Dec & mid-Jan–May; ☎) This superb waterfront restaurant is operated by seasoned restaurateurs who have created a lively menu of Icelandic dishes, with an emphasis on seafood and everything fresh. Desserts are delicious, and pretty too.

ⓘ GETTING THERE & AWAY

Strætó (p281) bus 82 Stykkishólmur–Hellissandur (920kr to Stykkishólmur, two daily mid-May to mid-September, continuing on to Arnarstapi once per day; the rest of the year it only goes from Stykkishólmur to Hellissandur four days per week).

SEYÐISFJÖRÐUR

Seyðisfjörður at a Glance...

If you visit only one town in the Eastfjords, this should be it. Made up of multi-coloured wooden houses and surrounded by snowcapped mountains and cascading waterfalls, super-picturesque Seyðisfjörður (pronounced 'say-this-fjurther') is the most historically and architecturally interesting town in East Iceland. It's also a friendly place with an international community of artists, musicians, craftspeople and students. The scenic Rte 93 drive from Egilsstaðir is a delight, climbing to a high pass then descending along the waterfall-filled river Fjarðará.

Two Days in Seyðisfjörður

Spend day one admiring the colourful houses on **Rainbow Street** (p165) then taking a **kayaking tour** (p159) on the fjord. In the evening hit the sushi bar at **Norð Austur** (p164). On day two hike up to **Tvísöngur** (p162) then spend the afternoon **boating** (p159) on the fjord or visiting the **Skaftfell – Center for Visual Art** (p163) and **technical museum** (p163).

Four Days in Seyðisfjörður

Drive north to **Borgarfjörður Eystri** (p160) for some hiking on the well-marked trails around the village. In summer, don't miss a visit to tiny **Hafnarhólmi** (p161) island, home to a large puffin colony. The following day, head to the dramatic **Dyrfjöll** (p161) mountain range for more hiking before returning to Seyðisfjörður for a dip in the local pool.

Previous page: Puffins
NINA B/SHUTTERSTOCK ©

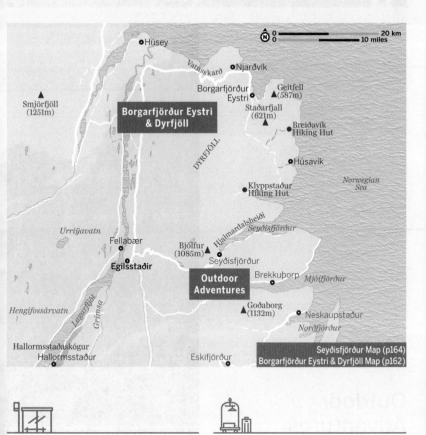

Seyðisfjörður Map (p164)
Borgarfjörður Eystri & Dyrfjöll Map (p162)

Arriving in Seyðisfjörður

Boat Smyril Line operates a weekly car ferry, the *Norröna*, on a convoluted year-round schedule from Hirsthals (Denmark) through Tórshavn (Faroe Islands) to Seyðisfjörður.

Bus SVAust (p165) runs a bus service between Egilsstaðir and Seyðisfjörður.

Where to Stay

Accommodation in town is of a high standard. Book well ahead for Wednesday nights in summer (the ferry to continental Europe leaves on Thursday mornings). If everything here is booked out, you may have to try Egilsstaðir, the main transport hub on the Ring Road (Rte 1), 27km west of Seyðisfjörður.

Waterfall in Vestdalur (p158)

Outdoor Adventures

Seyðisfjörður is a mini haven for outdoor adventure, whether kayaking on the fjord, hiking in the surrounding hills, skiing at Stafdalur or tackling the multiday trek to Borgarfjörður Eystri.

Great For...

ℹ **Need to Know**

The **Tourist Office** (📞472 1551; www.visitseydisfjordur.com; Ferjuleira 1; 🕘9am-5pm Mon-Fri May-Sep, 1-5pm Mon-Fri Oct-Apr) has information on booking tours.

☑ **Don't Miss**

Hiking in the scenic hills above
Seyðisfjörður.

Hiking

Short walking trails lead from the museum area uphill to waterfalls, and to the 'sound sculpture' Tvísöngur – five interconnected concrete domes. Another short walk leads from the road on the north shore of the fjord – about 6km beyond the Bláa Kirkjan (p162) – to the signposted **Dvergasteinn** (Dwarf Rock). According to folklore, this is a dwarf church that followed the people's church across the fjord.

The hills above Seyðisfjörður are the perfect spot for longer hiking. **Vestdalur** is a grassy valley north of town renowned for its glorious waterfalls. The hike begins just before the Langahlíð cottages. Following the Vestdalsá river, after two to three scenic hours you'll arrive at a small lake, **Vestdalsvatn**, which remains frozen most of the year (it's generally covered by snow until July).

Borgarfjörður to Seyðisfjörður Hike

Wildly wonderful and unexplored, the rugged country between Borgarfjörður and Seyðisfjörður makes for one of the best multiday hikes in the region.

To plan your journey, pick up a copy of the *Borgarfjörður Eystri & Víknaslóðir Hiking Map – Trails of the Deserted Inlets* (1000kr), and contact **Travel East Iceland** (Map p162; ☎471 3060; www.traveleast.is) or **Wild Boys** (☎864 7393; www.wildboys.is) if you're looking for a guide. For hiker huts along this route, see www.ferdaf.is.

In summer, **Icelandic Mountain Guides** (www.mountainguides.is) offers both a guided and a self-guided six-day package of this walk (called 'Hiking at the End of

Tvísöngur sculpture (p162)

the World') and arranges transfers, hut bookings etc. The complete trek is usually done over four days with overnight stops at campsites or trail huts.

Tvísöngur

A favourite walk takes explorers from a parking area south of Tækniminjasafn Austurlands (p163) about 15 or 20 minutes uphill to the 'sound sculpture' Tvísöngur (p162).

Other Activities

Kayaking

For a sublime outdoor experience, contact **Hlynur** (☑865 3741; hlynur@hotmail.de; Austurvegur 15b; ☺Jun-Aug), a charming Robert Redford–esque character who spends his summers around town and offers tailormade tours. Options on the fjord range from one to six hours, visiting a ship-

OLAF KRÜGER/ALAMY STOCK PHOTO ©

wreck or waterfalls (one/three hours 4000/8000kr). Experienced kayakers can choose longer trips (full day 25,000kr; minimum two people). Hlynur's tours begin from his base on the lagoon, behind Austurvegur.

Skiing

From about December to May there's downhill and cross-country skiing (and gear rental) at **Stafdalur** (Map p162; www.stafdalur.is; ☺5-8pm Tue-Fri, 11am-4pm Sat, 10am-4pm Sun Dec-May), 9km from Seyðisfjörður on the road to Egilsstaðir. Opening hours depend on the day's weather, with weekends being especially popular.

Boating & Fishing

Austursigling (☑899 2409; www.austursigling.is) takes passengers out on his 12-passenger boat. Standard tours are three hours (but shorter or longer trips can easily be arranged), and can take in sea angling, birdwatching, sunset, or Northern Lights hunting in winter. Contact Beggi to make arrangements – the price varies with numbers and trip duration (minimum is 15,000kr per hour for a small group).

From the small boat harbour, experienced fisherman Halli can take up to seven people in his boat for fishing and/or guided sightseeing around the fjord. Contact Seyðisfjörður Tours (p163) to make a booking.

🚶 Maps & Trails

Trails are marked on the widely available *Borgarfjörður Eystri & Víknaslóðir Hiking Map – Trails of the Deserted Inlets* map (1000kr), and the www.visitseydisfjordur.com website outlines some options, including the **Seven Peaks Hike** (trails climbing seven of the 1000m-plus peaks surrounding the town).

🚲 Mountain Biking

Seyðisfjörður Tours (p163) has mountain bikes for hire.

Hikers near Dyrfjöll mountains

ALLAN WATSON/SHUTTERSTOCK ©

Borgarfjörður Eystri & Dyrfjöll

The wee hamlet of Borgarfjörður Eystri, around 90km by road to the north of Seyðisfjörður, sits in a stunning location, framed by a backdrop of rugged rhyolite peaks and the spectacular Dyrfjöll mountains.

There's not much in the village itself, although driftwood sculptures, stories of hidden elves and crying seabirds exude a magical charm. As a bonus, this is one of Iceland's most accessible places for up-close viewing of nesting puffins. Hiking is the highlight here – this is the start or end point for the epic coastal Borgarfjörður to Seyðisfjörður hike (p158).

Hiking

There are loads of well-marked trails criss-crossing the area around Borgarfjörður – everything from easy one-hour strolls to serious mountain hiking. For a full array, get your hands on the *Borgarfjörður Eystri & Víknaslóðir Hiking Map – Trails of the Deserted Inlets* (1000kr). It's sold at most places in town, and also in Egilsstaðir visitor centres.

Great For...

☑ **Don't Miss**

Puffins on Hafnarhólmi.

- Njarðvík
- **Hafnarhólmi**
- **Stórurð**
- Borgarfjörður Eystri
- **Dyrfjöll Mountains**

❶ Need to Know

For local information, check out www. borgarfjordureystri.is.

✗ Take a Break

Stop by cafe-bar **Frystiklefinn** (Map p162; ☑846 0085; www.blabjorg.com; mains 1690-3200kr; ☺noon-10pm May-Sep, shorter hours winter; ☜) for fish stew or a beer.

★ Top Tip

For a post-hike soak, visit **Musterið Spa** (The Temple; Map p162; ☑861 1792; www. blabjorg.com; adult/child 3000/1000kr; ☺3-10pm or by appointment) at Blábjörg Guesthouse.

A good source of hiking information is the website of the Touring Club of Fljótsdalshérað: www.ferdaf.is. It has a summer program of walks and welcomes participants.

Dyrfjöll

One of Iceland's most dramatic ranges, the Dyrfjöll mountains rise precipitously to an altitude of 1136m between the marshy Héraðssandur plains and Borgarfjörður Eystri. The name Dyrfjöll means 'Door Mountain' and is due to the large and conspicuous notch in the highest peak – an Icelandic counterpart to Sweden's famous Lapporten.

There are walking tracks crossing the range, which allow for plentiful day hikes from Borgarfjörður Eystri. The prime draw in the range is the boulder-strewn oasis known as **Stórurð** (Map p162), an extraordi-

nary place scattered with huge rocks and small glacial ponds. The best time to hike the area is from mid-July (after snowmelt) to mid-September.

Contact Travel East Iceland (p158) in Borgarfjörður Eystri if you're looking for a guide or possible transfers to trailheads.

Hafnarhólmi

The photogenic small-boat harbour and islet of **Hafnarhólmi** (Map p162; www.puffins. is) is home to a large puffin colony. A staircase and viewing platforms allow you to get close to these cute, clumsy creatures (and other seabirds). The puffins arrive by mid-April and are gone by early to mid-August, but other species (including kittiwakes, fulmars and common eiders) may linger longer.

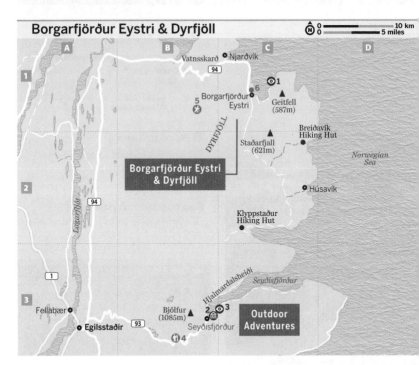

Borgarfjörður Eystri & Dyrfjöll

Seyðisfjörður Village

Seyðisfjörður is stuffed with 19th-century timber buildings, brought in kit form from Norway; several of these have been transformed into cosy ateliers where local artisans work on various projects. A quick loop around town will reveal half a dozen places to drop some krónur on art, handicrafts, knitwear and designer homewares.

◎ SIGHTS

Bláa Kirkjan   Church

(Map p164; Blue Church; www.blaakirkjan.is; Bjólfsgata 10) The star of many a tourist photo, the Blue Church has a dramatic mountain backdrop to add to its highly photogenic exterior. It's often locked, but opens for weekly summer concerts (p163).

Tvísöngur   Landmark

(Map p162) A favourite walk takes explorers from a parking area south of Tækniminjasafn

Austurlands about 15 or 20 minutes uphill to the 'sound sculpture' Tvísöngur, a concrete installation created by German artist Lukas Kühne. The piece comprises five interconnected domes of different sizes, and each is designed to resonate at a different harmonic.

Avalanche Monument Monument
(Map p164; Ránargata) The monument near the church dates from the 1996 avalanche, and is made from twisted girders from the factory demolished by the event. The girders were painted white and erected as they were found.

Skaftfell – Center for Visual Art Gallery
(Map p164; ☑472 1632; www.skaftfell.is; Austurvegur 42; ☺noon-6pm Jun-Aug, hours vary Sep-May) It's well worth a look in this gallery space above the Skaftfell Bistro. Skaftfell is a visual art centre with a focus on contemporary art, and it stages exhibitions and events, hosts workshops, and facilitates artist residencies.

Tækniminjasafn Austurlands Museum
(Map p162; www.tekmus.is; Hafnargata 44; adult/child 1000kr/free; ☺11am-5pm Mon-Fri Jun–mid-Sep) For insight into the town's fishing and telecommunications history, stop by this worthwhile technical museum. It's housed in two buildings on Hafnargata: the impressive 1894 home of Norwegian shipowner Otto Wathne (the old telegraph station), and a mechanical workshop from 1907.

🄶 TOURS
Seyðisfjörður Tours Tours
(Map p164; ☑785 4737; www.seydisfjordurtours.com; Norðurgata 6; ☺Jun–mid-Sep) From a central base, this friendly outfit offers bike rental and guided walking and hiking tours of the town and surrounds (lengths vary: the 75 minute 'Stories of Seyðisfjörður' is 4500kr; a two-hour easy scenic hike is 6000kr). Tailored biking and boating can be arranged. Confirm tour start times, as these also vary.

🄷 SHOPPING
Blóðberg Gifts & Souvenirs
(Map p164; www.blodberg.com; Bjólfsgata 4; ☺noon-6pm Tue-Fri, to 4pm Sat) Inside one of Seyðisfjörður's oldest houses, Erna hosts a pop-up shop in her living room, selling stylish Icelandic souvenirs including clothing, ceramics and skincare.

✪ ENTERTAINMENT
Blue Church Summer Concerts Live Music
(Map p164; www.blaakirkjan.is; Bjólfsgata 10; adult/child 2800kr/free) On Wednesday evenings from July to mid-August, the Bláa Kirkjan is the setting for a popular series of jazz, classical and folk concerts; see the website for the program. If you're leaving on the Thursday ferry, this is a lovely way to spend your final night in Iceland.

✖ EATING
There's a good array of options, including some high-quality restaurants serving fresh local produce.

Orkuskálinn Fast Food €
(Map p164; ☑471 2090; Hafnargata 2; meals 380-2200kr; ☺9am-9pm Mon-Fri, 11am-9pm Sat & Sun) The grill bar at the petrol station does fast-food regulars, as well as inexpensive hot lunch and dinner mains. As a completely unexpected treat; Pakistani food is served on Friday nights from 6.30pm to 8pm (thanks to the Pakistani owner).

Skaftfell Bistro International €€
(Map p164; ☑472 1633; http://skaftfell.is/en/bistro; Austurvegur 42; pizzas 1600-3500kr; ☺3-10pm; 🛜🖉🎮) This fabulous bistro-bar and cultural centre is perfect for chilling, snacking and/or meeting locals and artists. There's a short menu that changes weekly, plus popular pizza options (including 'reindeer bliss' and 'langoustine feast'). Be sure to check out the exhibitions in the gallery upstairs. Kitchen closes 9pm. Bookings recommended for larger groups.

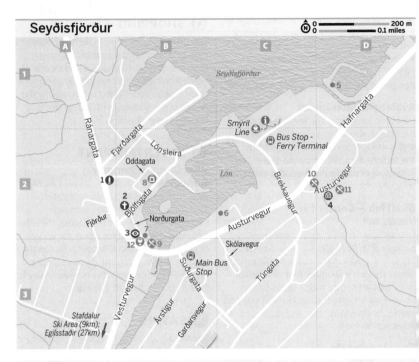

Seyðisfjörður

Norð Austur Sushi & Bar   Sushi €€

(Map p164; ☑787 4000; www.nordaustur.is; 2nd
fl, Norðurgata 2; small dishes 690-2190kr, maki
rolls 2190-2690kr; ⊙5-10pm Sun-Thu, to 11pm
Fri & Sat Jun-early Sep) Locals rave about this
place – and with good reason: the salmon,
trout and char come straight off the fishers'
boats and into the hands of accomplished
sushi chefs with international pedigree.
Set tasting menus offer excellent value

(five/seven courses for 6300/7500kr); the
decor is cool, as are the cocktails and sake.
Bookings recommended.

Nordic Restaurant   Icelandic €€

(Map p164; ☑472 1277; www.hotelaldan.is;
Norðurgata 2; lunch 1250-2650kr, dinner mains
2900-4600kr; ⊙noon-9pm; ☎) At the recep-
tion building for Hótel Aldan, coffee and
cakes are served all day in a country-chic

setting, and lunches feature the likes of goat's cheese salad or burger and fries. In the evening, flickering candles prettify the tables, and the menu showcases fine local ingredients (lamb, fish) with a contemporary touch. Dinner reservations advised.

🍸 DRINKING & NIGHTLIFE

Kaffi Lára – El Grilló Bar   Bar

(Map p164; 472 1703; Norðurgata 3; ⊘11am-1.30am Sun-Thu, to 3.30am Fri & Sat; 🛜) When you can't get a table elsewhere in town, there's usually space at this friendly, two-storey cafe-bar offering supremely tasty barbecue dishes and more than 20 different Icelandic beers. The must-try: El Grillo beer, brewed according to a recipe with a great backstory, and named after the bombed British tanker at the bottom of the fjord.

ℹ️ INFORMATION

The website www.visitseydisfjordur.com is invaluable.

Tourist office (472 1551; www.visitseydisfjordur.com; Ferjuleira 1; ⊘9am-5pm Mon-Fri May-Sep, 1-5pm Mon-Fri Oct-Apr) In the ferry terminal building, stocking local brochures, plus info on the entire country. Also open Tuesday mornings in winter (8am to noon) when the Smyril Line ferry docks, and during cruise-ship visits.

ℹ️ GETTING THERE & AWAY

BOAT

Smyril Line (Faroe Islands +298 345900; www.smyrilline.com; Ferjuleira 1) operates a weekly car ferry, the *Norröna*, on a convoluted year-round schedule from Hirsthals (Denmark) through Tórshavn (Faroe Islands) to Seyðisfjörður.

From mid-June to late August, the *Norröna* sails into town at 8.30am on Thursday, departing for Scandinavia two hours later. The rest of the year, the boat pulls in at 9am on Tuesday, leaving Wednesday at 8pm. Winter passage is possible

📷 Rainbow Street

Norðurgata street (Map p164) is supremely photogenic: a rainbow is painted on the pavement, and the Blue Church serves as a sweet backdrop. It features in many advertising campaigns and is a popular tourist photo opp.

MATTEO PROVENDOLA/SHUTTERSTOCK ©

(from October to March, departures are weather-dependent); see the website for more.

BUS

SVAust (893 2669, 472 1515; www.svaust.is) runs a bus service between Egilsstaðir and Seyðisfjörður (1080kr, around 45 minutes). Services operate year-round, one to three times daily from Monday to Saturday. An up-to-date schedule can be found on www.visitseydisfjordur.com or the site for SVAust.

The bus picks up from the **ferry terminal** only on ferry day; the main stop is outside the library on **Austurvegur**. In Egilsstaðir, the bus services the airport and campground.

ℹ️ GETTING AROUND

As well as offering walking, hiking and cycling tours, **Seyðisfjörður Tours** (p163) rents mountain bikes (one hour/half day 2000/4500kr).

VATNAJÖKULL
NATIONAL PARK

Vatnajökull National Park at a Glance...

Vatnajökull is the world's largest ice cap outside the poles. At 8100 sq km, it's more than three times the size of Luxembourg. Under this enormous blanket of ice lie countless peaks and valleys, including a number of live volcanoes and subglacial lakes, plus Iceland's highest point – the 2110m mountain Hvannadalshnúkur.

In 2008 the Vatnajökull National Park was formed when Jökulsárgljúfur National Park merged with Skaftafell National Park to the south, in an endeavour to protect the Vatnajökull ice cap and all of its glacial run-off under one super-sized reserve.

Two Days in Vatnajökull National Park

There are two very distinct sides to Vatnajökull, which means you can split your itinerary or spend more time in one place. Starting in the south you can easily spend two days exploring **Skaftafell National Park** (p170). There are numerous day hikes here, as well as overnight hikes with camping possible.

Four Days in Vatnajökull National Park

Your next two days can be spent at **Jökulsárgljúfur** (p176) in the far north. From Dettifoss in the south or Ásbyrgi in the north there are numerous day hikes and, in summer, free ranger-guided interpretive walks. A popular two-day hike is the 30km trail between Ásbyrgi and Dettifoss with an overnight camp at Vesturdalur.

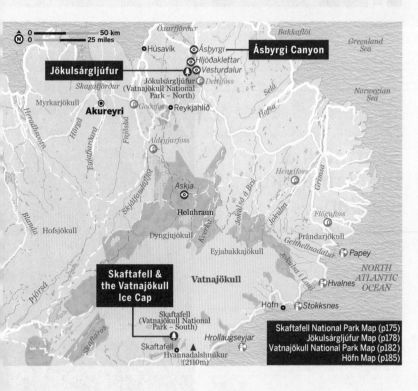

0 — 50 km
0 — 25 miles

Óxarfjörður

Bakkaflói

Greenland Sea

●Húsavík ◉Ásbyrgi

Ásbyrgi Canyon

◉Hljóðaklettar
◉Vesturdalur

Jökulsárgljúfur

Skagafjörður   Jökulsárgljúfur ◉Dettifoss
(Vatnajökull National Park – North)

Selá

Norwegian Sea

Myrkarjökull

Akureyri ◉Goðafoss●Reykjahlíð

Hofsá

Héraðsvötn

Hörgá

Eyjafjarðará

Fnjóská

Aldeyjarfoss

Skjálfandafljót

Hengifoss ◉

Grímsá

Askja ◉

Holuhraun

Jökulsá á Brú

Jökulsá

Flögufoss ◉

Blanda

Hofsjökull

Dyngjujökull

Kverká

Þrándarjökull

Geithellnadalur ◉ Papey

Þjórsá

Eyjabakkajökull

Jökulsá í Lóni

Dyngjujökull

Vatnajökull

NORTH ATLANTIC OCEAN

◉Hvalnes

Höfn ● ◉Stokksnes

Skaftafell (Vatnajökull National Park – South)

Skaftárós

Hrollaugseyjar

Skaftafell ▲
Hvannadalshnúkur (2110m)

Skaftafell & the Vatnajökull Ice Cap

Skaftafell National Park Map (p175)
Jökulsárgljúfur Map (p178)
Vatnajökull National Park Map (p182)
Höfn Map (p185)

Arriving in Vatnajökull National Park

Bus Skaftafell is a stop on Reykjavík–Höfn bus route and also a departure point for wilderness areas such as Landmannalaugar. In the north, bus services from Húsavík or Mývatn are less frequent.

Car It is mandatory for all visiting vehicles to pay parking fees at Skaftafell. In the north Rte 85 (sealed) takes you smoothly to the northern section of the park and the visitor centre at Ásbyrgi (from Húsavík it's 65km).

Where to Stay

Within the national park itself, camping is the only option. There's a campground in Skaftafell and hotels in nearby Hof or the larger town of Höfn. At Jökulsárgljúfur there's camping at Dettifoss, Vesturdalur and Ásbyrgi plus a few guesthouses in the surrounding area. Alternatively, make a base at Mývatn or Húsavík.

Svartifoss (p172)

Skaftafell & the Vatnajökull Ice Cap

Skaftafell is the jewel in the crown of Vatnajökull National Park, encompassing a breathtaking collection of peaks and glaciers, thundering waterfalls, rivers threading across the sandar, and the brilliant blue-white Vatnajökull.

Great For...

Vatnajökull

Skaftafell (Vatnajökull National Park – South)

Höfn

Skaftafell ▲ Hvannadalshnúkur (2110m)

❶ Need to Know

Skaftafellsstofa Visitor Centre (☎470 8300; www.vjp.is; ☉8am-7pm Jun-Sep, 9am-6pm Feb-May & Oct, 10am-6pm Nov-Jan; ☎) has an information desk and sells maps.

❶ Did You Know?

Note that from mid-June to mid-August, rangers usually guide free daily interpretive walks that depart from the visitor centre – a great way to learn about the area. Check the website or ask staff.

★ **Top Tip**
Stick to the marked paths to avoiding
damaging delicate plant life.

Skaftafell deserves its reputation, and few visitors – even those who usually shun the great outdoors – can resist it.

Walk & Hikes

Skaftafell is ideal for day hikes and also offers longer hikes through its wilderness regions. The park produces a good map outlining shorter hiking trails (350kr), and stocks larger topo maps from various publishers.

Most of Skaftafell's visitors keep to the popular routes on **Skaftafellsheiði**. Hiking in other accessible areas, such as the upper **Morsárdalur** and **Kjós** valleys, requires more time, motivation and planning. Before embarking on more remote routes, speak to the staff at the visitor centre, who are keen to impart knowledge and help you prepare, as well as make you aware of potential risks. You should enquire about river crossings along your intended route; you should also leave a travel plan at www. safetravel.is.

Other possibilities for hikes include the long day trip beyond Bæjarstaðarskógur into the rugged **Skaftafellsfjöll**. A recommended destination is the 862m-high summit of the **Jökulfell ridge**, which affords a commanding view of the vast expanses of **Skeiðarárjökull**. Even better is an excursion into the Kjós dell.

Svartifoss

Star of a hundred postcards, Svartifoss (Black Falls) is a stunning, moody-looking waterfall flanked by geometric black basalt columns. It's reached by a relatively easy 1.8km trail leading up from the visitor centre via the campground.

Ice cave, Skaftafell glacier

To take pressure off the busy trail to Svartifoss, park staff recommend you take an alternative path back to the visitor centre. From Svartifoss, continue west up the track to **Sjónarsker**, where there's a view disc that names the surrounding landmarks to help you get your bearings, plus an unforgettable vista across Skeiðarársandur. From here you can visit the traditional turf-roofed farmhouse **Sel**; this two-hour, 5.5km return walk (path S2) is classified as easy.

Alternatively, from Svartifoss head east over the heath to the viewpoint at **Sjónarnípa**, looking across Skaftafellsjökull. This walk (path S5/S6) is classified as challenging; allow three hours return (7.4km).

Skaftafellsjökull

A very popular trail is the easy one-hour walk (path S1; 3.7km return) to Skaftafellsjökull. The marked trail begins at the visitor centre and leads to the glacier face, where you can witness the bumps and groans of the ice (although the glacier is pretty grey and gritty here). The glacier has receded greatly in recent decades, meaning land along this trail has been gradually reappearing. Pick up a brochure that describes the trail's geology.

Skaftafellsheiði Loop

On a fine day, the five- to six-hour (path S3; 16.7km) walk around Skaftafellsheiði (Skaftafell Heath) is a hiker's dream. It begins by climbing from the campground to **Sjónarsker**, continuing across the moor to 610m-high **Fremrihnaukur**. From there it follows the edge of the plateau to the next rise, **Nyrðrihnaukur** (706m), which affords a superb view of Morsárdalur, and Morsárjökull and the iceberg-choked lagoon at its base. At this point the track turns southeast to an outlook point, **Gláma**, on the cliff

---

ⓘ Safety

When it comes to glaciers, the usual common-sense rules apply: don't get too close or walk on them without the proper equipment and guiding. The good news is that there is safe access to glaciated landscapes and a variety of walking trails that let you gape in wonder at glacier tongues and glacial lagoons (without the need to strap on crampons).

ANNA OM/SHUTTERSTOCK ©

🏃 Glacier Hikes & Climbing

The highlight of a visit to the southern reaches of Vatnajökull is a glacier hike. It's liberating to strap on crampons and crunch your way around a glacier, and there's much to see on the ice: waterfalls, ice caves, glacial mice (moss balls, not actual mice!) and different-coloured ash from ancient explosions. But take note: as magnetic as the glaciers are, they are also riven with fissures and are potentially dangerous, so don't be tempted to stride out onto one without the right equipment and guiding.

above Skaftafellsjökull. The route continues down to Sjónarnípa and then back to the campground.

Winter in Skaftafell

There has been a significant growth in winter travel to the region, with the strong draws of Northern Lights and ice caves (caves that form within the ice of a glacier, which become solid and safe for visiting in the coldest months). You can still do glacier walks in winter – and the glaciers look more pristine, taking on that blue hue so beloved by photographers. In the right conditions, Svartifoss freezes in January–February (on the flip side, in winter the falls are not always accessible, due to slippery, unsafe tracks). Between December and March, access to trails is weather dependent, and some may require crampons. There are also restricted daylight hours, so it pays to talk to park staff about your best options.

Ice Caves

In hot demand are winter visits to ice caves: glorious dimpled caverns of exquisite blue light, which are accessible (usually at glacier edges) only from around November to March – they can be viewed in cold conditions, and become unstable and unsafe in warmer weather. Temporary ice caves are created anew each season by the forces of nature, and are scouted by local experts. They *must* be visited with guides, who will ensure safety and correct equipment. As with glacier hikes, tours generally involve getting kitted out (crampons, helmets etc), then driving to the glacier edge and taking a walk to reach the destination. Reasonable fitness and mobility are required.

The largest and most accessible ice caves can become busy and crowded when tour groups arrive (from as far afield as Reykjavík). It is often the case that guided groups all visit the same cave – some tourists are disappointed to find queues of visitors waiting to enter. Catering to this, a few tour companies offer private tours to more remote caves: these tours are longer, more expensive, and generally require a higher level of fitness to reach.

Guides & Tours

Local Guide   Adventure

(☎894 1317; www.localguide.is; Freysnes) Local Guide is a family-owned business – the family has lived in the area for generations, so local knowledge is first-rate. Tours depart from the petrol station in Freysnes, about 5km from Skaftafell. From here, guides run year-round glacier hikes and ice climbs; the shortest tour offers one hour on the ice for adult/child 9490/8900kr (minimum age 10).

Arctic Adventures   Adventure

(Map p118; Glacier Guides; ☎562 7000; www.glacierguides.is) In addition to glacier walks of varying duration and difficulty, Arctic Adventures (formerly Glacier Guides) also offers ice climbing (24,990kr), plus wintertime ice-cave visits (adult/child 19,990/14,993kr) departing from Skaftafell and Jökulsárlón. The company's beginner-level glacier walk is the family-friendly 'Glacier Wonders', a 3½-hour tour with a one-hour walk on Falljökull (adult/child 10,750/5375kr; minimum age 10 years).

Icelandic Mountain
Guides   Adventure

(IMG; ☎Reykjavík 587 9999, Skaftafell 894 2959; www.mountainguides.is) IMG's best-selling walk is the family-friendly 'Blue Ice Experience', with 1½ to two hours spent on the ice (adult/child 10,900/7900kr, minimum age eight years). These tours run from Skaftafell four to eight times daily year-round. There are longer three-hour walks up the same glacier (16,900kr), and an option to combine it with an introduction to ice climbing (19,900kr).

☑ Don't Miss

For the best view of Skaftafellsjökull, Morsárdalur and the Skeiðarársandur, it's worth scaling the summit of **Kristínartindar** (1126m). The best way follows a well-marked 2km route (classified as difficult) up the prominent valley southeast of the Nyrðrihnaukur lookout, and back down near Gláma.

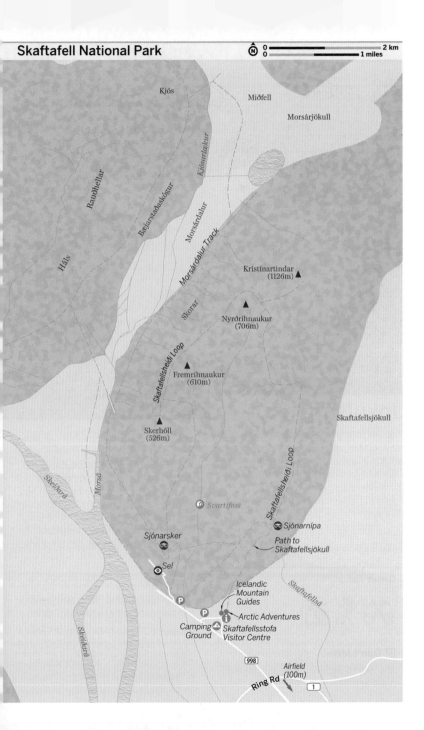

Skaftafell National Park

N 0 ————————————— 2 km
   0 ————————————— 1 miles

Kjós

Miðfell

Morsárjökull

Raudhellar

Kjósarlækur

Bæjarstaðaskógur

Morsárdalur

Háls

Morsárdalur Track

Kristínartindar
(1126m) ▲

Skorar

Nyrðrihnaukur
(706m) ▲

Skaftafellsheiði Loop

Fremrihnaukur
(610m) ▲

Skerhóll
(526m) ▲

Skaftafellsjökull

Sheiðará

Morsá

Svartifoss

Skaftafellsheiði Loop

Sjónarnípa

Path to
Skaftafellsjökull

Sjónarsker

Sel

Skaftafellsá

Icelandic
Mountain
Guides

P

P   i   Arctic Adventures

Camping   Skaftafellsstofa
Ground   Visitor Centre

Sheiðará

998

Airfield
(100m)

Ring Rd   1

Dettifoss

JOEL WUESTEHUBE/SHUTTERSTOCK ©

Jökulsárgljúfur

The Jökulsárgljúfur portion of Vatnajökull National Park protects a unique subglacial eruptive ridge and a 25km-long canyon carved out by the formidable Jökulsá á Fjöllum – the name literally means 'Glacier River Canyon'.

Jökulsá á Fjöllum starts in the Vatnajökull ice cap and flows just over 200km to the Arctic Ocean at Öxarfjörður. *Jökulhlaup* (flooding from volcanic eruptions beneath the ice cap) formed the canyon and has carved out a chasm that averages 100m deep and 500m wide. The canyon is well known for its waterfalls – Dettifoss is of course the most famous, but there are others.

Great For...

☑ Don't Miss

The hike to Dettifoss waterfall, Iceland's premier cascade.

The Park

Vatnajökull National Park's northern section can be roughly divided into three parts.

• **Ásbyrgi** The northern entry. A verdant, forested plain enclosed by vertical canyon walls. The visitor centre is here.

• **Vesturdalur** The middle section, with caves and fascinating geological anomalies.

Vesturdalur

MARTIN MEHES/SHUTTERSTOCK ©

Öxarfjörður

Húsavík

Jökulsárglúfur
(Vatnajökull National
Park – North) ○ ○ Dettifoss

Selá

Akureyri Reykjahlíð

❶ Need to Know

Gljúfrastofa Visitor Centre (📞470
7100; www.vjp.is; Rte 85, Ásbyrgi; ⊙9am-
6pm late May-Aug, 10am-4pm Sep-Oct,
shorter hours rest of year; 📶) has maps
and brochures.

✕ Take a Break

There's a shop on Rte 85 near the visitor
centre.

★ Top Tip

No buses currently serve Ásbyrgi, so
you'll need to arrange pick-up. Remember to log your hike with safetravel.is.

○ Dettifoss This mighty waterfall anchors
the park's southern entrance. From mid-
June to mid-August, rangers guide free daily interpretive walks that depart from the
parking place closest to Ásbyrgi canyon.

Dettifoss to Ásbyrgi Hike

The most popular hike in Jökulsárgljúfur is the two-day trip (roughly 30km)
between Dettifoss and Ásbyrgi, which
moves through birch forests, striking rock
formations, lush valleys and commanding vertical cliffs, while taking in all of the
region's major sights and offering awesome
canyon views.

The hike can be done in both directions;
however, the park rangers recommend
starting in Dettifoss and heading north.
Pick up information and a map from the
Gljúfrastofa Vsitor Centre in Ásbyrgi, or

download the map from the website and
consult with them over the phone.

The Dettifoss to Vesturdalur hike takes
an estimated six to eight hours. There are
two options on this stretch: the considerably more difficult route involves a steep
trail and a spectacular walk via the Hafragil
lowlands (18km); the easier takes a route
north of Hafragil (19.5km). The first trail is
not suitable for untrained hikers or people
afraid of heights.

On the second day of your walk, take
some trails around Vesturdalur's highlights,
then enjoy a leisurely hike to Ásbyrgi (12km,
three to four hours), opting for either the
rim of Ásbyrgi or walking along the Jökulsá
River. You'll return to hot showers at the
Ásbyrgi **campground** (📞470 7100; www.vjp.
is; site per adult/teen/child 1900/800kr/free;
⊙mid-May–Sep; 📶).

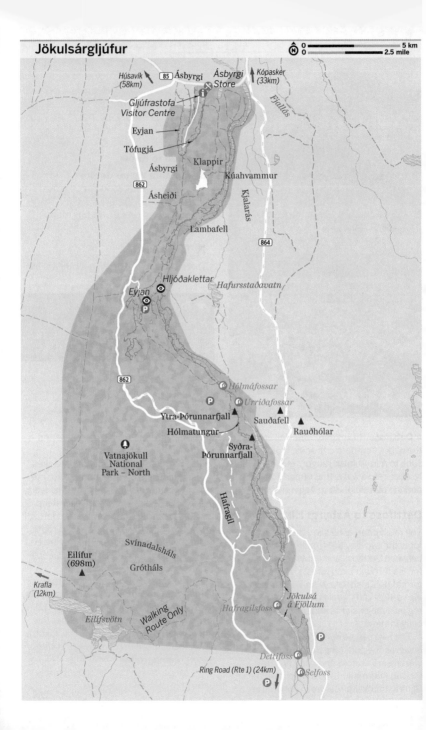

Jökulsárgljúfur

N
0 — 5 km
0 — 2.5 mile

Húsavík (58km)
85 Ásbyrgi
Ásbyrgi Store
Kópasker (33km)

Fjallás

Gljúfrastofa Visitor Centre

Eyjan

Tófugjá

Ásbyrgi
Klappir
Kúahvammur

862

Ásheiði

Kjalarás

Lambafell

864

Hljóðaklettar
Hafursstaðavatn

Eyjan
P

862

Hólmáfossar

Urriðafossar

P

Ytra-Þórunnarfjall
Sauðafell
Rauðhólar

Hólmatungur

Syðra-Þórunnarfjall

Vatnajökull National Park – North

Hafragil

Svínadalsháls

Eilífur (698m)

Grótháls

Krafla (12km)

Eilífsvötn

Walking Route Only

Jökulsá á Fjöllum

Hafragilsfoss

P

Dettifoss

Ring Road (Rte 1) (24km)
P

Selfoss

Fjaðrárgljúfur near Vatnajökull National Park

Ásbyrgi Canyon

Ásbyrgi Canyon

At the northern end of Vatnajökull National Park, the lush canyon Ásbyrgi extends in a massive horseshoe shape, measuring 3.5km from north to south and averaging 1km in width.

From the car park at the end of the access road, 3.5km south of the visitor centre, several easy short tracks lead through the forest to viewpoints of the canyon. Heading east the track leads to a spring near the canyon wall, while the western track climbs to a good view across the valley floor.

Creation of the Canyon

There are two stories about the creation of Ásbyrgi. The early Norse settlers believed that Óðinn's normally airborne eight-legged horse, Slættur (known in literature as Sleipnir), accidentally touched down on earth and left one hell of a hoof-print to prove it. The other theory, though more scientific, is also incredible. Geologists believe that the canyon was created by an enormous eruption of the Grímsvötn caldera beneath

Great For...

☑ Don't Miss

Hiking through the bizarre rock formations of Vesturdalur.

Hljóðaklettar

PEKY/SHUTTERSTOCK ©

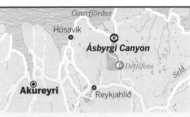

❶ Need to Know

Pick up maps and local tips at the **Gljúfrastofa Visitor Centre** (📞470 7100; www.vjp.is; Rte 85, Ásbyrgi; ⏰9am-6pm late May-Aug, 10am-4pm Sep-Oct, shorter hours rest of year; 📶).

✕ Take a Break

Ásbyrgi Store (📞465 2260; Rte 85; mains 900-2950kr; ⏰9am-10pm Jun-Aug, 10am-6pm Sep-May) sells groceries and simple meals.

★ Top Tip

The park map (350kr) is a useful 1:55,000 plan that ranks the local hikes by difficulty and is also available online.

distant Vatnajökull. It released a catastrophic *jökulhlaup* (glacial flood), which ploughed northward down the Jökulsá á Fjöllum and gouged out the canyon in a matter of days. The river then flowed through Ásbyrgi for about 100 years before shifting eastward to its present course.

Hiking

You can climb to the summit of **Eyjan**, the prominent outcrop at the centre of the canyon, from the Ásbyrgi campground (4.5km return), or take a trail from the visitor centre (from where it's easiest to take the route east along the golf course and turn south at the junction). This is also the northern end of the Dettifoss to Ásbyrgi hike (p177).

Vesturdalur

Off the beaten track and home to diverse scenery, Vesturdalur is a favourite destination for hikers. A series of weaving trails leads from the scrub around the campground to the cave-dotted pinnacles and rock formations of Hljóðaklettar, the Rauðhólar crater row, the ponds of Eyjan and the Jökulsárgljúfur canyon itself.

The bizarre swirls, spirals, rosettes, honeycombs and basalt columns at **Hljóðaklettar** (Echo Rocks) are a highlight of any hike around Vesturdalur and a puzzling place for amateur geologists. Dazzling concertina formations and repeat patterns occur throughout, and the normally vertical basalt columns show up on the horizontal here. A circular walking trail (3km) from the parking area takes around an hour to explore.

Vatnajökull National Park

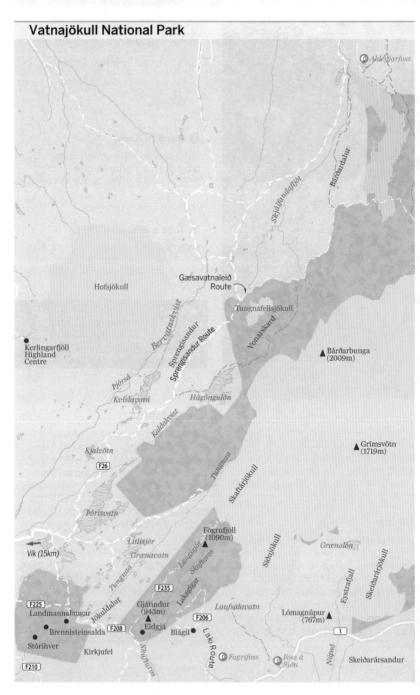

Aldeyjarfoss

Skjálfandafljót

Bárðardalur

Hofsjökull

Gæsavatnaleið
Route

Tungnafellsjökull

Vonarskard

Bárðarbunga
(2009m)

Berrugnskvisl

Sprengisandur
Sprengisandur Route

Kerlingarfjöll
Highland
Centre

Þjórsá

Kaldakvisl

Kvíslavatn

Hágöngulón

Grímsvötn
(1719m)

Kjalvötn

F26

Tungnaa

Skaftárjökull

Þórisvatn

Fögrufjöll
(1090m)

Síðujökull

Grænalón

Skeiðarárjökull

Vík (15km)

Lítlisjór

Grænavatn

Langisjór

Skaftáros

Eystrafjall

Tungnaá

Jökuldalur

F235

Lakagígar

Laufsálavatn

Lómagnúpur
(767m)

F225

Landmannalaugar

Gjátindur
(943m)

F208

Eldgjá

F206

Brennisteinsalda

Blágil

Laki Route

1

Stórihver

Kirkjufel

Skaftáros

Fagrifoss

Foss á
Síðu

Núpsá

Skeiðarársandur

F210

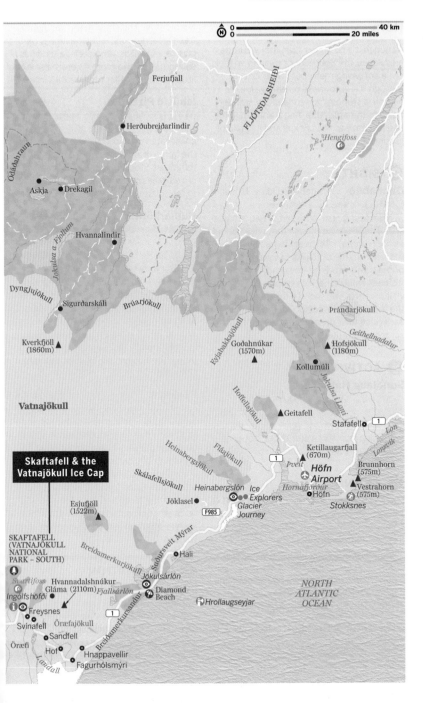

0 40 km
0 20 miles

Ferjufjall

FLJÓTSDALSHEIÐI

Herðubreiðarlindir

Hengifoss

Ódáðahraun

Askja   Drekagil

Hvannalindir

Jökulsá á Fjöllum

Dyngjujökull

Sigurðarskáli   Brúarjökull

Þrándarjökull

Geithellnadalur

Kverkfjöll
(1860m)

Goðahnúkar
(1570m)

Hofsjökull
(1180m)

Eyjabakkajökull

Kollumúli

Jökulsá í Lóni

Vatnajökull

Hoffellsjökull

Geitafell

Stafafell

Lón

Lónsvík

Heinabergsjökull

Fláajökull

Ketillaugarfjall
(670m)

Höfn
Airport

Þveit

Brunnhorn
(575m)

**Skaftafell & the
Vatnajökull Ice Cap**

Skálafellsjökull

Heinabergslón   Ice
Explorers
Glacier
Journey

Jöklasel

Hornafjörður

Höfn

Vestrahorn
(575m)

Stokksnes

Esjufjöll
(1522m)

F985

SKAFTAFELL
(VATNAJÖKULL
NATIONAL
PARK – SOUTH)

Svartifoss

Suðursveit   Mýrar

Hali

Breiðamerkurjökull

Jökulsárlón

Hvannadalshnúkur
Gláma (2110m) Fjallsárlón

Ingólfshöfði

Diamond
Beach

Hrollaugseyjar

NORTH
ATLANTIC
OCEAN

Freysnes

Svínafell   Öræfajökull

Breiðamerkursandur

Öræfi   Sandfell

Hof   Hnappavellir

Fagurhólsmýri

Landall

Höfn

Although it's no bigger than many European villages, the Southeast's main town feels like a sprawling metropolis after driving through the emptiness on either side. Its setting is stunning; on a clear day, wander down to the waterside, find a quiet bench and just gaze at Vatnajökull and its guild of glaciers.

◎ SIGHTS

Gamlabúð   Notable Building, Museum
(☑470 8330; www.vjp.is; Heppuvegur 1; ☺9am-7pm Jun-Aug, to 6pm May & Sep, to 5pm Oct-Apr) **FREE** The 1864 warehouse that once served as the regional folk museum has been moved from the outskirts of town to a prime position on the Höfn harbourfront. It's been refurbished to serve as the town's visitor centre, with good exhibits explaining the marvels of the region's flagship national park (including flora and fauna), and also screens documentaries.

✪ ACTIVITIES

Sundlaug Hafnar   Swimming
(☑470 8477; Víkurbraut 9; adult/child 900/200kr; ☺6.45am-9pm Mon-Fri, 10am-7pm Sat & Sun) The town's popular outdoor swimming pool has water slides, hot-pots and a steam bath.

✖ EATING

Hafnarbúðin   Fast Food €
(☑478 1095; Ránarslóð 2; snacks & meals 400-2600kr; ☺9am-10pm) A fabulous relic, this tiny old-school diner has a cheap-and-cheerful vibe, big breakfasts, a menu of fast-food favourites (hot dogs, burgers, toasted sandwiches) and a fine langoustine baguette – for the (relative) bargain price 2500kr. There's even a drive-up window!

Otto Matur & Drykkur   Icelandic €€
(☑478 1818; Hafnarbraut 2; mains 2890-5990kr; ☺noon-10pm) A new incarnation for the oldest house in Höfn (dating from 1897) has turned it into an elegant space high on Nordic style. The small menu spotlights fresh local produce – langoustine is here, of course, as well as simple, elegant dishes of salmon, lamb and more. There's also a cool little bar in the cellar (open until 1am).

Íshúsið Pizzeria   Pizza €€
(☑478 1230; http://ishusidpizzeria.is; Heppuvegur 2a; pizzas 1950-3500kr; ☺noon-10pm) In an elevated position by the harbour, the family-friendly Ice House doles out thin-crust, stone-baked pizzas with crowd-pleasing toppings, from Hawaiian to the 'lobster festival'.

Humarhöfnin   Icelandic €€€
(☑478 1200; www.humarhofnin.is; Hafnarbraut 4; mains 2900-7900kr; ☺noon-10pm May-Sep, to 9pm Oct-Nov) Humarhöfnin offers 'Gastronomy Langoustine' in a cute, cheerfully Frenchified space with great attention to detail: chequerboard tiled floor and herb pots on the windowsills. Mains that centre on pincer-waving critters cost around 7000kr, but there are also more budget-friendly dishes including a fine langoustine baguette (3900kr) or pizza (2900kr).

Pakkhús   Icelandic €€€
(☑478 2280; www.pakkhus.is; Krosseyjarvegur 3; mains 3100-6790kr; ☺noon-10pm) Hats off to a menu that tells you the name of the boat that delivers its star produce. In a stylish harbourside warehouse, Pakkhús offers a level of kitchen creativity you don't often find in rural Iceland. First-class local langoustine, lamb and duck tempt taste buds, while clever desserts end the meal in style; who can resist a dish called '*skyr volcano*'?

ℹ INFORMATION

Gamlabúð Visitor Centre (☑470 8330; www.visitvatnajokull.is; Heppuvegur 1; ☺9am-7pm Jun-Aug, to 6pm May & Sep, to 5pm Oct-Apr) Harbourfront Gamlabúð houses a national-park visitor centre with excellent exhibits, local tourist information and maps for sale. Ask about activities and hiking trails in the area.

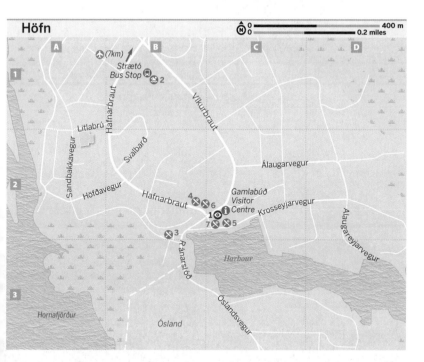

Höfn

❶ GETTING THERE & AWAY

Höfn is about 6km south of the Ring Road (Rte 1) on Rte 99. The nearest towns in either direction are Kirkjubæjarklaustur, 200km west, and Djúpivogur, 105km east.

AIR

Höfn's **airport** (www.isavia.is; Hwy 1) is 6.5km northwest of town. Eagle Air (www.eagleair.is) flies year-round between Höfn and Reykjavík Domestic Airport (ie not Keflavík International Airport). One-way fare from 20,000kr.

BUS

Strætó (☐540 2700; www.straeto.is) services pick up and drop-off from a **bus stop** (Vikurbraut 9) out the front of the swimming pool. Its bus 51 to/from Reykjavík (13,340kr, seven hours, two daily) stops at Jökulsárlón, Skaftafell, Kirkjubæjarklaustur, Vík, Skógar, Hvolsvöllur, Hella and Selfoss.

AKUREYRI

Akureyri at a Glance...

Akureyri stands strong as Iceland's second city, but a Melbourne, Manchester or Montréal it is not. And how could it be with only 18,600 residents? It's a wonder the city (a 'town' anywhere else) generates this much buzz. Expect cool cafes, quality restaurants, a handful of art galleries and even some late-night bustle – a far cry from other rural Icelandic towns. Akureyri nestles at the head of Eyjafjörður, Iceland's longest fjord (60km), at the base of snowcapped peaks. In summer flowering gardens belie the location, just a stone's throw from the Arctic Circle.

Two Days in Akureyri

Take a stroll along the seafront path before investigating Akureyri's trio of museums and the landmark **church** (p204). Spend a leisurely couple of hours in **Lystigarðurinn** (p204), the world's most northerly botanical gardens, then book a table at **Strikið** (p209). Later hit the streets to sample the local nightlife. On day two, either head to the ski slopes (winter) or line up some hiking, horse riding or golf (summer) or a boat tour to Eyjafjörður.

Four Days in Akureyri

Time to get out of the city for a morning of spectacular **whale watching** (p194) at Húsavík and a visit to Húsavík's engrossing whale museum. You'll be back in Akureyri in time for dinner at **Rub23** (p210) and a nightcap at **Ölstofa Akureyrar** (p211). Day four should be set aside for a day trip to **Grímsey** (p200) island, where you can spot puffins and other seabirds.

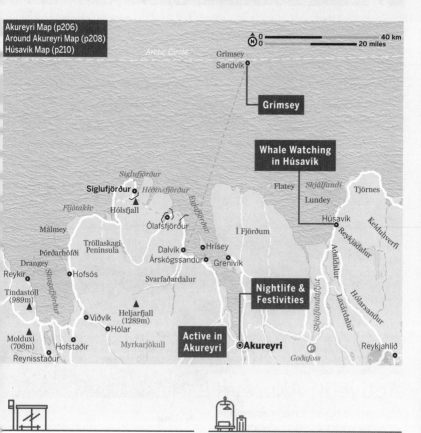

Akureyri Map (p206)
Around Akureyri Map (p208)
Húsavík Map (p210)

Arctic Circle

0 —— 40 km
0 —— 20 miles

Grímsey
Sandvík

Grímsey

Whale Watching in Húsavík

Siglufjörður
Siglufjörður Héðinsfjörður
Hólsfjall

Flatey Skjálfandi Tjörnes
Lundey
Húsavík Reykjadalur

Fljótaklv

Málmey
Tröllaskagi
Þórðarhöfði Peninsula
Drangey
Reykir
Tindastóll
(989m)

Ólafsfjörður Í Fjörðum
Eyjafjörður
Dalvík Hrísey
Árskógssandur Grenivík
Svarfaðardalur

Aðaldalur

Hólarsandur Keldhverfi
Laxárdalur
Skjálfandafljót

Nightlife & Festivities

Hofsós
Víðvík Heljarfjall
(1289m)
Hólar
Molduxi
(706m) Hofstaðir Myrkarjökull
Reynisstaður

Active in Akureyri **Akureyri**

Godafoss

Reykjahlíð

Arriving in Akureyri

Akureyri Airport Around 3km south of the city centre. Air Iceland Connect runs flights up to eight times daily between Akureyri and Reykjavík's domestic airport (45 minutes).

Bus Akureyri is the hub for bus travel in the North, provided by Strætó from a bus stop in front of Hof, with one summer route by SBA-Norðurleið.

Where to Stay

Akureyri's accommodation scene has undergone a transformation in recent years, with a slew of new, high-quality options. The town still fills up in summer so book ahead. There are plenty of options outside the town centre – Akureyri is surrounded by excellent rural farmstay properties (you'll need your own car for these). Consult Hey Iceland (www.heyiceland.is). Húsavík is an alternative accommodation base.

Hlíðarfjall

ARCTIC-IMAGES/GETTY IMAGES ©

Active in Akureyri

Akureyri is a base for many adventures, including winter skiing at Iceland's premier downhill slope, hiking, diving in Eyjafjörður, horse riding and midnight golf. Numerous adventure tour agents can organise trips from snowmobiling to hot-pot-hopping.

Great For...

☑ Don't Miss

Floodlit skiing down Iceland's longest slopes in the winter darkness.

Skiing

Iceland's premier downhill ski slope, **Hlíðarfjall Ski Centre** (Map p208; ☑462 2280; www.hlidarfjall.is; Rte 837; day pass adult/child 4900/1400kr;), is 5km west of town. The resort has a vertical drop of 537m; and a recently added lift has increased the longest trail to over 2.6km. There are eight lifts, 23 alpine slopes and also cross-country ski routes.

In the long hours of winter darkness, all of the main runs are floodlit.

There's ski and snowboard rental, two restaurants and a ski school. In season, buses usually connect the site with Akureyri; check the website for details and www.skiiceland.is for great passes.

In winter the **Kjarnaskógur** (Map p208;) forest is good for cross-country skiing (there's a 7km trail with lighting).

Hiking

For information on hiking in the area, contact **Ferðafélag Akureyrar** (Map p206; Touring Club of Akureyri; ☎462 2720; www.ffa.is; Strandgata 23; ☺2-5pm Mon-Fri May-Aug, 11am-1pm Mon-Fri Sep-Apr). Its website details (in English) the huts it operates in northern Iceland and the highlands, plus has notes on the Askja Trail and its program of hiking and skiing tours that travellers can join.

A pleasant but demanding day hike leads up the Glerárdalur valley to the summit of **Mt Súlur** (1213m). The trail begins on Súluvegur, a left turn off Þingvallastræti just before the Glerá bridge. Give yourself at least six hours to complete the return journey.

Golf

Up for a game of midnight golf? Only a few degrees south of the Arctic Circle, Akureyri's par-71 **Jaðarsvöllur** (Map p208; ☎462 2974; www.golficeland.org; Jaðar; per round 8500kr; ☺mid-May–Oct) basks in lengthy daylight from June to early August, and you can book ahead for the midnight tee-off. Clubs and trolleys can be hired. The course is home to the annual 36-hole **Arctic Open** (www.arcticopen.is), a tournament played under midnight sun over two nights in late June.

Horse Riding

Skjaldarvík (Map p208; ☎552 5200; www.skjaldarvik.is; horse rides from 11,900kr, buggy tours s/d 23,900/38,800kr) offers a couple of top-notch activities from its scenic fjordside locale 6km north of town: horse-riding tours (one hour) run along the fjord and into the surrounding hills, or you can take a fun, adrenaline-pumping buggy ride.

Nightlife & Festivities

Akureyri may be small by international standards, but it's second only behind Reykjavík for a good night out on the town as far as Iceland is concerned. An evening stroll down Hafnarstræti will present you with a few good options, and a chance to see where the crowds are.

Great For...

🍴 🍽️ 🍷🍸 ✨

☑ Don't Miss

Local beers at Ölstofa Akureyrar (p211).

Eating Out

Cafes and restaurants abound in Akureyri, but it pays to make dinner reservations in advance. Start the day with breakfast at timber-lined Berlin (p208), where you can linger over coffee and waffles. A good afternoon choice is Blaá Kannan (p208), the much-loved 'Blue Teapot' cafe with lunchtime specials.

In the evening, enjoy international and Icelandic specialities at Strikið (p209), or go for quality seafood dishes at quirky Noa Seafood Restaurant (p209).

On the Town

Your night out could begin at Götubarinn (p211), a local favourite, before moving on to Ölstofa Akureyrar (p211), the best place in town for draught beers thanks to its partnership with local brewery Einstök.

Call into the surprisingly convivial bar at
Akureyri Backpackers (p211), loved by
locals and travellers alike. Perhaps complete your night at cocktail bar Café Amour
(p211) – the upstairs club draws a crowd
on Friday and Saturday when it's open till
4am.

Festivals

Akureyri's biggest summertime fiesta is
Akureyri Town Festival, celebrating the
city's birthday on the last weekend of August with concerts, exhibitions and events.
Over six weeks from mid-July into August,
Akureyri celebrates the **Summer Arts Festival** (Listasumar; www.listasumar.is) with
exhibitions, events and concerts.

Golfers converge on Akureyri in June
for the annual 36-hole **Arctic Open** (www.
arcticopen.is).

Things don't stop in winter up here –
Akureyri is Iceland's winter-sports capital.
During the Iceland **Winter Games** (www.
icelandwintergames.com), snowy activities
take centre stage, including international
freeskiing and snowboarding competitions.
Tour operators offer ways to get out into
gloriously wintry landscapes (such as dog
sledding, snowmobiling, and super-Jeep or
helicopter tours).

Whale Watching in Húsavík

Iceland's whale-watching capital is Húsavík, around 92km northeast of Akureyri, where sightings are near-guaranteed between June and August. There are also whale-watching opportunities in Eyjafjörður and from the hamlet of Hauganes.

Great For...

ⓘ Need to Know

The best time to see whales is between June and August. Check www.visithus avik.is for info.

★ **Top Tip**

Consider taking an early-morning or evening cruise (bus groups visit in the middle of the day).

Whales of Húsavík

The first to arrive are humpback whales (*Megaptera novaeangliae*) and minke whales (*Balaenoptera acutorostrata*). The humpback whale is known for its curious nature, equanimity and spectacular surface displays, whereas the minke whale is famous for its elegant features: a streamlined and slender black body and white-striped pectoral fin.

Several minke and humpback whales stay in the bay throughout the year, but most migrate south during winter, returning again and again. The enormous blue whale (*Balaenoptera musculus*), undoubtedly the most exciting sight in Skjálfandi, usually starts coming in mid-June and stays until the middle of July.

Other summer sightings in Skjálfandi include the orca, also known as the killer whale (*Orcinus orca;* some come to the bay to feed on fish, others come to hunt mammals), northern bottlenose whales (*Hyperoodon ampullatus;* a mysterious, deep-diving beaked whale), fin whales (*Balaenoptera physalus*), sei whales (*Balaenoptera borealis*), pilot whales (*Globicephala melas*) and sperm whales (*Physeter macrocephalus*).

Húsavík Whale Museum

The excellent **Húsavík Whale Museum** (Hvalasafnið; Map p210; ☎414 2800; www.whalemuseum.is; Hafnarstétt 1; adult/child 1900/500kr; ☉9am-6pm May-Sep, shorter hours rest of year) provides all you need to know about the impressive creatures that visit Skjálfandi bay. Housed in an old harbourside slaughterhouse, the museum interprets the ecology and habits of whales, conservation

Húsavík

and the history of whaling in Iceland through beautifully curated displays, including several huge skeletons (they're real).

Whale-Watching Tours

Although there are other Iceland locales where you can do whale-watching tours (Reykjavík and Eyjafjörður), Húsavík has become Iceland's premier whale-watching destination, with up to 11 species coming here to feed in summer.

CANADASTOCK/SHUTTERSTOCK ©

Four whale-watching companies operate from Húsavík harbour. Don't stress *too* much over picking an operator; prices are similar and services comparable for standard three-hour tours (warm overalls supplied). When puffins are nesting (roughly mid-April to mid-August), all companies offer tours combining whale watching with a sail past puffin-thronged Lundey.

Where the differences are clear, however, is in the excursions that go beyond the standard. **North Sailing** (Map p210; ☑464 7272; www.northsailing.is; Garðarsbraut; 3hr tours adult/child 10,500/3500kr) has an atmospheric old schooner and hoists sails when conditions are right. **Gentle Giants** (Map p210; ☑464 1500; www.gentlegiants. is; Garðarsbraut; 3hr tours adult/child 10,400/4400kr) can zoom between points in a high-speed rigid inflatable boat (RIB), and has a tour that takes in idyllic Flatey.

Trips depart throughout the day (June to August) from around 8am to 8pm, and large signs at the ticket booths advertise the next departure time. Boats also run frequently in April, May, September and October, but drop way off in March, November and December. In winter, boats operate as Northern Lights cruises. You can't miss the offices on the waterfront.

● **Ambassador** (Map p206; ☑462 6800; www. ambassador.is; Torfunefsbryggja dock; 3hr tour adult/child 10,990/5495kr) Ambassador has a growing range of tours on Eyjafjörður, from three-hour whale-watching cruises to fast-paced explorations on RIBs (rigid inflatable boats; two hours, adult 19,990kr). Also runs winter Northern Lights cruises, though sightings cannot be guaranteed.

● **Elding** (Map p206; ☑519 5000; www. elding.is; Akureyri harbour; 3hr tour adult/child 10,990/5495kr) From a base on the harbour behind the Hof cultural centre, Reykjavík company Elding operates a three-hour whale-watching cruise, with year-round sailings, plus an 'express tour' on a RIB (20,000kr per person; no children under 10) from April to September. They also have a Northern Lights tour in winter.

○ **Whale Watching Hauganes** (Map p208;
📞 867 0000; www.whales.is; Hafnargata 2,
Hauganes; 3hr tour adult/child 9900/4500kr;
🕑 May–mid-Nov) From the hamlet of
Hauganes, climb aboard one of two oak
former fishing boats for a carbon-neutral
adventure that includes fishing and whale
watching (this is Iceland's oldest whale-
watch operator).

Other Tours

○ **Fjallasýn** (📞 464 3941; www.fjallasyn.is) This
well-established Húsavík-based company
does tours in the area – day or multiday,
4WD, hiking, birdwatching etc – both in
Húsavík and further afield to various parts
of northeast Iceland and the highlands.

○ **Húsavík Adventures** (Map p210; 📞 853
4205; www.husavikadventures.is; Garðarsbraut
5; 2hr RIB tours adult/child 17,900/11,900kr)
This company offers racy two-hour RIB
tours, three to seven times a day from May
to September and partners with Mývatn
Activity – Hike&Bike (p102) to offer ATV
tours year-round.

○ **Saltvík Horse Farm** (Map p208; 📞 847
9515; www.saltvik.is; Rte 85; 2hr tours 9900kr)
Two-hour coastal rides with glorious
views over Skjálfandi bay are available at
Saltvík Horse Farm, 5km south of Húsavík.
No special riding experience is required.
Saltvík also offers week-long rides (around
Mývatn, into the more-remote northeast, or
along the highland Sprengisandur route),
plus farmhouse accommodation.

Not Just Whales

Don't rush off after your whale-watching
trip; beautiful Húsavík has a few surprises
up its sleeve.

○ **Húsavíkurkirkja** (Map p210; 📞 464 1317;
www.husavikurkirkja.is; Garðarsbraut 9a; 🕑 9am-
5pm) Húsavík's beloved church is quite
different from anything else seen in Iceland.
Constructed in 1907 from Norwegian
timber, the delicately proportioned red-
and-white church would look more at home
in the Alps. Its cruciform shape becomes
apparent inside and is dominated by a

depiction of the resurrection of Lazarus
(from lava) on the altarpiece. It's open most
days in summer.

○ **Skrúðgarður** (Map p210) A walk along the
duck-filled stream of the endearing town
park, which is as scenic as the waterfront
area, offers a serene break. Access is via
a footbridge on Ásgarðsvegur, or beside
Árból guesthouse.

○ **Culture House** (Safnahúsið; Map p210;
📞 464 1860; www.husmus.is; Stórigarður 17;
adult/child 1000kr/free; 🕑 10am-6pm Jun–mid-
Sep, to 4pm Mon-Fri mid-Sep–May) A folk, maritime and natural-history museum rolled
into one, the Culture House is one of the
North's most interesting regional museums.
'Man and Nature' nicely outlines a century
of life in the region, from 1850 to 1950 (lots
of local flavour), while the stuffed animals

Whale watching near Húsavík

include a frightening-looking hooded seal, and a polar bear that was welcomed to Grímsey in 1969 with both barrels of a gun.

Exploration Museum (Map p210; ☑464 2328; www.explorationmuseum.com; Héðinsbraut 3; adult/child 1000/500kr; ☺2-6pm Jun-Aug, noon-3pm Sep, by appointment rest of year) Opened in 2014, this museum salutes the history of human exploration, covering Viking voyages and polar expeditions, but its most notable exhibition focuses on the Apollo astronauts in Iceland in the 1960s, who received geology training in the lunar-like landscapes near Askja.

GeoSea (Map p208; ☑860 0202; www.geosea.is; Vitaslóð 1; adult/child 4300/1800kr; ☺9am-midnight May-Sep, noon-10pm Oct-Apr) Brand-new salt-water spa GeoSea fills the point near the lighthouse on the north edge of town, looking over the broad bay and the snow-capped peaks across the way. Geothermally heated sea water fills pools with perfectly warm (38° to 39°C) soaking waters. The modern cafe allows for ocean-view dining.

ⓘ Need to Know

Strætó (☑540 2700; www.straeto.is) services (departing from the N1 service station) include bus 79 to Akureyri (2760kr, 1¼ hours, three daily Monday to Friday, one Saturday, two Sunday).

🚗 Driving to Húsavík

From the Ring Road there are two options to head north to Húsavík: Rte 85 is the shorter route, covering 45km. From northern Mývatn, take Rte 87 55km north. Note that Rte 87 is partially gravel, but fine for small cars.

RNDMS/SHUTTERSTOCK ©

Puffin

OLEG SENKOV/SHUTTERSTOCK ©

Grímsey

Best known as Iceland's only true piece of the Arctic Circle, the remote island of Grímsey, 40km from the mainland, is a serene little place where birds outnumber people by about 10,000 to one. The island is small (5 sq km) but the welcome is big and the relaxation deep.

Great For...

☑ **Don't Miss**

Diving or snorkelling with the swooping seabirds.

Visiting Grímsey

Grímsey's appeal to many lies in what it represents. Tourists flock here to snap up their 'I visited the Arctic Circle' certificate and appreciate its windswept setting. Though the Arctic Circle is shown on maps at a fixed 66.5°, it actually moves with the wobble of the Earth's tilt (2.4° every 40,000 years). As of 2017, a 7980kg concrete sphere marks the actual spot on the island, currently about a 45-minute hike north of the airstrip. So, unless you are a runner, the best way to ensure you actually get to the real Arctic Circle is by coming by boat (longer layover) or staying the night. Reach Grímsey by ferry or flight – guided tours to the island are usually available in summer months. Norlandair (www.norlandair.is) operates flights to and from Akureyri. The 25-minute journey takes

❶ Need to Know

See www.grimsey.is, or ask at the island shop.

✕ Take a Break

Krían (☏467 3112; ⊘noon-9pm mid-May– early Sep, hours vary rest of year) is the island's only restaurant, with a deck overlooking the harbour.

★ Top Tip

Puffins are not guaranteed beyond early August (viewing is best from May to July); terns (May to September) are pretty aggressive in July.

n the full length of Eyjafjörður and is an experience in itself.

There is year-round ferry service between Dalvík and Grímsey: the Sæfari ferry (three hours, adult/child 3500kr/ free) departs from Dalvík at 9am Monday, Wednesday, Thursday and Friday. From June to August there is also a service on Sunday.

Seabirds & Coastal Cliffs

Scenic coastal cliffs and dramatic basalt formations make a popular home for dozens of species of seabirds, including loads of puffins, plus the kamikaze Arctic tern. We're particularly fond of the anecdote that the airport runway has to be cleared of the terns a few minutes before aircraft arrive. Take care walking around cliff edges. Note that puffins are best seen from May to July.

Arctic Trip

Local guide Halla and her team at **Arctic Trip** (☏848 1696; www.arctictrip.is) offer unique island insights, including a Grímsey day tour (28,000kr) via ferry from Dalvík. Once-in-a-lifetime underwater adventure – Arctic diving in the presence of swimming puffins and guillemots – requires Open Water scuba dive certification (PADI or equivalent) and drysuit experience. Check website for myriad tours.

Staying on Grímsey

To soak up Grímsey's Arctic Circle relaxation two guesthouses offer accommodation. There's a small campground (800kr per person) by the community centre with very basic facilities.

Akureyri Walking Tour

Akureyri is a compact waterfront town, ideal for walking. This tour can be done in as little as an hour, but with time spent enjoying the botanical gardens and soaking in the local pool, allow half a day.

Start Hof
Distance 3km
Duration Three to four hours

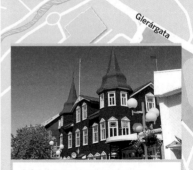

6 On the way back to the waterfront stop at **Götubarinn** (p211), a favourite local bar.

5 Time for a dip: head north to the local geothermal pool, **Sundlaug Akureyrar** (p205).

4 Continue 700m south to **Lystigarðurinn** (p204), the world's most northerly botanic garden.

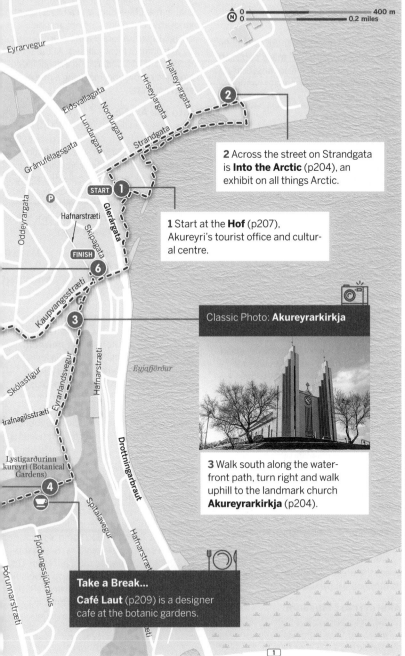

N
0 | 400 m
0 | 0.2 miles

Eyrarvegur

Hjalteyrargata

Hríseyjargata

Eiðsvallagata

Norðurgata

Lundargata

Gránufélagsgata

Strandgata

2

2 Across the street on Strandgata is **Into the Arctic** (p204), an exhibit on all things Arctic.

Oddeyrargata

P

START **1**

Hafnarstræti

Glerárgata

Skipagata

FINISH
6

1 Start at the **Hof** (p207), Akureyri's tourist office and cultural centre.

Kaupvangsstræti

3

Skólastígur

Hrafnagilsstræti

Eyrarlandsvegur

Hafnarstræti

Eyjafjörður

Classic Photo: **Akureyrarkirkja**

3 Walk south along the waterfront path, turn right and walk uphill to the landmark church **Akureyrarkirkja** (p204).

Lystigarðurinn Akureyri (Botanical Gardens)

4

Drottningarbraut

Spítalavegur

Hafnarstr

Fjórðungssjúkrahús

Þórunnarstræti

Take a Break...
Café Laut (p209) is a designer cafe at the botanic gardens.

1

3 MYCATISNOTFAT/SHUTTERSTOCK © 4 GESTUR GISLASON/SHUTTERSTOCK © 6 AIMINTANG/GETTY IMAGES©

Akureyri

◎ SIGHTS

The Akureyri Art Trail brochure (available at the tourist office; p211) maps public art around town. There are also museums dedicated to aviation, local industry, antique toys and motorbikes.

Lystigarðurinn — Gardens

(Map p206; ☏462 7487; www.lystigardur.akureyri. is; Eyrarlandsholt; ☺8am-10pm, from 9am Sat & Sun Jun-Sep) FREE The most northerly botanical garden in the world makes a delightful spot for a fragrant wander on sunny days. The wealth of plant life on display is truly astonishing considering the gardens' proximity to the Arctic Circle. You'll find examples of every species native to Iceland, as well as a host of high-latitude and high-altitude plants from around the world. There's also the beautifully situated Café Laut (p209).

Akureyrarkirkja — Church

(Map p206; ☏462 7700; www.akureyrarkirkja.is; Eyrarlandsvegur; ☺generally 10am-4pm Mon-Fri) Dominating the town from high on a hill, Akureyri's landmark church was designed by Guðjón Samúelsson, the architect responsible for Reykjavík's Hallgrímskirkja. Although the basalt theme connects them, Akureyrarkirkja looks more like a stylised 1920s US skyscraper than its big-city sibling.

Built in 1940, the church contains a large 3200-pipe organ and a series of rather untraditional reliefs of the life of Christ. There's also a suspended ship hanging from the ceiling, reflecting an old Nordic tradition of votive offerings for the protection of loved ones at sea. Perhaps the most striking feature is the beautiful central stained-glass window above the altar, which originally graced Coventry Cathedral in England.

The church admits visitors most days; check the board outside for opening times, as they change frequently.

Akureyri Art Museum — Museum

(Listasafnið á Akureyri; Map p206; ☏461 2610; www.listak.is; Kaupvangsstræti 8; 1500kr; ☺10am-5pm Jun-Aug, noon-5pm Tue-Sun Sep-May) Stimulate your senses at the Akureyri Art Museum, which hosts eclectic, innovative exhibitions – from graphic design to portraiture – and is surrounded by a handful of local galleries. At the time of research, it was undergoing a major extension and renovation, including a museum shop and cafe.

Into the Arctic — Museum

(Map p208; Norðurslóð; ☏588 9050; www. nordurslod.is; Strandgata 53; adult/child 1500kr/ free; ☺11am-6pm, to 5pm Sat & Sun) Akureyri's newest entry on the exhibition scene, Into the Arctic's displays cover the great north's wildlife, settlement, explorers and culture, from dog sledding and aviation to handicrafts. The founders' extensive map collection is on display as well.

Akureyri Museum — Museum

(Map p208; Minjasafnið á Akureyri; ☏462 4162; www.akmus.is; Aðalstræti 58; adult/child 1500kr/ free; ☺10am-5pm Jun-Sep, 1-4pm Oct-May) This sweet, well-curated museum houses art and historical items relating to town life, including maps, photos and recreations of early Icelandic homes. The **museum garden** became the first place in Iceland to cultivate trees when a nursery was established here in 1899. Next door is a tiny, black-tarred timber **church** dating from 1846.

A combined ticket including neighbouring Nonnahús and several town museums costs 2000kr.

Nonnahús — Museum

(Map p208; ☏462 4162; www.nonni.is; Aðalstræti 54; adult/child 1400kr/free; ☺10am-5pm Jun-Aug, Thu-Sun Sep-May) The most interesting of the artists' residences in Akureyri, Nonnahús was the childhood home of renowned children's writer Reverend Jón Sveinsson (1857–1944), known to most as Nonni. His old-fashioned tales of derring-do have a rich local flavour. The house dates from 1850; its cramped rooms and simple furnishings provide a poignant insight into life in 19th-century Iceland.

A combined ticket for Nonnahús, neighbouring Akureyri Museum and several town museums costs 2000kr.

🌀 ACTIVITIES

Sundlaug Akureyrar   Swimming

(Map p206; ☑461 4455; www.visitakureyri. is; Þingvallastræti 21; adult/child 950/250kr; ⊗6.45am-9pm Mon-Fri, 8am-9pm Sat, 8am-7.30pm Sun; 🐾) The hub of local life, Akureyri's outdoor swimming pool is one of Iceland's finest. It has three recently refurbished heated pools, plus hot-pots, water slides, saunas and steam rooms.

🌀 TOURS

Saga Travel   Adventure Tour

(Map p208; ☑558 8888; www.sagatravel.is; Fjölnisgata 6a; ⊗booking office 8am-4pm Mon-Fri, to 2pm Sat & Sun) Saga offers a rich and diverse year-round program of excursions and activities throughout the north. It includes obvious spots such as Mývatn, Húsavík (for whale watching) and Askja in the highlands, but also offers innovative tours along themes such as food or art and design.

Winter tours include snowmobiling, snowshoeing and Northern Lights viewing (of course, weather dependent). Private itineraries can be arranged; guides are local and well connected. Tours have a maximum of 19 participants (and minimum of two).

Nonni Travel   Tours

(Map p206; ☑461 1841; www.nonnitravel.is; Brekkugata 5; ⊗9am-5pm Mon-Fri May-Sep, 10am-3pm Mon-Fri Oct-Apr) Travel agency able to hook you up with just about any tour in the area, as well as tours further afield (to Greenland and the Faroe Islands).

Circle Air   Flight Tour

(Map p208; ☑588 4000; www.circleair.is) Operating out of Akureyri Airport, this company offers flightseeing starting at 42,000kr for an 1½-hour flight over Dettifoss and Mývatn, plus the central highlands (52,000kr) or a one-hour stop on Grímsey (54,000kr).

📖 First Settlers

The first permanent inhabitant of Eyjafjörður was Norse-Irish settler Helgi Magri (Helgi the Lean), who arrived in about 890. By 1602 a trading post had been established at present-day Akureyri. There were still no permanent dwellings though, as all the settlers maintained rural farms and homesteads. By the late 18th century the town had accumulated a whopping 10 residents, all Danish traders, and was granted municipal status. The town soon began to prosper and by 1900 Akureyri's population numbered 1370.

Today Akureyri is thriving. Its fishing company and shipyard are the largest in the country, and the city's university (established in 1987) gives the town a youthful exuberance.

Traveling Viking   Adventure Tour

(☑896 3569; www.ttv.is; 🐾) Offers plenty of tours, from the expected (Mývatn, Dettifoss, Húsavík) to the offbeat, including a four-hour family-friendly option focusing on the 'hidden people', or winter ice-fishing. Also a *Game of Thrones* tour of the Mývatn region and kayaking.

🛍️ SHOPPING

Several shops on Hafnarstræti sell traditional *lopapeysur* Icelandic woollen sweaters, books, knick-knacks and souvenirs. Remember to look for Icelandic-made knitwear (some is now mass-produced in China) and ask about the tax-free scheme.

The Glerártorg shopping mall, on Rte 1 about 1km north of the town centre, is home to a large Nettó supermarket and other shops and services.

Geysir   Clothing

(Map p206; ☑519 6040; www.geysir.com; Hafnarstræti 98; ⊗10am-6pm, noon-5pm Sun) We covet everything in this shop, from the woollen

Akureyri

N 0 —————————— 200 m
    0 —————————— 0.1 miles

SBA-Norðurleið
(100m)

Eyrarvegur

⊗15

Glerárgata

Grænagata

Sports
Stadium

Eiðsvallagata

Byggðavegur

Klappastígur

Pórunnarstræti

Brekkugata

Munkaþverárstræti

Laxagata

Hólabraut

Grófargilsgata

Gránufélagsgata

Geislagata

Norðurgata

Lundargata

Into the Arctic
(100m)

Strandgata

Helgamagrastræti

⊗6

🅿

Strætó

●5

Bjarkarstígur

Oddeyrargata

Hofsbót

Glerárgata

⭐27
ℹ
Hof

Ásvegur

7
● Ráðhústorg
🅿

22
21 17 25 13
18 Hafnarstræti

Skipagata

12
10 🔒 20
26 23

●4

Hamarstígur

Bjarmastígur

Oddagata

19

Kaupvangsstræti

Lögbergsgata

Gilsbakkavegur

🏛2
24 🔒11

⬆1

⭐9

Hafnarstræti

Eyjafjörður

Pingvallastræti

16
⊗

8
⊗

Laugargata

Móðuvallastígur

Skólastígur

Eyrarlandsvegur

⭐28

Pórunnarstræti

Vanabyggð

Hrafnagilsstræti

Byggðavegur

Drottningarbraut

Lystigarðurinn
Akureyri (Botanical
Gardens)

3 ◉

⊗14

Noa Seafood Restaurant (150m);
Brynja (300m); Nonnahús (500m);
Akureyri Museum (550m)

Jaðarsvöllur
(2.3km)

Akureyri

blankets to the hipster-chic *lopapeysur* and the old Iceland maps.

Flora
Design
(Map p206; ☎661 0168; www.facebook.com/flora.akureyri; Hafnarstræti 90; ◷10am-7pm, from noon Sun) This artist-run collective selling creative designware and handicrafts strives for sustainability and reuse in the materials in its goods.

Sjoppan
Design
(Map p206; ☎864 0710; www.facebook.com/sjoppanvoruhus; Kaupvangsstræti 21; ◷hours vary) Cute as a button, this tiny shop dispenses cool design items and gifts from a hutch out the front (ring the bell for service). It's across from the art museum (p204). Check out its Facebook page for hours and other details.

✪ ENTERTAINMENT

Græni Hatturinn
Live Music
(Map p206; ☎461 4646; http://graenihatturinn.is; Hafnarstræti 96) Tucked down a lane beside Blaá Kannan (p208), this intimate venue is the best place in town to see live music – and one of the best in the country. If you get the chance, buy a ticket to anything going.

Hof
Music, Performing Arts
(Map p206; ☎450 1000; www.mak.is; Strandgata 12) Modern Hof is a cultural centre designed for music and other performing arts. Along with conference and exhibition facilities and a good daytime restaurant (1862 Nordic Bistro), it's also home to Akureyri's tourist office (p211); ask here about any scheduled performances, or check the website.

Leikfélag Akureyrar
Theatre
(Map p206; ☎450 1000; www.mak.is; Hafnarstræti 57) The only professional theatre company outside the Reykjavík area performs drama, musicals, dance and opera, with its main season running from September to May. It is mainly based in the 1906 wooden Samkomuhúsið building, but also performs at Hof. Check the website for upcoming performances.

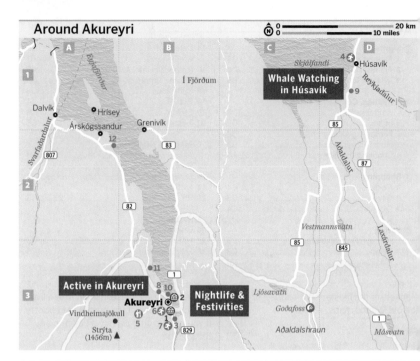

Around Akureyri

⊙ **Sights**

✖ EATING

Berlin   Cafe €

(Map p206; 📞772 5061; www.facebook.com/
berlinakureyri; Skipagata 4; breakfast 800-
1700kr; ⏰8am-6pm; 🛜🍴) Breakfast served
all day? Hello Berlin! If you need a fix of bacon and eggs or avocado on toast, this cosy
timber-lined cafe is your spot. Good coffee
is a bonus, and you can linger over waffles
with caramel sauce too. From 11.30am
the menu adds lunch-y offerings such as
vegetable dhal and chicken wings.

Blaá Kannan   Cafe €

(Map p206; 📞461 4600; www.facebook.com/
blaakannan; Hafnarstræti 96; lunchtime buffet
1800kr; ⏰9am-10.30pm, from 10am Sat &
Sun) Prime people-watching is on offer at
this much-loved cafe (the Blue Teapot, in
the dark-blue Cafe Paris building) on the
main drag. The interior is timber-lined and
blinged up with chandeliers; the menu
offers panini and bagels, and there's a
cabinet full of sweet treats.

Café Laut Cafe €

(Map p206; ☑461 4601; www.facebook.com/
cafelaut; Eyrarlandsvegur 30; dishes 1000-
2600kr; ⊙10am-10pm Jun-Sep) What could be
better than a designer cafe in a botanical
garden (p204)? This cafe has gorgeous
picture windows, good coffee, a big sun
terrace and a lunchtime soup-and-bread
buffet (1590kr), as well as bagels, salads
and panini.

Kaffi Ilmur Cafe €

(Map p206; ☑571 6444; www.kaffiilmur.com;
Hafnarstræti 107b; dishes 1500-2500kr, lunch
buffet 2400kr; ⊙8am-11pm, to 7pm Fri-Sun)
In a charming historical building painted
butter yellow (and once a saddlery), this
welcoming cafe offers a tasty range of
bodacious breakfast and lunch options
and a substantial lunch buffet. The kitchen
closes at 3.30pm, and then cakes, snacks
and drinks are served.

Strikið International €€

(Map p206; ☑462 7100; www.strikid.is; Skipagata 14; mains lunch 2000-3200kr, dinner 4000-
5500kr; ⊙11.30am-10pm) Huge windows
with fjord views lend a magical glitz to this
5th-floor restaurant, and the cool cocktails
help things along. The menu showcases
prime Icelandic produce (reindeer burgers,
super-fresh sushi, lamb shoulder, shellfish
soup). The four-course signature menu is
9000kr. Reserve ahead.

Greifinn International €€

(Map p206; ☑460 1600; www.greifinn.is;
Glerárgata 20; mains 1700-5000kr; ⊙11.30am-
10pm; ▣) Family friendly and *always* full to
bursting, Greifinn is one of the most popular
spots in town. The menu favours comfort
food above all: ribs and wings, juicy burgers,
pizzas, pastas, milkshakes and devilish ice-
cream desserts. Takeaway available.

Noa Seafood
Restaurant Seafood €€

(Örkin hans Nóa; ☑461 2100; www.noa.is;
Hafnarstræti 22; mains 3800-7400kr; ⊙4-9pm)
Part gallery, part furniture store, part res-
taurant – 'Noah's Ark' is certainly unique,

New
Tunnel

A new 7.5km-long road tunnel is being
built on the eastern side of Eyjafjörður,
which will shorten the Rte 1 journey
to Húsavík by about 16km. Drivers will
be able to avoid the mountain pass
Víkurskarð (often blocked by winter
snows). The tunnel is being built under
Vaðlaheiði mountain; it's had a few
hiccups since construction began, but is
expected to be completed in 2019.

and offers a simple food concept done well.
The menu features a selection of fresh fish
options, which are pan-fried and served
with vegetables, with the pan brought to
the table. Classic, effective and tasty. There
are quality beef and lamb dishes for non-
fish-fans. Bookings recommended.

Akureyri Fish
Restaurant Fish & Chips €€

(Map p206; ☑414 6050; www.facebook.com/
pg/Akureyri-fish-and-chips; Skipagata 12;
mains 1500-2500kr; ⊙11.30am-10pm; ☎) The
short blackboard at this bustling, casual
place highlights piscatorial pleasures:
fish and chips is the bestseller, or there's
oven-baked salmon, crumbed cod, fish
soup, fish burger, mussels (in season) and
plokkfiskur (a tasty, traditional, creamy
mashed-fish stew served with rye bread).

Icelandair Hotel
Akureyri Desserts €€

(Map p206; www.icelandairhotels.com; Þingvallastræti 23; high tea 2750kr; ⊙high tea 2-5pm)
Suffering afternoon sluggishness?
Get your sugar rush courtesy of the
great-value high tea served every afternoon
in the smart lounge of the hotel. You'll
be served a three-tiered tray of delights:
savoury, sweet and more sweet. Coffee or
tea included; champagne optional. You're
welcome.

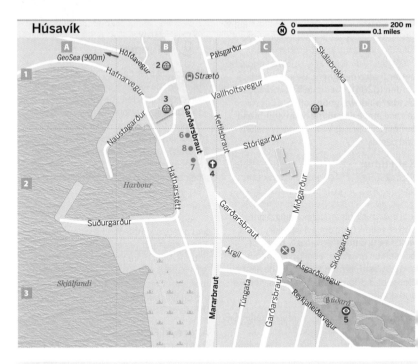

Húsavík

Indian Curry House   Indian €€

(Map p206; ☑461 4242; www.facebook.com/
IndianCurryHutAkureyri; Ráðhústorg 3; dishes
1900-2500kr; ⊙11.30am-1.30pm & 5.30-9pm
Tue-Fri, 5.30-9pm Sat & Sun) Add a little heat
to a chilly evening with a flavourful curry
from this family-run restaurant.

Rub23   International €€€

(Map p206; ☑462 2223; www.rub23.is; Kaupvang
sstræti 6; mains lunch 2600-3200kr, dinner
5000-5900kr; ⊙11.30am-2pm & 5.30-10pm
Mon-Fri, 5.30-10pm Sat & Sun) This sleek,
seafood-showcasing restaurant has a

decidedly Japanese flavour, but also promotes its use of 'rubs' or marinades (along
the lines of sweet mango chilli or citrus
rosemary). The food is first-rate, and at dinner there's an array of menus (including a
sushi menu and tasting menus). Bookings
advised.

T-Bone Steakhouse   Steak €€€

(Map p206; ☑469 4020; www.tbone.is;
Brekkugata 3; mains lunch 2500-2700kr, dinner
4000-6200kr; ⊙11.30am-2pm & 5-10pm Mon-Fri,
5-10pm Sat & Sun) Wearing its carnivorous
heart on its sleeve ('We bloody love steak' is

on the menu, and the exterior signage), this steakhouse gets mixed reviews, but may appeal if you're tiring of lamb and fish.

🍷 DRINKING & NIGHTLIFE

Ölstofa Akureyrar Bar
(Map p206; ☎663 8886; www.facebook.com/ olstofak; Kaupvangsstræti 23; ☺6pm-1am, to 3am Fri & Sat, to 10pm Sun) *The* place in town for draught and local beers, this convivial spot has recently partnered with local (and well-loved) brewery, Einstök, to create a brewer's lounge (www.brewerslounge.is) where you sample their delicious wares, fresh from the brewery.

Akureyri Backpackers Bar
(Map p206; ☎571 9050; www.akureyriback packers.com; Hafnarstræti 98; ☺7.30am-11pm, to 1am Fri & Sat) Always a hub of convivial main-street activity, the fun timber-clad bar at this place is beloved of both travellers and locals for its occasional live music, good-value burgers and weekend brunches, and a wide beer selection – this is a fine spot to sample local microbrews Kaldi and Einstök.

Götubarinn Bar
(Map p206; ☎462 4747; www.facebook.com/ gotubarinn; Hafnarstræti 96; ☺1.30-9pm Tue, 5pm-1am Thu, 5pm-3am Fri & Sat) The locals' favourite drinking spot, fun and central Götubarinn (Street Bar) has a surprising amount of cosiness and charm for a place that closes so late.

Café Amour Bar
(Map p206; ☎461 3030; www.facebook.com/ kaffiamour; Ráðhústorg 9; ☺6pm-1am Mon-Thu, to 4am Fri, 1pm-4am Sat, 1pm-1am Sun) Café Amour lures Akureyri's bright young things with its lengthy cocktail list and New World wines. The small club upstairs is pretty garish but draws the crowds at weekends. Occasional live music, too.

R5 Bar
(Map p206; ☎412 9933; www.r5.is; Ráðhústorg 5; ☺5pm-1am, to 3am Fri & Sat) An easy-breezy stop for an evening drink, convivial R5 has

a mixed bag of decor (tiles, carpeted ban-quettes, timber tables) and an array of Euro brews, including local drops.

ℹ️ INFORMATION

Tourist Office (☎450 1050; www.visitakureyri. is; Hof, Strandgata 12; ☺8am-6.30pm Jun–mid-Sep, 8am-4pm Mon-Fri mid-Sep–Apr, 8am-4pm May; 🛜) This friendly, efficient office inside **Hof** (p207) offers loads of brochures, maps, inter-net access and a great design store. Knowledge-able staff advise on tours and transport.

ℹ️ GETTING THERE & AWAY

AIR
Air Iceland Connect (☎460 7000; www.air icelandconnect.is) runs flights up to eight times daily between Akureyri and Reykjavík's domestic airport (45 minutes).

Norlandair (www.norlandair.is) has flights from Akureyri to Grímsey island (30 minutes).

Super Break (www.superbreak.com) has winter flights serving the UK.

BUS
Akureyri is the hub for bus travel in the North, provided by **Strætó** (☎540 2700; www.straeto. is) from a bus stop in front of Hof, with one sum-mer route by **SBA-Norðurleið** (Map p208; ☎550 0700; www.sba.is; Hjalteyrargata 10).

CAR
All the major car-hire firms have representation at the airport. For a fee, most will let you pick up a car in Akureyri and drop it off in Reykjavík or vice versa. Check out www.samferda.is for information about car-pooling, or check hostel noticeboards.

ℹ️ GETTING AROUND

Central Akureyri is quite compact and easy to get around on foot. If you plan to park a car in the town centre you'll need to get a free **parking clock** from the tourist office, banks or petrol stations.

WESTFJORDS

The Westfjords at a Glance...

The Westfjords is where Iceland's dramatic landscapes come to a riveting climax and where mass tourism disappears – only about 10% of Iceland's visitors ever see the region. Jagged bird cliffs and broad multihued dream beaches flank the south. Rutted dirt roads snake north along jaw-dropping coastal fjords and over immense central mountains, revealing tiny fishing villages embracing traditional ways of life.

Leave plenty of time: unpaved roads weave around fjords and over pothole-pitted mountain passes, but the scenery is never short of breathtaking.

Two Days in the Westfjords

Start in **Ísafjörður** (p223), the Westfjords' main town and a good base to find adventure tour guides. Spend some town wandering the **Old Town** (p223) and check out the **Museum of Everyday Life** (p223) and/or the **Westfjords Heritage Museum** (p223). On day two head south to **Þingeyri** (p229) for some serious hiking, mountain biking or horse riding.

Four Days in the Westfjords

Westfjords is so big and spread out that possible choices are myriad. If you're interested in wildlife, head to **Látrabjarg Bird Cliffs** (p216) for some puffin viewing, day-trip to **Vigur island** (p227) or book a whale-watching tour with **Láki Tours** (p217). Serious hikers should head to **Hornstrandir Peninsula** (p220).

Map labels:

Hornstrandir Nature Reserve

Hornstrandir Nature Reserve

Búrfell (498m)

Hesteyri

Jökulfirðir

Grunnavík

Reykjarfjörður

GREENLAND SEA

Óshlíð

Tungudalur

Ísafjörður

Drangajökull

DENMARK STRAIT

Ísafjörður Airport

Lóndjúp

Reykjanes

Reykjanes

Djúpavík

Lambatindur (854m)

Selárdalur

Dýrafjörður

Þingeyri

Lambadalsfjall (957m)

Sjónfríð (920m)

Hólsfjall (469m)

Húnaflói

Arnarfjörður

Kaldbakur (998m)

Ketildalur

Dynjandi

Reiphólsfjöll (881m)

Bjarnarfjarðarháls

Hólmavík

Drangsnes

Steingrímsfjörður

Kollsvík

Gláma

Waterfall

Vaðalfjöll (508m)

Patreksfjörður

Foss

Hvallátur

Sauðlauksdalur

Brjánslækur

Þorskafjörður

Bjarkalundur

Reykjanes

Barðaströnd

Breiðafjörður

Reykhólar

40 km
20 miles

Hornstrandir Map (p222)
The Westfjords (p224)
Ísafjörður Map (p228)

Arriving in the Westfjords

Air From Reykjavík's domestic airport, Air Iceland Connect has twice-daily flights to Ísafjörður; Eagle Air flies from Reykjavík to Bíldudalur and Gjögur.

Ferry Take a ferry from Stykkishólmur in West Iceland and Brjánslækur in the Westfjords, from where you can connect to a summertime-only bus.

Bus Strætó buses run from Hólmavík on the Strandir Coast to Borgarnes; there are connections to Reykjavík, Akureyri and Staðarskáli from there.

Where to Stay

There's a surprisingly good range of hotels, guesthouses and campgrounds in the Westfjords, though they are generally of a low-key and simple nature. Book ahead in the most remote regions so you don't get caught out in the middle of the countryside. Ísafjörður is the main town, while Þingeyri and Patreksfjörður are also good bases.

Razorbill

LOUIELEA/SHUTTERSTOCK ©

Westfjords Wildlife Watching

You'll likely see more nesting birds and breaching whales than you will people in the remote and wild Westfjords, from the crazy puffin colonies of Látrabjarg to the shy Arctic foxes of Hornstrandir.

Great For...

☑ Don't Miss

The Látrabjarg Bird Cliffs.

Látrabjarg Bird Cliffs

These renowned, dramatic **cliffs** (Map p224) on the headland beside **Bjargtan-gar Lighthouse** (Map p224) extend for 12km. They're mobbed by nesting seabirds in early summer when unbelievable numbers of puffins, razorbills, guillemots, cormorants, fulmars, gulls and kittiwakes nest here from June to mid-August. It's best to visit in the evening, when the birds return to their nests. On calm days, seals are often seen basking on the skerries around the lighthouse.

Ísafjarðardjúp

The largest of the fjords in the Central Peninsulas, 75km-long Ísafjarðardjúp takes a massive swath out of the Westfjords' landmass. Highlights for wildlife watchers are the day trip to Vigur island (p227),

Bjargtangar Lighthouse

STUDIO DAGDAGAZ/SHUTTERSTOCK ©

with its puffin colonies and whale-watching opportunities, and the roadside **Seal Viewpoint** (Map p224; Rte 61; ⊘24hr) FREE about 75km east of Ísafjörður.

Wildlife Centres & Tours

Arctic Fox Center · Visitor Center

(Melrakkasetur; Map p224; ☑456 4922; www.arcticfoxcenter.com; Eyrardalur; adult/child 1200kr/free; ⊘9am-6pm Jun-Aug, 10am-4pm Sep & May, 10am-2pm Mon-Fri Oct-Apr) The study of the Arctic fox has been under way on nearby Hornstrandir for years, and this locally loved exhibition details the life of the creatures, their relationship with humans and their habitat. It also has a wealth of stuffed foxes in realistic poses plus some cute-looking live ones, who were orphaned, in a pen outside. The centre sits inside the renovated farmstead of **Eyrardalur** – one of the oldest buildings in the area.

White-Tailed Eagle Centre · Museum

(Map p224; ☑894 1011; www.visitreykholah reppur.is; Króksfjarðarnes; adult/child 600kr/ free; ⊘11am-6pm mid-Jun–mid-Aug) The White-Tailed Eagle Centre highlights the attempts to increase the population of the struggling species, which peaked in 2011 at 66 nests. It also has a handicrafts market. The centre is just north of the causeway on Rte 60 that crosses Gilsfjörður.

Láki Tours · Whale Watching

(Map p224; ☑546 6808; www.lakitours.com; Hafnarbraut 14; adult/child 7300/3650kr; ⊘mid-Jun–Aug) You've a good chance of spotting playful humpbacked whales on these trips onto sheltered Steingrímsfjörður, run by a responsible, small-scale operator. Also look out for minke and pilot whales, white-beaked dolphins, and even orcas and sperm whales.

Hot spring pools at Pollurinn

MARTIN MOOS/GETTY IMAGES ©

Westfjords Activities

The Westfjords offers up dramatic landscapes and unrivalled coastal scenery, and one of the best ways to see it is via the slow pace of a mountain bike, a kayak or your own two feet.

Great For...

☑ **Don't Miss**
Soaking in one of the many Westfjords hot-pots.

Hiking & Cycling

There are many opportunities for hiking in the Westfjords, but if you're going it alone (without a tour) you must be well prepared. Easy walks include the beaches of **Ingjaldssandur** (Map p224) and **Rauðasandur** (Map p224) – a 20km coastal path runs between Rauðasandur and the Látrabjarg bird cliffs – or the trek to the top of the spectacular waterfall, Dynjandi. Challenging treks include the Royal Horn on Hornstrandir Peninsula or the remote Strandir coast.

Þingeyri Peninsula

West of Þingeyri, the **peninsula** (Map p224) and its dramatic peaks offer spectacular hiking and cycling. You can rent fat bikes and mountain bikes and follow the dirt road that runs northwest along

the northern edge of the peninsula and along Dýrafjörður to the scenic valley at Haukadalur, an important Viking site.

Inland, the Westfjords' highest peak, **Kaldbakur** (998m), is a good hiking spot. The steep trail to the summit begins from the road about 2km west of Þingeyri town.

Adventure Tours

The best (and safest) way to get out hiking, cycling, kayaking or horse riding is to join an organised adventure tour. Ísafjörður has numerous operators, including the following:

- West Tours (p226)
- Borea (p226)
- Simba Horses & Bike Rental (p230)
- Westfjords Adventures (p231)
- **Kayak Flateyri** (Map p224; ☑863 7662; www.facebook.com/kajakleiga; Ólafstúni 7; trips from 7000kr)

Hot-Pots

Soaking in a geothermal pool or hot-pot after a day of activity is the quintessential Icelandic experience and the Westfjords has some of the country's best. Our favourites in the region include the following:

Hellulaug (Map p224; Rte 62; by donation) in Flókalundur.

Seaweed baths (Sjávarsmiðjan; Map p224; ☑577 4800; www.sjavarsmidjan.is; Vesturbraut; adult/child 3900kr/free; ⊘hours vary) at Reykhólar.

Reykjarfjarðarlaug (Map p224) **FREE**, which has glorious geothermal pools.

Pollurinn (Map p224; ⊘24hr) **FREE** at Tálknafjörður.

Hot-pot (Map p224; Aðalbraut; by donation) at the waterfront seawall of Drangsnes.

Krossneslaug (Map p224; adult/child 650/200kr; ⊘24hr), a spectacular geothermal infinity pool of in Norðurfjörður.

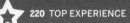

110MM/SHUTTERSTOCK ©

Hornstrandir Nature Reserve

Craggy mountains, precarious sea cliffs and plunging waterfalls ring Hornstrandir peninsula and nature reserve, one of Europe's last true wilderness areas, and offer excellent opportunities for spotting Arctic foxes, seals, whales and teeming bird life.

Great For...

☑ Don't Miss
The remote Royal Horn hike.

The best time to visit Hornstrandir is in July. Outside the summer season (which runs from late June to mid-August; ferry boats run June to August) there are few people around and the weather is even more unpredictable.

Hiking the Royal Horn

Locals and tourists agree that the Royal Horn (or 'Hornsleið') is the best hike on the peninsula. This four- to five-day hike from Veiðileysufjörður to Hesteyri can also be easily modified if you run into bad weather. The trail is partially marked with cairns, but there are very few tourists, so keep track of the route. It's a great way to experience this remote land. Make sure you're fully prepared, prebook your return boat, and check with the rangers for the latest conditions before setting out.

ⓘ Need to Know

(☑591 2000; www.ust.is/hornstrandir)

✕ Take a Break

Old Doctor's House (☑845 5075, Jun-Aug 899 7661; www.hesteyri.net; Hesteyri; d incl breakfast & dinner 16,000kr; ◷mid-Jun–late Aug) is the area's most developed cafe-guesthouse.

★ Top Tip

If entering Hornstrandir Nature Reserve between September and 15 June it is mandatory to register with a **park ranger** (Environmental Agency of Iceland; ☑591 2000; www.ust.is/hornstrandir).

Other Hikes

You can take the ferry to Veiðileysufjörður, hike up to Hornvík and spend a couple of nights there, ensuring there's time to explore **Hornbjarg**. From there you can backtrack to Veiðileysufjörður to link up with the boat, *but only if you've prebooked it*.

Alternatively, just sail in and use Hesteyri as a day-hike base. Prebook at the Old Doctor's House if you want sleeping-bag accommodation.

Camping

Camping in Hornstrandir is free. Carry out all rubbish, and stick to designated campgrounds: wild camping is prohibited in the nature reserve. All campgrounds have dry latrines. Latrine doors are weighed down with heavy timber to prevent near-certain wind damage if they are left open, so be sure to secure the door after use.

Camping on private grounds with facilities costs from around 1500kr per person. Expect to pay upwards of 5000kr for sleeping-bag space, which must be reserved well in advance, especially in Hesteyri.

Hornstrandir

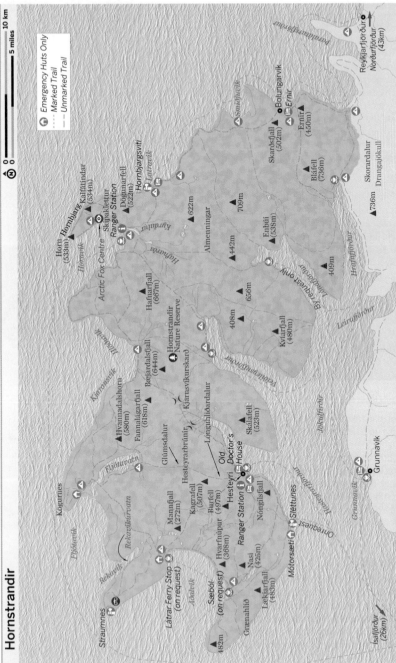

Ísafjörður

Hub of the Westfjords' adventure tours, and by far the region's largest town, Ísafjörður (www.isafjordur.is) is a pleasant and prosperous place and an excellent base for travellers. The town is set on an arcing spit that extends out into Skutulsfjörður, and is hemmed in on all sides by towering peaks and the dark waters of the fjord.

The centre of Ísafjörður is a charming grid of old timber and tin-clad buildings, many unchanged since the 18th century, when the harbour was full of tall ships and Norwegian whaling crews. Today it is a surprisingly cosmopolitan place, and after some time spent travelling in the Westfjords, it'll feel like a bustling metropolis with its tempting cafes and fine choice of restaurants.

There's hiking in the hills around the town, skiing in winter and regular summer boats ferry hikers across to the remote Hornstrandir Peninsula.

◎ SIGHTS

Westfjords Heritage Museum
Museum

(Byggðasafn Vestfjarða; Map p228; ☑456 3293; www.nedsti.is; Neðstikaupstaður; adult/child 1200kr/free; ⊙9am-5pm mid-May–Sep) Part of a cluster of historical wooden buildings by the harbour, this museum is in the **Turnhús** (1784), which was originally a warehouse. It's crammed with fishing and nautical exhibits, tools from the whaling days, fascinating old photos depicting town life over the centuries, and accordions. To the right is the **Tjöruhús** (1781), now an excellent seafood restaurant. The **Faktorhús** (1765), which housed the manager of the village shop, and the **Krambúð** (1757), originally a storehouse, are now private residences.

Museum of Everyday Life
Museum

(Hversdagssafn; Map p228; ☑694 4266; www.everydaylife.is; Hafnarstræti 5; ⊙10am-5pm Mon-Fri, 11am-2pm Sat; adult/child 700kr/free) Celebrating the magic of the mundane is the aim of the powerful, creative displays here, where shoes, books and mini movies each come with personal narratives and story fragments. As an intriguing insight into life in the Westfjords, it's poetic, thought-provoking and beautifully done.

Old Town
Area

(Map p228; Tangagata) Ísafjörður's historical quarter borders it's eastern edges. Start explorations in Tangagata to see gabled, tin-clad homes, often brightly painted in patriotic russet red or blue and trimmed with white. Look out for the dates from the late 1890s and early 1900s above the doors.

Culture House
Cultural Centre

(Map p228; ☑450 8220; Eyrartúni; ⊙1-6pm Mon-Fri, to 4pm Sat) FREE The intensely close-knit nature of Westfjords life is evoked in the 2nd-floor displays in what was once the town hospital. Look out for vintage scales for newborns, a disturbing hacksaw and an eye-watering enema device, and the touching testimonies of former patients.

✪ ACTIVITIES

Path Towards Óshlíð
Hiking, Cycling

(Map p224) A precarious path leads around the point from Ísafjörður towards Bolungarvík and the mountain Óshlíð. The teeny track, which is prone to rockfalls and avalanches, was once the only route to Bolungarvík. Check with the tourist office for current conditions – with caution, you can often walk or cycle the bit nearest the tunnel to Bolungarvík and see Hornstrandir and Snæfjallaströnd in the distance.

Swimming Pool
Swimming

(Map p228; ☑450 8480; Austurvegur 9; adult/child 620/320kr; ⊙7-8am & 6-9pm Mon-Fri, 10am-5pm Sat & Sun) Although plain by Icelandic standards, the town swimming pool makes a good retreat on a wet day. It has indoor hot-pots and a tiny sauna.

Fosshestar
Horse Riding

(☑842 6969; www.fosshestar.is) Short riding tours (from 15,000kr) for all skill levels in the nearby Engidalur Valley. Also offers horse feeding and petting (3500kr). Book ahead; cash only. The price includes pick-up and drop-off from Ísafjörður.

Westfjords

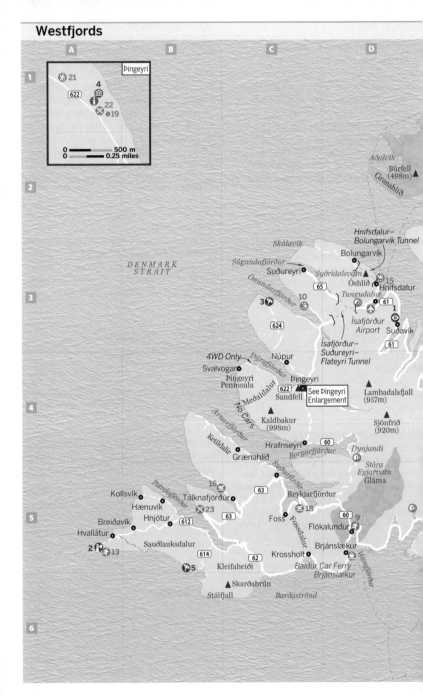

A B C D

Þingeyri

☒ 21
4
622
ⓘ
22
✕ ●19

0 ——— 500 m
0 ——— 0.25 miles

*DENMARK
STRAIT*

Aðalvík

Búrfell
(498m) ▲
Granahlíð

Skálavík

Hnifsdalur–
Bolungarvík Tunnel

Súgandafjörður → Bolungarvík
Suðureyri ● *Syðridalsvatn* ▲
Önundarfjörður 10 *Tungudalur* 15
3 ○ Óshlíð ● Hnifsdalur
65 61 1

624 Ísafjörður
Airport Suðavík

*Ísafjörður–
Suðureyri–
Flateyri Tunnel* 61

4WD Only *Dýrafjörður* Núpur ●
Svalvogar ●
Þingeyri
Peninsula Þingeyri
622 ▲ **See Þingeyri**
Sandfell **Enlargement** Lambadalsfjall
(957m) ▲

Arnarfjörður *Meðaldalur* Kaldbakur
(998m) Sjónfríð
(920m) ▲

Ketildalur Hrafnseyri ● 60
Græna hlíð ● *Borgarfjörður* *Dynjandi*
Suðurfjörður *Stóra
Eyjarvatn*
Gláma

Patreksfjörður 16 ☒
Kollsvík ● Tálknafjörður ● 63
Hænuvík ● Reykjarfjörður ●
Breiðavík ● Hnjótur ● 18
Hvallátur ● 612 Foss ● 60 9
2 ○ ○13 *Fossdalur* Flókalundur ●
Sauðlauksdalur Brjánslækur ●
614 Krossholt ● *Vatnsfjörður*
☒5 Kleifaheiði 62 *Baldur Car Ferry -
Brjánslækur*

▲ Skarðabrún
Stálfjall *Barðaströnd*

N

40 km

20 miles

E   **F**   **G**   **H**

1

Hornbjarg

Hornvík   Hornbjargsviti

Hornstrandir
Nature Reserve   Latravík

Hesteyri

Jökulfirðir

Bolungarvík

GREENLAND
SEA

2

Grunnavík

Reykjarfjörður

Furufjörður

Bjarnarfjörður

Snæfjallaströnd

Drangajökull

Drangar

Drangavík

3

Æðey   Dalbær

Vigur

Kaldalón

14

Ögur

6

Sela

Norðurfjörður   11

20

Melgraseyri

Lóndjúp

Árnes   643   Reykjanes

Litlibær

Skötufjörður

Reykjarfjörður

Reykjanes

633

Djúpavík

Veiðileysa

Strandir
Coast   Lambatindur
(854m)

4

61

Reykjarfjörður

Mjóifjörður

Ísafjörður

Selárdalur

Bjarnarfjörður

Kaldbaksvík

Heydalur

Hólsfjall
(469m)

Staður

Hvammsvatn

643

Bjarnarfjörður

Húnaflói

12   Bjarnarfjarðarháls

Hólmavík   645   Bær

Reiphólsfjöll
(881m)   *Þiðriksvallavatn*

8   Drangsnes

Grímsey

68

Vaðalfjöll
(508m)

Kirkjuból

Djúpidalur

60

Broddanes

690   68

Bjarkalundur

Króksfjörður

Þorskafjörður

711

Reykjanes

607

60

Bitrufjörður

17   Reykhólar   7

Breiðafjörður

Króksfjarðarnes

5

6

60

↓ Búðardalur (25km);
Reykjavík (95km)

68

Staðarskáli (40km);
Akureyri (110km);
Reykjavík (110km)

Westfjords

ⓖ TOURS

Borea Adventure

(Map p228; ☑456 3322; www.borea.is; Aðalstræti 18; ☺8am-6pm Mon-Fri, 9am-7pm Sat, 10am-4pm Sun Jun-Aug, shorter hours rest of year) An adventure outfitter offering fjord kayaking (from 13,900kr), excellent hiking in Hornstrandir (from 41,900kr) and mountain biking (from 13,900kr). It also runs ferry services to Hornstrandir and operates Kviar, its private cabin in the reserve.

West Tours Adventure Tour

(Vesturferðir; Map p228; ☑456 5111; www.westtours.is; Aðalstræti 7; ☺8am-6pm Mon-Fri, 8.30am-4.30pm Sat, 10am-3pm Sun Jun-Aug, 8am-4pm Mon-Fri Sep-May) Popular, professional West Tours organises a mind-boggling array of trips throughout the Westfjords including tours of Vigur island (p227) (11,000kr), hiking in Hornstrandir (from 32,900kr) and kayaking trips (from 7000kr), plus cycling, horse riding, boat and angling tours, birdwatching and cultural excursions. Kids are generally half-price.

Wild Westfjords Adventure Tour

(Map p228; ☑456 3300; www.wildwestfjords.com; Hafnarstræti 9; ☺9am-5.30pm May-Sep, shorter hours rest of year) Operates multiday guided or self-drive tours around the fjords and Iceland, as well as day tours, including trips to **Dynjandi waterfall** (adult/child 28,000/14,000kr), kayaking tours (from 12,800kr), hiking in Hornstrandir (from 33,000kr), and more challenging, adult-only treks to the iconic Hornbjarg cliffs (44,000kr).

ⓐ SHOPPING

Ísafjörður has good shopping opportunities, from souvenirs, knitting supplies and clothing to books, arts and design ware.

Karitas Clothing

(Map p228; Aðalstræti 20; ☺11am-6pm Mon-Thu, to 4pm Fri & Sat) A small seasonal pop-up selling traditional, handcrafted Icelandic jumpers, plus knitted socks, hats, shawls and jewellery.

Rammagerð Ísafjarðar Arts & Craft

(Map p228; ☑456 3041; Aðalstræti 14; ☺1-6pm Mon-Fri, noon-2pm Sat) Rammagerð Ísafjarðar sells quality knitting and other local crafts.

✕ EATING

Ísafjörður has an excellent restaurant, some great bistros, a batch of tempting fast-food outlets and some big supermarkets – ideal for stocking up with supplies before heading to remote areas.

Gamla Bakaríð Bakery

(Map p228; ☑456 3226; www.facebook.com/gamlabakariid; Aðalstræti 24; ☺7am-6pm Mon-Fri am-4pm Sat & Sun) For breakfast, lunch or mid-morning sugar fix, Gamla is the best akery in town and is usually packed for its ull range of sweet treats (cookies, dough-uts and cakes) as well as fresh bread.

Gata Cafe €

Map p228; ✆897 0942; www.facebook.com/pg/ataverslun; Aðalstræti 22b; snacks from 650kr; ⊗hours vary; 🛜🅿) Check to see if friendly Gata – part cafe, part outdoors store – is open for coffee, cake, paninis and fresh juice.

Thai Koon Thai €

Map p228; ✆456 0123; Hafnarstræti 9, Neisti centre; mains from 1800kr; ⊗11.30am-8pm, -8pm Sun) After a stretch of limited food options in remote Iceland, this small Thai canteen seems decidedly exotic. There's no grand ambience, but the curries and noodles are reliably tasty and served up in heaped portions.

Tjöruhúsið Seafood €€

Map p228; ✆456 4419; www.facebook.com/joruhusid; Neðstakaupstaður 1; mains 2600-700kr; ⊗noon-2pm & 7-9pm Jun-Sep) Set in a building from 1781, warm, rustic Tjöruhúsið offers some of the best seafood around. The set-course, serve-yourself dinner includes soup, catches of the day (fresh off the boat from the nearby harbour), and dessert such as chocolate mousse. There's outdoor eating on benches when it's sunny. Dinner starts promptly at 7pm and they're deserv-dly popular so book in advance.

Húsið International €€

Map p228; ✆456 5555; Hrannargata 2; mains 890-3590kr; ⊗kitchen 11am-10pm; 🛜) Sidle up to the rough-hewn wood tables inside this tin-clad house, or kick back on the sunny terrace for flavourful, relaxed meals and local beer on tap. Groovy tunes play as staff serve fish, burgers, pizza and Icelandic lamb. It's a fun hang-out with regular live music and DJs.

Við Pollinn Icelandic, Seafood €€€

Map p228; ✆456 3360; www.vidpollinn.is; Silfurtorg 2; mains 2700-5900kr; ⊗11am-9pm May-Sep, shorter hours rest of year) Although the minimalist decor at Hótel Ísafjörður's

🐦 Visiting Vigur Island

Charming **Vigur** (Map p224) is a popular destination for day trippers from Ísafjörður. In season it's a nesting site for hundreds of puffins, and the rest of the year it's a peaceful spot, sitting in the mouth of Hestfjörður andoffering sweeping fjord views in every direction, with seals splashing in the water and the chance to spot whales and dolphins.

Besides wildlife watching and taking a scenic stroll, you can take a snap of Iceland's oldest lighthouse (1837) and enjoy delicious cakes in the cafe, one of a scattering of ridiculously pretty buildings on the island (if the cinnamon buns are available, don't miss them). **West Tours** (p226) in Ísafjörður and **Ögur Travel** (Map p224; ✆857 1840; www.ogurtravel.com; Rte 61 ⊗May-Sep) in Ögur run boat tours and kayaking trips to the island.

Windmill on Vigur

restaurant lacks pizzazz, the food more than makes up for it. The strong selection of local cuisine, especially fish, is prepared with flair and the windows offer great views over the fjord – you might even see your next meal getting hauled into the harbour.

🍸 DRINKING & NIGHTLIFE

Edinborg Cafe, Bar

(Map p228; ✆456 8335; Aðalstræti 7; ⊗noon-11pm Mon-Thu, to 3am Fri, 4pm-3am Sat, 4-11pm Sun; 🛜) There's a mellow feel to Edinborg, where a relaxed bar with a pool table sits

Ísafjörður

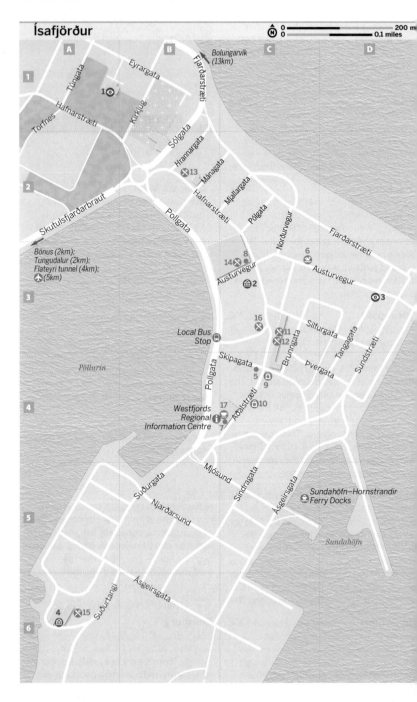

N 0 ⎯⎯⎯⎯⎯⎯⎯⎯ 200 m
0 ⎯⎯⎯⎯⎯⎯⎯⎯ 0.1 miles

Bolungarvík
(13km)

Tungata

Eyrargata

Fjarðarstræti

Kirkjubó

Hafnarstræti

Torfnes

1

Sólgata

Hrannargata

Mánagata

13

Skutulsfjarðarbraut

Pollgata

Hafnarstræti

Mjallargata

Pólgata

Norðurvegur

Fjarðarstræti

Bónus (2km);
Tungudalur (2km);
Flateyri tunnel (4km);
(5km)

8
14
Austurvegur

2

6

Austurvegur

3

16

11
Silfurgata

Local Bus
Stop

12
Brunngata

Tangagata

Sundstræti

Skipagata

Pvergata

Pöllurin

5

Pollgata

9

Aðalstræti

10

Westfjords
Regional
Information Centre

17

7

Mjósund

Sindragata

Ásgeirsgata

Suðurgata

Njarðarsund

Sundahöfn–Hornstrandir
Ferry Docks

Sundahöfn

Ásgeirsgata

Suðurtangi

4
15

Ísafjörður

side by side with a restaurant serving great burgers and fish. That makes it popular, as does occasional live music and having the local brew – zesty, amber-coloured Dokkan – on tap.

ⓘ INFORMATION

Westfjords Regional Information Centre
(Map p228; ☏450 8060; www.isafjordur.is; Aðalstræti 7, Edinborgarhús; ☉8am-6pm Mon-Fri, 8am-3pm Sat & Sun Jun-Aug, 8am-4pm Mon-Fri Sep-May) By the harbour in the Edinborgarhús (1907). Helpful staff have loads of info on the Westfjords and Hornstrandir Nature Reserve. Internet terminal with free 10-minute session; luggage storage 200kr per day.

ⓘ GETTING THERE & AWAY

AIR

Air Iceland Connect (p283) flies between **Ísafjörður Airport** (IFJ; Map p224; ☏570 3000; www.airicelandconnect.com), 5km south on the fjord, and Reykjavík's domestic airport twice daily. It also offers day tours.

A Flybus, timed to meet flights, runs between Ísafjörður and the airport (1000kr); it stops near Hótel Ísafjörður. The bus also goes onto Bolungarvík (1500kr).

BOAT

In summer, West Tours (p226) and Borea (p226) ferries to Hornstrandir depart from the **Sundahöfn docks** (Map p228) on the eastern side of the town promontory.

BUS

Ísafjörður is the major bus hub in the Westfjords. The long-distance bus stop is at the **tourist information centre**. Main services run by **Westfjords Adventures** (☏456 5006; www.westfjords adventures.com) go to Patreksfjörður and Brjánslækur (the terminal for the Stykkishólmur ferry) via Þingeyri, Dynjandi and Flókalundur. Other services go to Hólmavík. Services are reduced or nonexistent between mid-September and May.

For Reykjavík and Akureyri you'll need to make a number of changes. Check with the **information centre** or www.westfjords.is for current schedules.

ⓘ GETTING AROUND

City buses (350kr) operate from 7.30am to 6.15pm and connect the town centre with Hnífsdalur and Holtahverfi on the town's edges; they **stop** (Map p228; Pollgata) along the waterfront.

West Tours (p226) rents out bikes (75000/10,000kr for four/12 hours).

Þingeyri

A tiny village on the southern side of beautiful Dýrafjörður, Þingeyri sits on the fringes of an important Viking site and celebrates that connection with a Viking-themed festival and replica sailing ship. The town (www.thingeyri.is) is also a good jumping-off point for hiking, cycling and horse riding on the Þingeyri Peninsula (p218), just to the west.

Westfjords Heritage Museum (p223)

SIGHTS

Old Blacksmith's Workshop   Museum

(Gamla Smiðjan Þingeyri; Map p224; ☑456 3291; www.nedsti.is; Hafnarstræti 14; adult/ child 1200/950kr; ⊙9am-5pm mid-May–Aug) It was the first of its kind in Iceland when it was created in 1913, and today Þingeyri's atmospheric Old Blacksmith's Workshop is still crammed with original machinery and tools. It's part of Ísafjörður's Westfjords Heritage Museum (p223); the ticket includes admission to both sights.

ACTIVITIES

Simba Horses & Bike Rental   Horse Riding

(Simbahöllin Cafe; Map p224; ☑869 5654; www.westfjords-horseriding.com; Fjarðargata 5; ⊙mid-May–mid-Sep) You will get deep into the remote Þingeyri Peninsula on Simba's high-quality, small-group horse riding tours. Choose from a two-hour meander through the tranquil Sandar valley (9900kr) or trek across rivers to black-sand beaches (12,900kr). Or rent a classic mountain bike

(from 7500kr) or all-terrain fat bike (from 9000kr) for self-guided explorations of rugged trails.

TOURS

Reykjavík Viking Adventure   Boatin

(Map p224; ☑842 6660; www.reykjavikviking adventure.is; Old Harbour; per 12 people 125,000kr; ⊙Jun-Aug) ✔ Having relocated from the capital, Reykjavík Viking Adventure now offers trips in a reconstruction of Viking ship *Gaukstad* from Þingeyri Harbour. Operates group bookings only.

EATING

Simbahöllin   Cafe €€

(Map p224; ☑899 6659; www.simbahollin.is; Fjarðargata 5; mains 1400-3100kr; ⊙10am-10pm mid-Jun–Aug, noon-6pm mid-May–mid-Jun & early Sep; 🛜) Simbahöllin is a cool cafe in a restored 1915 general store with friendly staff serving tasty Belgian waffles during the day and hearty lamb tagines at night. Outdoor seating, fjord views and a cosy vibe ensure this is one of the Westfjords best boltholes.

ℹ️ INFORMATION

ingeyri Tourist Office (Map p224; 📞456
304; www.thingeyri.is; Hafnarstræti 6; ⏱️10am-
pm mid-May–early Sep) On the main road.

ℹ️ GETTING THERE & AWAY

Iunicipal bus (📞456 5518; www.isafjordur.is)
ervices go to Flateyri and Ísafjörður (350kr, one
our, three to four daily Monday to Friday).

From June to August Westfjords Adven-
ures (p229) has services along the route
atreksfjörður–Brjánslækur (the terminal for the
tykkishólmur ferry)–Flókalundur–Ísafjörður.
: stops in Þingeyri and runs once a day in each
irection on Monday, Wednesday and Friday.

Patreksfjörður

The largest village in this part of the
Vestfjords, zippy little Patreksfjörður on
he fjord of the same name is a convenient
umping-off point for visits to the Látrabjarg
Peninsula. The no-frills town has dramat-
c views to the bluffs and good services
or those preparing to head out to more
emote fjords. The town was named after
St Patrick of Ireland, who was the spiritual
uide of Örlygur Hrappson, the first settler
n the area.

🏃 ACTIVITIES

Patreksfjörður Pool   Swimming
Map p224; 📞456 1301; Aðalstræti 55; adult/
hild 700kr/free; ⏱️8am-9.30pm Mon-Fri, 10am-
pm Sat & Sun mid-May–mid-Sep, shorter hours
vinter) Patreksfjörður's swim spot is an
bsolute beauty – the infinity pool sits on
2nd-story terrace overlooking the fjord.
here's a sauna and two hot-pots too.

🎫 TOURS

**Westfjords
Adventures**   Hiking Tour, Jeep Tour
Map p224; 📞456 5006; www.wa.is; Þórsgata
a; ⏱️8.15am-5pm Mon-Fri, 10am-noon Sat & Sun
nid-May–mid-Sep, 9am-noon mid-Sep–mid-May)
he area's top tour provider offers

Þingeyri Viking Festival

The big local party is the **Dýrafjarðard-
agar Viking Festival**, held on either the
last weekend of June or the first weekend of July. It features staged fights and
celebrates the area's Viking heritage
and the saga of local man Gísli Súrsson.

everything from birdwatching and hikes
on the Látrabjarg Peninsula (eight hours,
29,500kr) to day-long jeep tours around
the fjords (34,000kr) or along the remote
Kjaran's Ave (39,900kr), a rough gravel
track hewn into the fjord. There's a range
of boat, whale-watching and fishing tours
(from 13,900kr) on Patreksfjörður, as well
as tours further afield.

🍴 EATING

Stúkuhúsið   Bistro €€
(Map p224; 📞456 1404; www.stukuhusid.is;
Aðalstræti 50; mains 1300-4990kr; ⏱️11am-11pm
mid-May–Aug, noon-4pm Wed-Sat rest of year;
📶🚻) In this cool eatery friendly staff serve
up filling salads, chicken soup, Icelandic
lamb and their speciality: succulent fish
fresh from the fjord outside the window –
the cod with hints of wasabi is superb.

ℹ️ GETTING THERE & AWAY

From June to August Westfjords Adventures
(p229) runs bus services to Brjánslækur,
Flókalundur, Dynjandi, Þingeyri and Ísafjörður.
A bus links Patreksfjörður with Látrabjarg,
Rauðasandur and Brjánslækur, reaching
Brjánslækur in time for the ferry to Stykkishól-
mur. It has to be booked in advance.

Get to Reykjavík by catching the **Baldur Car
Ferry** (Map p224; 📞433 2254; www.seatours.is;
Rte 62) from Brjánslækur to Stykkishólmur, then
taking Strætó (p281) bus 58 to Borgarnes and
transferring to bus 57 to Reykjavík.

Ice cave under a glacier

In Focus

Iceland Today

Iceland's booming tourism has helped the country stabilise its economy and lift capital controls following the 2008 banking crash. Tourism has also brought a host of changes, from crowds to more foreign-born workers. Meanwhile the populace is pressuring the government to respond to the country's changing situation, protect the environment and recover from high-profile scandals.

Tourism Boom

Curious travellers started to arrive en masse following the 2010 Eyjafjallajökull eruption and a smart publicity campaign led by the Iceland tourism board, which helped spread word of Iceland's charms. Tourism saw a 444% increase from 2010 to 2017, with about 2.2 million visitors arriving in 2017. There are some signs of a slowdown, as the strong króna and higher prices have made travel (and life) in Iceland expensive – also potentially shortening visitor stays. Even so, places like the North, East and Westfjords still remain relatively undervisited.

belief systems
(% of population)

70

6   4   1   6   13

angelical   Other   Roman   Ásatrú   No religion   Other
utheran   Lutheran   Catholic   (Norse gods)

celand were 100 people

91 would be Icelandic
4 would be Polish
4 would be other European
1 would be other

pulation per sq km

♦ ≈ 3 people

eland   USA

Tourism Repercussions

The strengthening of the economy as a result of tourism income is indisputable, and many locals appreciate the new services, increase in international profile and wage increases that the industry brings. However, short-term apartment rentals in the centre of Reykjavík are pushing locals out of the market and a hotel-building explosion in the capital is bringing new changes.

News reports consistently feature the destruction of the environment, or rescues of stranded tourists from glaciers, mountainsides and wave-swept beaches. Responses include limits on short-term apartment rentals, additional cautionary signs and barriers at sights, restrictions on free camping and improved methods for learning about safety and registering hikes (www.safetravel.is).

Protecting Iceland

Important debate is taking place about how Iceland's fragile environment can withstand the pressure it's under. The country's unspoilt natural landscape is both beloved by Icelanders and a major tourist draw. There's also concern about foreign interests buying vast swaths of land, including important salmon-fishing rivers.

Tourism authorities are currently placing huge emphasis on promoting responsible travel and preparing visitors for how to experience and protect the unusual environment. There is also a move to create a Highland National Park, which would protect a full 40% of the country, and a popular initiative that promotes whale watching over eating whale.

Iceland also benefits from its copious sources of renewable energy (primarily geothermal and hydro power). This helps fuel life on the island and also attracts large energy users – (controversial) aluminium smelters are already in place for cheap power, and lower-impact computing 'server farms' are on the rise.

Political Hijinks

One of the world's few nations to prosecute the bankers held responsible for the financial collapse in 2008, Icelanders maintain a sharp watch on their leaders. From the April 2016 Panama Papers scandal that brought down Prime Minister Sigmundur Davíð Gunnlaugsson to the 2017 controversy that brought down the coalition of Prime Minister Bjarni Benediktsson (when his father defended a convicted paedophile), Icelanders hold their leaders to account.

Despite the resulting drama, capital controls (measures limiting the movement of cash and capital in and out of the country) put in place during the recovery after the financial collapse were finally lifted in 2018, and that same year Iceland made grand news when it became the first nation in the world to legislate parity in pay for men and women.

Recreation of the Battle of Orlygsstathir, Saga Museum (p56)

JONATHAN SMITH/LONELY PLANET ©

History

Geologically young, staunchly independent and frequently rocked by natural disaster, Iceland has a turbulent and absorbing history of Norse settlement, literary genius, bitter feuding and foreign oppression. Life was never going to be easy, but the challenges have cultivated a modern Icelandic spirit that's remarkably resilient, fiercely individualistic and justifiably proud.

AD 600–700
Irish monks voyage to uninhabited Iceland, becoming the first (temporary) settlers.

850–930
Norse settlers from Norway and Sweden arrive, calling the island Snæland (Snow Land) and later Ísland (Iceland).

871
Norwegian Viking Ingólfur Arnarson, credited as the country's first permanent inhabitant, sails to the southwest coast.

Traditional house, Varmahlíð

DALUSH/SHUTTERSTOCK ©

Early Travellers & Irish Monks

A veritable baby in geological terms, Iceland was created around 20 million years ago. It was only around 330 BC, when the Greek explorer Pytheas wrote about the island of Ultima Thule, six days north of Britain by ship, that Europeans became aware of a landmass beyond the confines of their maps, lurking in a 'congealed sea'.

For many years rumour, myth and fantastic tales of fierce storms, howling winds and barbaric dog-headed people kept explorers away from the great northern ocean, *oceanus innavigabilis*. Irish monks were the next to stumble upon Iceland: they regularly sailed to the Faroes looking for solitude and seclusion. It's thought that Irish *papar* (fathers) settled in Iceland around the year AD 700. The Irish monk Dicuil wrote in 825 of a land where there was no daylight in winter, but on summer nights 'whatever task a man wishes to perform, even picking lice from his shirt, he can manage as well as in clear daylight'. This almost certainly describes Iceland and its long summer nights. The *papar* fled when the Norsemen began to arrive in the early 9th century.

930
The world's oldest existing parliament, the Alþingi, is founded at Þingvellir. The law code is memorised by an elected law speaker.

986
Erik the Red founds the first permanent European colony in Greenland.

999–1000
Iceland officially converts to Christianity under pressure from the Norwegian king, though pagan beliefs and rituals remain.

The Vikings Are Coming?

After the Irish monks, Iceland's first permanent settlers came from Norway. The Age of Settlement is traditionally defined as the period between 870 and 930, when political strife on the Scandinavian mainland caused many to flee. Most North Atlantic Norse settlers were ordinary Scandinavian citizens: farmers, herders and merchants who settled right across Western Europe, marrying Britons, Westmen (Irish) and Scots.

It's likely that the Norse accidentally discovered Iceland after being blown off course en route to the Faroes. The first arrival, Naddoddr, sailed from Norway and landed on the east coast around 850. He named the place Snæland (Snow Land) before backtracking to his original destination.

Iceland's second visitor, Garðar Svavarsson, circumnavigated the island and then settled in for the winter at Húsavík on the north coast. When he left in the spring some of his crew remained, or were left behind, thus becoming the first Norse to stay.

Around 860 the Norwegian Flóki Vilgerðarson uprooted his farm and family and headed for Snæland. He navigated via ravens, which, after some trial and error, led him to his destination and provided his nickname, Hrafna-Flóki (Raven-Flóki). Hrafna-Flóki sailed to Vatnsfjörður on the west coast; but became disenchanted after seeing icebergs floating in the fjord. He renamed the country Ísland (Iceland) and returned to Norway; although he did eventually come back to Iceland, settling in the Skagafjörður district on the north coast.

Credit for the first intentional permanent settlement, according to the 12th-century *Íslendingabók*, goes to Ingólfur Arnarson, who fled Norway with his blood brother Hjörleifur. He landed at Ingólfshöfði (Southeast Iceland) in 871, then continued around the coast and set up house in 874 at a place he called Reykjavík (Smoky Bay), named after the steam from thermal springs there. Hjörleifur settled near the present town of Vík, but was murdered by his slaves shortly after.

As for Ingólfur, he was led to Reykjavík by a fascinating pagan ritual. It was traditional for Viking settlers to toss their high-seat pillars (a symbol of authority and part of a chieftain's paraphernalia) into the sea as they approached land. The settler's new home was established wherever the gods brought the pillars ashore – a practice imitated by waves of settlers who followed from the Norwegian mainland.

Assembling the Alþingi

By the time Ingólfur's son Þorsteinn reached adulthood, the whole island was scattered with farms, and people began to feel the need for some sort of government. Iceland's landowners gathered first at regional assemblies to trade and settle disputes, but it became apparent that a national assembly was needed. This was a completely novel idea at the time, but Icelanders reasoned that it must be an improvement on the oppressive system they had experienced under the Nordic monarchy.

1100–1230	1104	1200
Iceland's literary Golden Age takes place, during which the Old Norse sagas are written. Several are attributed to Snorri Sturluson.	Hekla's first recorded eruption in human-historical times, covers Þjórsárdalur valley and its medieval farms with a thick layer of ash.	Iceland descends into anarchy during the Sturlung Age. The government dissolves and, in 1281, Iceland is absorbed by Norway.

In the early 10th century Þorsteinn Ingólfsson held Iceland's first large-scale district assembly near Reykjavík, and in the 920s the self-styled lawyer Úlfljótur was sent to study Norway's law codes and prepare something similar for Iceland.

At the same time Grímur Geitskör was commissioned to find a location for the Alþingi (National Assembly). Bláskógar, near the eastern boundary of Ingólfur's estate, with its beautiful lake and wooded plain, seemed ideal. Along one side of the plain was a long cliff with an elevated base (the Mid-Atlantic Ridge), from where speakers and representatives could preside over people gathered below.

In 930 Bláskógar was renamed Þingvellir (Assembly Plains). Þorsteinn Ingólfsson was given the honorary title *allsherjargoði* (supreme chieftain) and Úlfljótur was designated the first *lögsögumaður* (law speaker), who was required to memorise and annually recite the entire law of the land. It was he, along with the 48 *goðar* (chieftains), who held the actual legislative power.

Although squabbles arose over the choice of leaders, and allegiances were continually questioned, the new parliamentary system was a success. At the annual convention of the year 999 or 1000, the

The Viking Age

Scandinavia's greatest impact on world history probably occurred during the Viking Age. In the 8th century, an increase in the numbers of restless, landless young men in western Norway coincided with advances in technology, as Nordic shipbuilders developed fast, manoeuvrable boats sturdy enough for ocean crossings.

The Viking Age officially began in bloodshed in 793, when Norsemen plundered St Cuthbert's monastery on Lindisfarne, an island off Britain's Northumberland coast. The Vikings took to monasteries with delight, realising that speedy raids could bring handsome rewards.

In the following years Viking raiders returned with great fleets, terrorising, murdering, enslaving and displacing local populations, and capturing whole regions across Britain, Ireland, France and Russia. Icelandic tradition credits the Norse settlement of Iceland to tyrannical Harald Hårfagre (Harald Fairhair), king of Vestfold in southeastern Norway.

assembled crowd was bitterly divided between pagans and Christians, and civil war looked likely. Luckily Þorgeir, the incumbent law speaker, was a master of tact. The *Íslendingabók* relates that he retired to his booth, refusing to speak to anyone for a day and a night while he pondered the matter. When he emerged, he decreed that Iceland should accept the new religion and convert to Christianity, although pagans (such as himself) were to be allowed to practise their religion in private. This decision gave the formerly divided groups a semblance of national unity, and soon the first bishoprics were set up at Skálholt in the southwest and Hólar in the north.

Over the following years, the two-week national assembly at Þingvellir became the social event of the year. All free men could attend. Single people came looking for partners,

1397	1402–04	1550
On 17 June the Kalmar Union is signed in Sweden, uniting the countries of Norway, Sweden and Denmark under one king.	The Black Death sweeps across Iceland and kills around half of the population.	Lutheranism is imposed after the Catholic bishop Jón Arason is captured in battle and beheaded at Skálholt.

★ **Best Viking Experiences**

National Museum (p42), Reykjavík

Settlement Exhibition (p41), Reykjavík

Þingvellir National Park (p78), near Selfoss

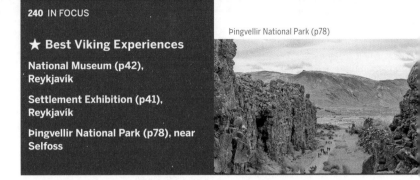

Þingvellir National Park (p78)

marriages were contracted and solemnised, business deals were finalised, duels and executions were held, and the Appeals Court handed down judgements on matters that couldn't be resolved in lower courts.

Anarchy & the Sturlung Age

The late 12th century kicked off the Saga Age, when epic tales of early settlement, family struggles, romance and tragic characters were recorded by historians and writers. Much of our knowledge of this time comes from two weighty tomes: the *Íslendingabók,* a historical narrative from the Settlement Era written by 12th-century scholar Ari Þorgilsson (Ari the Learned), and the detailed *Landnámabók,* a comprehensive account of the settlement.

Despite the advances in such cultural pursuits, Icelandic society was beginning to deteriorate. By the early 13th century the enlightened period of peace that had lasted 200 years was waning. Constant power struggles between rival chieftains led to violent feuds and a flourishing of Viking-like private armies, which raided farms across the country. This dark hour in Iceland's history was known as the Sturlung Age, named for the Sturlungs, the most powerful family clan in Iceland at the time. The tragic events and brutal history of this 40-year era is graphically recounted in the three-volume *Sturlunga Saga.*

As Iceland descended into chaos, the Norwegian king Hákon Hákonarson pressured chieftains, priests and the new breed of wealthy aristocrats to accept his authority. The Icelanders, who saw no alternative, dissolved all but a superficial shell of their government and swore their allegiance to the king. An agreement of confederacy was made in 1262. In 1281 a new code of law, the *Jónsbók,* was introduced by the king, and Iceland was absorbed into Norwegian rule.

Norway immediately set about appointing Norwegian bishops to Hólar and Skálholt and imposed excessive taxes. Contention flared as former chieftains quibbled over high offices, particularly that of *járl* (earl), an honour that fell to the ruthless Gissur Þorvaldsson, who in 1241 murdered Snorri Sturluson, Iceland's best-known historian and writer.

1602	1625–85	1703
Denmark imposes a trade monopoly, giving Danish and Swedish firms exclusive trading rights in Iceland.	During the notorious Westfjords witch hunts; 21 Icelanders are executed, beginning with Jón Rögnvaldsson.	Iceland's first census reveals a population of 50,358; 55% are female.

Meanwhile the volcano Hekla erupted three times, covering a third of the country in ash; a mini–ice age followed, and severe winters wiped out livestock and crops. The Black Death arrived, killing half the population, and the once indomitable spirit of the people seemed broken.

Enter the Danes

Iceland's fate was now in the hands of the highest Norwegian bidder, who could lease the governorship of the country on a three-year basis. In 1397 the Kalmar Union of Norway, Sweden and Denmark brought Iceland under Danish rule. After disputes between Church and state, the Danish government seized Church property and imposed Lutheranism in the Reformation of 1550. When the stubborn Catholic bishop of Hólar, Jón Arason, resisted and gained a following, he and his two sons were taken to Skálholt and beheaded.

In 1602 the Danish king imposed a crippling trade monopoly whereby Swedish and Danish firms were given exclusive trading rights in Iceland for 12-year periods. This resulted in large-scale extortion, importation of spoilt or inferior goods, and yet more suffering that would last another 250 years. However, one positive eventually emerged from the monopoly. In an attempt to bypass the embargo and boost local industry, powerful town magistrate Skúli Magnússon built weaving, tanning and wool-dyeing factories, which would become the foundations of the modern city of Reykjavík.

Even More Misery

If impoverishment at the hands of Danish overlords was not enough, Barbary pirates got in on the action, raiding the Eastfjords and the Reykjanes Peninsula before descending on Vestmannaeyjar in 1627. The defenceless population attempted to hide in Heimaey's cliffs and caves, but the pirates ransacked the island, killing indiscriminately and loading 242 people onto their ships. The unfortunate Icelanders were taken to Algiers, where most were sold into slavery. Back home, money was scrimped and saved for ransom, and eventually 13 of the captives were freed. The most famous was Guðríður Símonardóttir, who returned to Iceland and married Hallgrímur Pétursson, one of Iceland's most famous poets – the three bells in Hallgrímskirkja are named after the couple and their daughter.

During the same period, Europe's witch-hunting craze reached Icelandic shores. Icelandic witches were mostly men – of the 130 cases that appear in the court annals, only 10% involve women. The luckiest defendants were brutally flogged; 21 of the unluckiest were burned at the stake, mostly for supposedly making their neighbours sick or for possessing magical writing or suspicious-looking amulets.

It may have been the Age of Enlightenment in Europe, but it's a wonder any Icelanders survived the 18th century. In this remote outpost in the North Atlantic, the population of 50,000 was holding on for dear life in the face of a powerful smallpox epidemic, which

1783–84	1786	1855–90
The Laki crater row erupts, pouring out poisonous gas clouds that kill 25% of the population and more than 50% of livestock.	Reykjavík is officially founded (inhabited at the time by fewer than 200 souls). The settlement is granted a trade charter.	Iceland moves towards independence, with free trade and a draft constitution. Many Icelanders emigrate to North America.

arrived in 1707 and killed an estimated 18,000 people, along with a series of volcanic erup-tions: Katla in 1660, 1721 and again in 1755; Hekla in 1693 and 1766; and Öræfajökull in 1727.

Things got worse. In 1783 the Laki crater row erupted, spewing out billions of tonnes of lava and poisonous gas clouds for a full eight months. Fifty farms in the immediate area were wiped out, and the noxious dust and vapours and consequent Haze Famine went on to kill around 9000 Icelanders; first plants died, then livestock, then people. Ash clouds from the eruption affected the whole of Europe, causing freak weather conditions, includ-ing acid rain and floods. Authorities in Denmark contemplated relocating the remaining Icelandic population, which by 1801 numbered just 47,000, to Denmark.

Return to Independence

After five centuries of oppressive foreign rule, Icelandic nationalism flourished in the 19th century, conscious of a growing sense of liberalisation across Europe. By 1855 Jón Sig-urðsson, an Icelandic scholar, had successfully lobbied for restoration of free trade, and by 1874 Iceland had drafted a constitution and regained control of its domestic affairs.

Iceland's first political parties were formed during this period, and urban development began in this most rural of countries. Still, it wasn't enough to stave off the wave of emigra-tion that had started: between 1870 and 1914, some 16,000 Icelanders left to seek a better life in North America. Reasons for emigrating included lack of opportunity – the growing fishing industry could not employ all the workers who wished to escape the hard labour of rural life and move to the new urban centres – and yet another volcanic eruption, Askja, in 1875, which spewed livestock-poisoning ash.

By 1918 Iceland had signed the Act of Union, which effectively released the country from Danish rule, making it an independent state within the Kingdom of Denmark.

Iceland prospered during WWI as wool, meat and fish exports gained high prices. When WWII loomed, however, Iceland declared neutrality in the hope of maintaining its important trade links with both Britain and Germany.

On 9 April 1940 Denmark was occupied by Germany, prompting the Alþingi to take control of Iceland's foreign affairs once more. A year later, on 17 May 1941, Icelanders requested complete independence. The formal establishment of the Republic of Iceland finally took place at Þingvellir on 17 June 1944 – now celebrated as Independence Day.

WWII & the USA Moves In

Wartime Iceland's complete lack of military force worried the Allied powers and so in May 1940 Britain, most vulnerable to a German-controlled Iceland, sent in forces to occupy the island. Iceland had little choice but to accept the situation, but ultimately the country's economy profited from British construction projects and spending.

When the British troops withdrew in 1941 the government allowed US troops to move in on the understanding they would move out at the end of the war. Although the US military

1918
Denmark's grip on Iceland gradually loosens. Following Home Rule in 1904, the Act of Union is signed on 1 December 1918.

1940–41
After the Nazis occupy Den-mark, the UK sends troops to occupy neutral Iceland. A US base is later established.

1944
A majority of Icelanders vote for independence from Denmark; the Republic of Iceland is established on 17 June.

left in 1946, it retained the right to re-establish a base at Keflavík should war threaten again. Back under their own control, Icelanders were reluctant to submit to any foreign power. When the government was pressured into becoming a founding member of NATO in 1949, riots broke out in Reykjavík. The government agreed to the proposition on the conditions that Iceland would never take part in offensive action and that no foreign military troops would be based in the country during peacetime.

These conditions were soon broken. War with Korea erupted in 1950, and at NATO's request in 1951 the USA, jumpy about the Soviet threat, once again took responsibility for the island's defence. US military personnel and technology at the Keflavík base continued to increase over the next four decades, as Iceland served as an important Cold War monitoring station. The controversial US military presence in Iceland only ended in September 2006, when the base at Keflavík finally closed.

Modern Iceland

In the 20th century Iceland transformed itself from one of the poorest countries in Europe to one of the most developed.

Following the Cold War, Iceland went through a period of growth, rebuilding and modernisation. The Ring Road was completed in 1974 – opening up transport links to the remote southeast – and projects such as the Krafla power station in the northeast and the Svartsengi power plant near Reykjavík were developed. A boom in the fishing industry saw Iceland extend its fishing limit in the 1970s to 200 miles (322km). This, however, precipitated the worst of the 'cod wars', as the UK refused to recognise the new zone. During the seven-month conflict, Icelandic ships cut the nets of British trawlers, shots were fired, and ships on both sides were rammed.

The fishing industry has always been vital to Iceland, although it's had its ups and downs – quotas were reduced in the 1990s so stocks could regenerate after overfishing. The industry went into recession, leading to an unemployment rate of 3% and a sharp drop in the króna. The country slowly began a period of economic regeneration as the fishing industry stabilised. Today the industry still provides 33.6% of exports and 12% of GDP, and employs 4% of the workforce. It remains sensitive to declining fish stocks.

In 2003 Iceland resumed whaling as part of a scientific research program, despite a global moratorium on hunts. In 2006 Iceland resumed commercial whaling, in spite of condemnation from around the world. Hunting of minke whales continues, drawing further international rebukes; hunting of endangered fin whales was suspended in 2016 but resumed in 2018.

Financial Crash & Volcanic Eruptions

Iceland's huge dependence on its fishing industry and on imported goods means that the country has always had relatively high prices and a currency prone to fluctuation. Its vulnerability was brought into focus in September 2008, when the global economic crisis

1974	1975	1986
The Ring Road around the island is completed when the Skeiðarárbrú bridge opens on 14 July.	The third in a series of 'cod wars' takes place between Iceland and the UK.	General Secretary Mikhail Gorbachev and President Ronald Reagan agree to meet at a summit in Reykjavík.

Iceland's Economic Meltdown

Between 2003 and early 2008, Iceland was full of confidence and riding high. But much of the country's wealth was built over a black hole of debt – its banks' liabilities were more than 10 times the country's annual GDP. The ripples of the worldwide financial crisis became a tidal wave by the time they reached Icelandic shores, washing away the country's entire economy.

By October 2008 the Icelandic stock market had crashed; the króna plummeted, losing almost half its value overnight; all three national banks went into receivership; and the country teetered on the brink of bankruptcy. Help came for Iceland in November 2008 with a US$2.1 billion International Monetary Fund (IMF) loan and a US$3 billion bailout from Scandinavian neighbours.

hit the country with a sledgehammer blow. Reykjavík was rocked by months of fierce protest, as the then-government's popularity evaporated along with the country's wealth.

Prime Minister Geir Haarde resigned in January 2009. His replacement, Jóhanna Sigurðardóttir, hit international headlines as the world's first openly gay prime minister. Her first major act was to apply for EU membership, with the eventual aim of adopting the euro as the country's new currency, in an effort to stabilise the economy. EU membership was then and continues to be a contentious issue.

Iceland again hit global headlines in April 2010, when ash cloud from the eruption under Eyjafjallajökull ice cap shut down European air traffic for six days, causing travel chaos across much of the continent. In comparison, the Grímsvötn volcano, which erupted the following year, was a mere trifle – its ash cloud caused just three days of air-traffic disruption. In 2014 Bárðarbunga's rumblings shone a spotlight onto Iceland's volatility once again, as have Katla's jolts in 2016. In 2018 seismic activity was on the increase in Öræfajökull and continues in Bárðarbunga.

Tourism Boom & Political Scandals

Events in Iceland have proved there's no such thing as bad publicity. Triggered by the 2010 eruption and the free press it generated for Iceland, plus a concerted Icelandic effort to build airline routes and exposure, tourism has boomed, increasing 440% from 2010 to 2017. The country has become the fastest-growing travel destination in Europe, with all the benefits (economic growth and employment) and headaches (infrastructure issues and environmental impact) that such status entails.

Icelanders went to the polls in April 2013 with the national economy on the path to recovery, but the population smarting from the government's tough austerity measures (including higher taxes and spending cuts). The results showed a backlash against the ruling Social Democrats; the centre-right camp (comprising the Progressive Party and

2006	**2008**	**2009**
The controversial US military base at Keflavík closes down after 45 years in service; commercial whaling resumes.	The worldwide financial downturn hits Iceland particularly hard, precipitating the country's worst ever national banking crisis.	Iceland formally applies for EU membership – the application is withdrawn by a new government in 2014.

the Independence Party) successfully campaigned on promises of debt relief and a cut in taxes, as well as opposition to Iceland's application to join the EU.

The two parties formed a coalition government. In early 2014 the government halted all negotiations with the EU – despite promising a referendum on whether or not to proceed with membership negotiations. Although polls show a majority of Icelanders still oppose joining the EU, making such a move without the promised referendum was deeply unpopular.

In April 2016 the Panama Papers document leak from the law firm Mossack Fonseca revealed financial improprieties implicating three Icelandic ministers, including Prime Minister Sigmundur Davíð Gunnlaugsson. As a result of massive protests, Gunnlaugsson stepped aside as prime minister. Sigurður Ingi Jóhannsson became the acting prime minister, and early elections produced no clear coalition.

In June 2016, on a wave of anti-establishment sentiment, Iceland elected its first new president in 20 years: historian and author Guðni Thorlacius Jóhannesson.

In January 2017 a short-lived coalition formed with only 32 MPs out of 63, headed by the Independence Party and Bjarni Benediktsson, but in September a scandal surrounding Benediktsson's father's defence of a convicted paedophile brought down that government.

A new government coalition was formed in late 2017, led by Prime Minister Katrín Jakobsdóttir, the chair of the Left-Green Party, in partnership with the Independence Party and the Progressive Party (Framsóknarflokkurinn), an agrarian-based party.

2010
The volcano under Eyjafjallajökull glacier begins erupting, bringing European flights to a standstill for six days.

2013
The number of international visitors to Iceland numbers 807,000 (up from 320,000 in 2003). In 2017 it's 2.2 million.

2016
As a result of financial improprieties, Prime Minister Sigmundur Davíð Gunnlaugsson steps aside.

Hot spring, Reykjavík

SAM SPICER/GETTY IMAGES ©

Natural Wonders

It's difficult to remain unmoved by the amazing diversity of the Icelandic landscape. Prepare to explore everything from a lunar-like terrain of ornate lava flows and towering volcanoes with misty ice caps to steep-sided glistening fjords, lush emerald-green hills, glacier-carved valleys, bubbling mudpots and vast, desert-like expanses. It's a rich mix of extraordinary scenery and extremes.

Volatile Iceland

Situated on the Mid-Atlantic Ridge, a massive 18,000km-long rift between two of the earth's major tectonic plates, Iceland is a shifting, steaming lesson in schoolroom geology. Suddenly you'll be racking your brains to remember long-forgotten homework on how volcanoes work, what a solfatara is (spoiler: it's a volcanic vent emitting hot gases), and why lava and magma aren't quite the same thing.

Iceland is one of the youngest landmasses on the planet, formed by underwater volcanic eruptions along the joint of the North American and Eurasian plates around 20 million years ago. The earth's crust in Iceland is only a third of its normal thickness, and magma (molten rock) continues to rise from deep within, forcing the two plates apart. The result is clearly

Dynjandi waterfall (p226)

JULES_KITANO/SHUTTERSTOCK ©

visible at Þingvellir, where the great rift Almannagjá broadens by between 1mm and 18mm per year, and at Námafjall (near Mývatn), where a series of steaming vents mark the ridge.

Volcanoes

Thin crust and grating plates are responsible for a host of exciting volcanic situations in Iceland. The country's volcanoes are many and varied – some are active, some are extinct, and some are dormant and dreaming, no doubt, of future destruction. Fissure eruptions and their associated craters are probably the most common type of eruption in Iceland. The still-volatile Lakagígar crater row around Laki mountain is the country's most extreme example. It produced the largest lava flow in human history in the 18th century, covering an area of 565 sq km to a depth of 12m.

Several of Iceland's liveliest volcanoes are found beneath glaciers, which makes for dramatic eruptions as molten lava and ice interact. The main 2010 Eyjafjallajökull eruption was of this type: it caused a *jökulhlaup* (flooding caused by volcanic eruption beneath an ice cap) that damaged part of the Ring Road, before throwing up the famous ash plume that grounded Europe's aeroplanes. Iceland's most active volcano, Grímsvötn, which lies beneath the Vatnajökull ice cap, behaved in a similar fashion in 2011.

Iceland not only has subglacial eruptions, but also submarine ones. In 1963 the island of Surtsey exploded from the sea, giving scientists the opportunity to study how smouldering chunks of newly created land are colonised by plants and animals. Surtsey is off limits to visitors, but you can climb many classical-looking cones such as Hekla, once thought to be the gateway to Hell; Eldfell, which did its best to bury the town of Heimaey in 1974; and Snæfellsjökull on the Snæfellsnes Peninsula.

★ **Best Puffin Viewing**

Borgarfjörður Eystri (p160)

Grímsey (p200)

Heimaey (p123)

Látrabjarg Bird Cliffs (p216)

Puffins

Recent eruptions in Iceland have tended to be fairly harmless – they're often called 'tourist eruptions' because their fountains of magma, electric storms and dramatic ash clouds make perfect photos but cause relatively little damage. This is partly due to the sparsely populated land, and partly because devastating features such as fast-flowing lava, lahars (mudslides) and pyroclastic surges (like the ones that obliterated Pompeii and Herculaneum) are usually absent in this part of the world.

The main danger lies in the gases that are released: suffocating carbon dioxide, highly acidic sulphur-based gases, and the deadly fluorine that poisoned people and livestock during the Laki eruptions of 1783. The **Icelandic Met Office** (Veðurstofa Íslands; www.vedur.is) keeps track of eruptions and the earthquakes that tend to precede them, plus the emissions that follow. Its work during 2014–15 Bárðarbunga seismic events and volcanic activity included daily factsheets. As of 2018, the volcanoes to watch are Katla, Hekla and Öræfajökull – all well overdue for eruption.

Geysers, Springs & Fumaroles

Iceland's Great Geysir gave its name to the world's spouting hot springs (it comes from the Icelandic for 'to gush'). It was once very active, frequently blowing water to a height of 80m, but earthquakes have altered the pressures inside its plumbing system and today it is far quieter. Its neighbour, Strokkur, now demonstrates the effect admirably, blasting a steaming column into the air every five to 10 minutes.

Geysers are reasonably rare phenomena, with around a thousand existing on earth. However, in Iceland, water that has percolated down through the rock and been superheated by magma can emerge on the surface in various other exciting ways. Some of it boils into hot springs, pools and rivers – you'll find naturally hot water sources all around Iceland, including the springs at Landmannalaugar, the river at Hveragerði and the warm blue-white pool in the bottom of Víti crater at Askja. Icelanders have long harnessed these soothing gifts of nature, turning them into geothermal swimming pools and spas. The country's smartest spas are Mývatn Nature Baths and the Blue Lagoon, but note that they are not natural hot springs – they are human-made lagoons fed by the water output of the nearby geothermal power plants.

Fumaroles are places where superheated water reaches the surface as steam – the weirdest Icelandic examples are at Hverir, where gases literally scream their way from sulphurous vents in the earth. Lazier, messier bloops and bubblings take place at mudpots, at Seltún (Krýsuvík) on the Reykjanes Peninsula, where heated water mixes with mud and clay. The colourful spatterings around some of the mudpots are caused by various minerals (sulphurous yellow, iron-red), and also by the extremophile bacteria and algae that somehow thrive in this boiling-acid environment.

Ice & Snow

Glaciers and ice caps cover around 11% of Iceland; many are remnants of a cool period that began 2500 years ago. Ice caps are formed as snow piles over millennia in an area where it's never warm enough to melt. The weight of the snow causes it to slowly compress into ice, eventually crushing the land beneath the ice cap.

Iceland's largest ice cap, Vatnajökull in the southeast, covers about 8% of the country and is the largest in the world outside the poles. This immense glittering weight of ice may seem immovable, but around its edges, slow-moving rivers of ice – glaciers – flow imperceptibly down the mountainsides. Like rivers, glaciers carry pieces of stony sediment, which they dump in cindery-looking moraines at the foot of the mountain, or on vast gravelly outwash plains such as the Skeiðarársandur in Southeast Iceland. This can occur very quickly if volcanoes under the ice erupt and cause a *jökulhlaup* (flood): the *jökulhlaup* from the 1996 Grímsvötn eruption destroyed Iceland's longest bridge and swept jeep-sized boulders down onto the plain.

Several of Iceland's glaciers have lakes at their tips. Jökulsárlón is a stunning place to admire icebergs that have calved from Breiðamerkurjökull. Luminous-blue pieces tend to indicate a greater age of ice, as centuries of compression squeeze out the air bubbles that give ice its usual silvery-white appearance. Icebergs may also appear blue due to light refraction.

Glaciers have carved out much of the Icelandic landscape since its creation, forming the glacial valleys and fjords that make those picture-postcard photos of today. The ice advances and retreats with the millennia, and also with the seasons, but there are worrying signs that Iceland's major ice caps – Vatnajökull, Mýrdalsjökull in the southwest, and Langjökull and Hofsjökull in the highlands – have been melting at an unprecedented rate since 2000. Glaciologists believe the ice cap Snæfellsjökull in the west (with an average ice thickness of only 30m), as well as some of the outlet glaciers of the larger ice caps, could disappear completely within a few decades. Others have lost their glacier status due to melting, such as West Iceland's Ok (formerly Okjökull) in 2014.

Fire & Ice

'Land of fire and ice' might be an overused marketing slogan, but it's not hyperbole. Serene, majestic scenery belies Iceland's fiery heart – there are some 30 active volcanoes, and many of them lie under thick ice.

Vatnajökull The island's ice queen is Europe's largest ice cap and the namesake for its largest national park.

Eyjafjallajökull The treacherous eruption spewed impenetrable tufts of ash over Europe in 2010, causing the cancellation of thousands of flights.

Hekla & Katla Like wicked stepsisters from some Icelandic fairy tale, Hekla and Katla are volatile beasts that dominate many of the southern vistas.

Snæfellsjökull Jules Verne's famous *Journey to the Centre of the Earth* starts here – the Snæfellsnes Peninsula's prominent glacial fist.

Magni & Móði Iceland's newest mountains were formed during the eruptions of 2010.

Wildlife

Mammals & Marine Life

Apart from birds, sheep and horses, you'll be lucky to have any casual sightings of animals in Iceland. The only indigenous land mammal is the elusive Arctic fox, best spotted in remote Hornstrandir in the Westfjords – wildlife enthusiasts can apply in advance to monitor

Geologically Speaking

Everywhere you go in Iceland you'll be bombarded with geological jargon to describe the landscape. These terms will let you one-up geological neophytes.

Basalt The most common type of solidified lava. This hard, dark, dense volcanic rock often solidifies into hexagonal columns.

Igneous A rock formed by solidifying magma or lava.

Moraine A ridge of boulders, clay and sand carried and deposited by a glacier.

Obsidian Black, glassy rock formed by the rapid solidification of lava without crystallisation.

Rhyolite Light-coloured, fine-grained volcanic rock similar to granite in composition.

Scoria Porous volcanic gravel that has cooled rapidly while moving, creating a glassy surface with iron-rich crystals that give it a glittery appearance.

Tephra Solid matter ejected into the air by an erupting volcano.

these creatures while volunteering at the **Arctic Fox Center** (www.arcticfoxcenter. com). In East Iceland, herds of reindeer can sometimes be spotted from the road. Reindeer were introduced from Norway in the 18th century and now roam the mountains in the east. Polar bears very occasionally drift across from Greenland on ice floes, but armed farmers make sure they don't last long.

In contrast, Iceland has a rich marine life, particularly whales. On whale-watching tours from Húsavík in North Iceland, you'll have an excellent chance of seeing cetaceans, particularly dolphins, porpoises, minke whales and humpback whales. Sperm, fin, sei, pilot, orca and blue whales also swim in Icelandic waters and have been seen by visitors. Seals can be seen in the Eastfjords, on the Vatnsnes Peninsula in northwest Iceland, in the Mýrar region on the southeast coast (including at Jökulsárlón), in Breiðafjörður in the west, and in the Westfjords.

Birds

Bird life is prolific, at least from May to August. On coastal cliffs and islands around the country you can see a mind-boggling array of seabirds, often in massive colonies. Most impressive for their sheer numbers are gannets, guillemots, gulls, razorbills, kittiwakes, fulmars and puffins. Less numerous birds include wood sandpipers, Arctic terns, skuas, Manx shearwaters, golden plovers, storm petrels and Leach's petrels. In the southern Westfjords you can occasionally spot endangered white-tailed eagles. In addition, there are many species of ducks, ptarmigans, whooping swans, redwings, divers and gyrfalcons, and two species of owls.

Flowers & Fungi

Although Iceland was largely deforested long ago, its vegetation is surprisingly varied – you just need to get close to see it. Most vegetation is low-growing, spreading as much as possible to get a better grip on the easily eroded soil. Wind erosion and damage from off-road drivers are big conservation issues. Even the trees, where there are any, are stunted. As the old joke goes, if you're lost in an Icelandic forest, just stand up.

If you're visiting in summer, you'll be treated to incredible displays of wildflowers blooming right across the country. Most of Iceland's 450 flowering plants are introduced species – especially the ubiquitous purple lupin, once an environmental help, but now a hindrance. A nationwide poll held in 2004 voted for the mountain avens (*Dryas octopetala*), known as *holtasóley* (heath buttercup) in Icelandic, as the national flower. Look out for it on gravel stretches and rocky outcrops – its flowers are about 3cm in diameter, each with eight delicate white petals and an exploding yellow-sun centre.

Coastal areas are generally character-ised by low grasses, bogs and marshlands, while at higher elevations hard or soft tundra covers the ground.

Another common sight when walking almost anywhere in Iceland is fungi. There are about 2000 types growing here, and you'll see everything from pale white mush-rooms to bright orange flat caps as you walk along trails, by roadsides or through fields.

In southern and eastern Iceland new lava flows are first colonised by mosses, which create a velvety green cloak across the rough rocks. Older lava flows in the east and those at higher elevations are generally first colonised by lichens. Confusingly, Icelandic moss (Cetraria islandica), the grey-green or pale brown frilly growth that you'll see absolutely everywhere, is actually lichen.

National Parks & Reserves

Iceland has three national parks and more than 100 nature reserves, natural monu-ments and country parks, with a protected area of 18,806 sq km (about 18% of the entire country). A proposed **Highland National Park** (www.halendid.is) would protect a vast section of Iceland's interior (40,000 sq km), comprising a full 40% of the country.

Umhverfisstofnun (Environment Agen-cy of Iceland; www.ust.is) is responsible for protecting many of these sites. Its website contains information on its work to promote the protection as well as sustainable use of Iceland's natural resources, including ways travellers can tread lightly. The agency also recruits summer volunteers each year to work in conservation projects within the parks.

Þingvellir National Park (p78), Iceland's oldest national park, protects a scenic 84-sq-km lake and the geologically significant Almannagjá rift, and is the site of the original Alþingi (National Assembly). The park is a Unesco World Heritage Site.

Snæfellsjökull National Park (p140) in West Iceland was established in June 2001. The park protects the Snæfellsjökull glacier (made famous by author Jules Verne) and the surrounding lava fields and coast.

Vatnajökull National Park (p114) is the largest national park in Europe and covers roughly 13% of Iceland. It was founded in 2008 by uniting two previously established national parks: Skaftafell (p170) in Southeast Iceland, and Jökulsárgljúfur (p176) further north. The park protects the entirety of the Vatnajökull ice cap, the mighty Dettifoss water-fall and a great variety of geological anomalies.

Whaling in Iceland

In the late 19th century, whale hunting became a lucrative commercial pros-pect with the arrival of steam-powered ships and explosive harpoons. Norwegian hunters built 13 large-scale whaling stations in Iceland, and hunted until stocks practically disappeared in 1913. Icelanders established their own whaling industry in 1935, until whale numbers again became dangerously low and commercial hunting was banned by the International Whaling Commission (IWC) in 1986. Iceland resumed com-mercial whaling in 2006, to the conster-nation of environmentalists worldwide. The question of why Iceland is whaling today is not a simple one to answer.

Iceland's authorities stress that the country's position has always been that whale stocks should be utilised in a sustainable manner like any other living marine resource. Its catch limits for common minke whales and fin whales follow the advice given by the Marine Research Institute of Iceland regarding sustainability – the quota for the 2018 season was for an annual maximum catch of 217 minke whales and 209 fin whales.

Puffins

Cute, clumsy and endearingly comic, the puffin (*Fratercula arctica,* or *lundi* as they're called in Icelandic) is one of Iceland's best-loved birds. The puffin is a member of the auk family and spends most of its year at sea. For four or five months it comes to land to breed, generally keeping the same mate and burrow (a multiroom apartment!) from year to year.

Until very recently, 60% of the world's puffins bred in Iceland, and you could see them in huge numbers around the island from late May to August. However, over the last decade, the puffin stock has gone into a sudden, sharp decline in the south of Iceland. They still visit the south – Vestmannaeyjar Islands' puffins are the largest puffin colony in the world – but in smaller numbers and with considerably less breeding success. The reason is uncertain, but it's thought that warming ocean temperatures have caused their main food source – sand eels – to decline. It's also possible that hunting and egg collection have had an effect. In 2018 BirdLife International reported that puffins are threatened with extinction globally.

Energy Agendas

Iceland's small population, pristine wilderness, lack of heavy industry and high use of geothermal and hydroelectric power (81.2% of their energy use came from renewable sources in 2017) give it an enviable environmental reputation. Its use of geothermal power is one of the most creative in the world, and the country's energy experts are now advising Asian and African industries on possible ways to harness geothermal sources.

However, power supplies provided free by bountiful nature are not just of interest to Icelanders. Foreign industrialists in search of cheap energy also have their eye on the country's glacial rivers and geothermal hot spots. Alcoa, an American aluminium-smelting company, was responsible for one of Iceland's most controversial schemes: the Kárahnjúkar hydroelectric station in East Iceland, completed in 2009, was the biggest construction project in Iceland's history. It created a network of dams and tunnels, a vast reservoir, a power station and miles of power lines to supply electricity to a fjord-side smelter 80km away in Reyðarfjörður.

Alcoa makes much of its efforts to reduce its carbon footprint including the fact that the aluminium it manufactures in Iceland uses cheap, green energy from renewable sources (this was the whole point of closing two US smelters and setting up here). Environmentalists, however, raised serious objections to the project on a number of grounds, not least that the mega-dam built specifically to power the Alcoa plant has devastated the landscape. Locals though were less vocal – many were grateful for work opportunities coming to the area.

The Power of Power

The Kárahnjúkar dam and aluminium smelter are dramatic illustrations of the dilemma Iceland faces.

To ensure economic prosperity, Iceland is seeking to shore up its position as a green-energy superpower. Thanks to its rich geothermal and hydroelectric energy sources, and new wind turbines (read more at www.nea.is), Iceland generates more electricity per capita than any other country in the world – and twice as much as second-placed Norway. Iceland and the UK have moved through the initial feasibility studies of exporting clean hydroelectric energy via a 1500km subsea power cable running from Iceland to the UK (read more at www.atlanticsuperconnection.com). Iceland is also continuing to expand its power-intensive industries, including becoming a global data-centre hub, home to servers housing digitised information.

But if such initiatives go ahead, the power must still be harnessed, and power plants and power lines must be built for such a purpose. Where will these be located? What tracts of Iceland's highland wilderness may be threatened by industrial megaprojects? NGO organisation **Landvernd** (www.landvernd.is), the Icelandic Environment Association, has proposed that the central highlands be protected with the establishment of a national park. Economic profit versus the preservation of nature – it's an age-old battle. Watch this space.

The Impact of Tourism on Nature

Icelanders are voicing a valid concern that the population of 350,000 and its existing infrastructure is ill-equipped to handle the demands and behaviour of over 2.2 million visitors per year. Media consistently reports instances of tourists disrespecting nature or taking dangerous risks: hiking in poor weather without proper equipment, getting vehicles stuck in rivers, driving cars onto glaciers, falling off cliffs or being swept off beaches.

The people on the hook for rescues are the extraordinarily competent and well-respected **Icelandic Association for Search and Rescue** (ICE-SAR; www.icesar.com). It is an all-volunteer operation funded by donations. Icelanders have responded by erecting more signs; ropes along some walkways – which some visitors continue to flout; and an educational campaign (www.inspiredbyiceland.com/icelandacademy). The government has also instituted camping rules requiring campervans to spend the night in organised campgrounds rather than on roadsides or in car parks, in part to address the problem of people using the roadside as their toilet. Laws are slightly more relaxed for hikers and cyclists, but they are bound by rules regarding obtaining landowner permission, being an acceptable distance from official campgrounds, ensuring they don't set up more than the allowed number of tents, and ensuring they're not camping on cultivated land.

Ultimately the protection of Iceland's environment will be a joint project between Icelanders and visitors. Icelanders must build on their infrastructure and rules, and foster an attitude of environmental protection, and visitors must heed local advice and respect the country they are visiting.

Waiting by artist Aðalheiður S. Eysteinsdóttir, in Siglufjörður

BENJAMIN ABRAM/SHUTTERSTOCK ©

Icelandic Culture

Iceland blows away concerns such as isolation and its small population with a glowing passion for all things cultural. The country's unique literary heritage begins with high-action medieval sagas and stretches to today's Nordic Noir bestsellers. Every Icelander seems to play in a band, and the country produces a disproportionate number of world-class musicians.

Literature

Bloody, mystical and nuanced, the late 12th- and 13th-century sagas are some of Iceland's greatest cultural achievements. Reverend Hallgrímur Pétursson's 1659 *Passíusálmar* (Passion Hymns) were an Icelandic staple, sung or read at Lent. Nobel Prize–winning author Halldór Laxness put Iceland on the 20th-century literary map. But Icelanders aren't resting on their laurels: today the country produces the most writers and literary translations per capita of any country in the world.

Hallgrímskirkja (p44)

The Sagas

Iceland's medieval prose sagas are some of the most imaginative and enduring works of early literature – epic, brutal tales that flower repeatedly with wisdom, magic, elegiac poetry and love.

Written down during the 12th to early 14th centuries, these sagas look back on the disputes, families, doomed romances and larger-than-life characters (from warrior and poet to outlaw) who lived during the Settlement Era. Most were written anonymously, though *Egil's Saga* has been attributed to Snorri Sturluson. Some are sources for historical understanding, such as the *Saga of the Greenlanders* and *Saga of Erik the Red,* which describe the travels of Erik and his family, including his son Leif (a settler in North America).

The sagas, written over the long, desperate centuries of Norwegian and Danish subjugation, provided a strong sense of cultural heritage at a time when Icelanders had little else. On winter nights, people would gather for the *kvöldvaka* (evening vigil). While the men twisted horsehair ropes and women spun wool or knitted, a family member would read the sagas and recite *rímur* (verse reworkings of the sagas).

The sagas are very much alive today. Icelanders of all ages can (and do) read them in Old Norse, the language in which they were written 800 years ago. Most people can quote chunks from them, know the farms where the characters lived and died, and flock to cinemas to see the latest film versions of these eternal tales. Check out the **Icelandic Saga Database** (www.sagadb.org) for more.

Carving of a character from *Egil's Saga*

★ **Top Icelandic Sagas**

Egil's Saga

Laxdæla Saga

Njál's Saga

Gisli Sursson's Saga

Völsungasaga (Saga of the Völsungs)

Eyrbyggja Saga

Eddic & Skaldic Poetry

The first settlers brought their oral poetic tradition with them from other parts of Scandinavia, and the poems were committed to parchment in the 12th century.

Eddic poems were composed in free, variable metres with a structure very similar to that of early Germanic poetry. Probably the most well known is the gnomic *Hávamál*, which extols the virtues of the common life – its wise proverbs on how to be a good guest are still quoted today.

Skaldic poems were composed by *skalds* (Norwegian court poets) and are mainly praise-poems of Scandinavian kings, with lots of description packed into tightly structured lines. As well as having fiercely rigid alliteration, syllable counts and stresses, Skaldic poetry is made more complex by *kennings*, a kind of compact word-riddle. Blood, for instance, is 'wound dew', while an arm might be described as a 'hawk's perch'.

The most renowned *skald* was saga anti-hero Egil Skallagrímsson. In 948, after being captured and sentenced to death, Egil composed the ode *Höfuðlausn* (Head Ransom) for his captor Eirík Blood-Axe. Flattered, the monarch released Egil unharmed.

Modern Literature

Nobel Prize–winner Halldór Laxness is Iceland's modern literary genius. Also well known is the early-20th-century children's writer Reverend Jón Sveinsson (nicknamed Nonni), whose old-fashioned tales of derring-do have a rich Icelandic flavour and were once translated into 40 languages; *At Skipalón* is the only one readily available in English, or you can read his 1894 memoir, *A Journey Across Iceland: The Ministry of Rev. Jon Sveinsson S.J.* Sveinsson's house in Akureyri is now an interesting museum. Two other masters of Icelandic literature are Gunnar Gunnarsson (1889–1975; look for *The Sworn Brothers, a Tale of the Early Days of Iceland*, 2012) and Þórbergur Þórðarson (1888–1974; look for *The Stones Speak*, 2012).

For more contemporary fare, try Einar Kárason's outstanding *Devil's Island*, the first of a trilogy about Reykjavík life in the 1950s; unfortunately, the other two parts haven't yet been translated into English. Hallgrímur Helgason's *101 Reykjavík* is the book on which the cult film was based. It's a dark comedy following the torpid life and fertile imagination of out-of-work Hlynur, who lives in central Reykjavík with his mother. Even blacker is *Angels of the Universe*, by Einar Már Gudmundsson, which is about a schizophrenic man's spells in a psychiatric hospital. Svava Jakobsdóttir's *Gunnlöth's Tale* blends contemporary life with Nordic mythology.

Surfing the Nordic Noir tidal wave is Arnaldur Indriðason, whose Reykjavík-based crime fiction permanently tops the bestseller lists. Many of his novels are available in English, including *Voices*, the award-winning *Silence of the Grave*, *The Draining Lake* and, possibly the best, *Tainted Blood* (also published as *Jar City*, and the inspiration for a film of the same

ame). Yrsa Sigurðardóttir's thrillers have also been widely translated – her latest are *The Absolution* and *The Hole*. Dip into Ragnar Jónasson's Dark Iceland series with the first, *Snowblind*, set in remote Siglufjörður. Viktor Arnar Ingólfsson's *The Flatey Enigma* has been made into a TV series.

Also look for Guðrún Eva Mínervudóttir's *The Creator*, a dark psychological novel. Former Sugarcube collaborator Sjón's *The Blue Fox* is a fantasy-adventure tale set in the 19th century; or try his most recent: *Moonstone – The Boy Who Never Was*.

Diverse Talents

Many Icelandic painters and musicians are serious creative artists in multiple disciplines. Some are making a splash overseas, such as Ragnar Kjartansson, who represents a new breed of Icelandic artist: painter, actor, director and musician. Reykjavík Art Museum's Hafnarhús and Reykjavík galleries do a great job showcasing such artists.

Music

Pop, Rock & Electronica

Iceland punches above its weight in the pop- and rock-music worlds. Internationally famous Icelandic musicians include (of course) Björk and her former band, the Sugarcubes. From her platinum album *Debut* (1993) to her most recent, *Utopia* (2017), Björk continues to be a force.

Sigur Rós, stars on the international stage, garnered rave reviews with albums such as *Ágætis Byrjun* (1999) and *Takk* (2005). Their most recent, *Route One* (2017), was assembled from music created while they drove the entire Ring Road in midsummer 2016. The band's concert movie *Heima* (2007) is a must-see. Lead singer Jónsi had success with his joyful solo album *Go* (2010).

Indie-folk Of Monsters and Men stormed the US charts in 2011 with their debut album, *My Head is an Animal*. The track 'Little Talks' from that album reached number one on the Billboard US Alternative Songs chart in 2012. Their latest album, *Beneath the Skin* (2015), debuted at number three on the US Billboard 200.

Ásgeir Trausti, who records simply as Ásgeir, had a breakout hit with *In the Silence* (2014) and sells out concerts internationally. His latest is *Afterglow* (2017).

Reykjavík has a flourishing music scene with a constantly changing line-up of new bands and sounds – see www.icelandmusic.is for an idea of the variety.

Seabear, an indie-folk band, have spawned several top music-makers such as Sin Fang (try *Flowers* from 2013 or *Spaceland* from 2016) and Sóley (*We Sink* from 2012, *Ask the Deep* from 2015 and *Endless Summer* from 2017). Árstíðir record minimalist indie-folk, and had a 2013 YouTube hit when they sang a 13th-century Icelandic hymn a cappella in a train station in Germany. Their album, *Nivalis*, was released in 2018. Kiasmos is a duo mixing moody, minimalist electronica; check out their album also called *Kiasmos* (2014) or the several EPs they've released since.

GusGus, a local pop-electronica act, have 10 studio albums to their credit and opened for Justin Timberlake at his sold-out 2014 concert in Reykjavík. In September 2016, Sturla Atlas, the Icelandic hip-hop/R&B phenom opened for the other Justin (Bieber); Bieber's video *I'll Show You* was shot in Iceland. Another well-known Icelandic rapper is Gísli Pálmi.

Kaleo, a popular blues-folk-rock band from Mosfellsbær, has hit the international stage with a splash – the song 'No Good' from their 2016 debut studio album *A/B* garnered a Grammy award nomination.

Vestmannaeyjar Islands–born Júníus Meyvant's 2016 debut, *Floating Harmonies,* is a creative blend of beautifully orchestrated folk, funk and soul.

FM Belfast, an electronica band, set up their own recording label to release their first album, *How to Make Friends* (2008); their latest is *Island Broadcast* (2017). Múm makes experimental electronica mixed with traditional instruments (*Smilewound,* 2013).

Prins Póló, named after a candy bar, records lyric-heavy dance-pop. Also check out Hafdís Huld, whose latest pop album is called *Dare to Dream Small,* and ebullient garage-rockers Benny Crespo's Gang. Just Another Snake Cult heads towards the psychedelic with *Cupid Makes a Fool of Me* (2013). Or check out Singapore Sling for straight-up rock and roll.

Traditional Music

Until rock and roll arrived in the 20th century, Iceland was a land practically devoid of musical instruments. The Vikings brought the *fiðla* and the *langspil* with them from Scandi navia – both a kind of two-stringed box rested on the player's knee and played with a bow. They were never solo instruments but merely served to accompany singers.

Instruments were generally an unheard-of luxury and singing was the sole form of music. The most famous song styles are *rímur* (poetry or stories from the sagas performed in a low, eerie chant; Sigur Rós have dabbled with the form), and *fimmundasöngur* (sung by two people in harmony). Cut off from other influences, the Icelandic singing style barely changed from the 14th century to the 20th century; it also managed to retain harmonies that were banned by the church across the rest of Europe on the basis of being the work of the devil.

Cinema & TV

Iceland's film industry is young and strong – regular production started around the early 1980s – and it creates distinctive work. Both short-form and feature-length Icelandic films receive international awards and prestige, and they often feature thought-provoking material and superb cinematography, using Iceland's powerful landscape as a backdrop.

In 1992 the film world first took notice of Iceland when *Children of Nature* was nominated for an Academy Award for Best Foreign Film. In it, an elderly couple forced into a retirement home in Reykjavík make a break for the countryside. The director, Friðrik Þór Friðriksson, is something of a legend in Icelandic cinema circles. *Cold Fever* (1994), *Angels of the Universe* (2000) and *The Sunshine Boy* (2009) are well worth watching, and he also produces many films.

Another film to put Reykjavík on the cinematic map was *101 Reykjavík* (2000), directed by Baltasar Kormákur and based on the novel by Hallgrímur Helgason. This dark comedy explores sex, drugs and the life of a loafer in downtown Reykjavík. Kormákur's *Jar City* (2006) stars the ever-watchable Ingvar E Sigurðsson as Iceland's favourite detective, Inspector Erlendur, from the novels by Arnaldur Indriðason. Kormákur's 2012 film, *The Deep,* based on a true story of a man who saved himself from a shipwreck in the Vestmannaeyjar Islands, was a hit, and in 2013 he launched into Hollywood with *2 Guns,* starring Denzel Washington and Mark Wahlberg. *Everest* (2015) starred Keira Knightley, Robin Wright and Jake Gyllenhaal. Kormákur has established RVK Studios, which also produces the hit TV series *Ófærð* (Trapped, 2015), an excellent, moody crime drama set in Seyðisfjörður in East Iceland (though filmed in Siglufjörður in the north). His latest includes thriller *The Oath* (*Eiðurinn,* 2016) and *Adrift* (2018), starring Shailene Woodley and Sam Claflin.

Director Dagur Kári achieved international success with films including *Nói Albínói* (2003), the story of a restless adolescent in a snowed-in northern fjord town, and the

Interior of Harpa concert hall (p57)

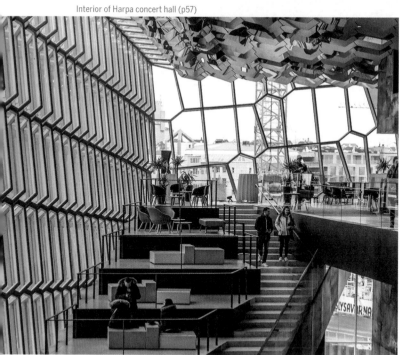

English-language *The Good Heart* (2009). Another RVK Studios production, Kári's *Virgin Mountain* (*Fúsi,* 2015), is a touching portrait of a gentle, isolated man, and played in art houses around the world.

Also look out for Hilmar Oddsson's *Cold Light* (*Kaldaljós,* 2004), a slow-moving, poignant film about life in an isolated fjord town, with a stunning performance from the little boy on whom it centres. And the quirky 2012 documentary *The Final Member* details the bizarre quest for a *Homo sapiens* penis for the Icelandic Phallological Museum in Reykjavík.

Hafsteinn Gunnar Sigurðsson's first feature film *Either Way* (2011), about two road workers painting stripes on the highway, was remade in the US by David Gordon Green as *Prince Avalanche* (2013). Sigurðsson's *Paris of the North* (2014), a father-son comedy-drama set in remote East Iceland, was a hit at film festivals, and his latest is *Under the Tree* (2017).

Painting & Sculpture

Many of Iceland's most successful artists have studied abroad before returning home to wrestle with Iceland's enigmatic soul. The result is a European-influenced style, but with Icelandic landscapes and saga-related scenes as key subjects. Refreshingly, you'll find museums stocked with wonderful works by men and women alike.

The first great Icelandic landscape painter was the prolific Ásgrímur Jónsson (1876–1958), who produced a startling number of Impressionistic oils and watercolours depicting Icelandic landscapes and folk tales. You can see his work at the National Gallery in Reykjavík.

One of Ásgrímur's students was Johannes Kjarval (1885–1972), Iceland's most enduringly popular artist, who grew up in the remote East Iceland village of Borgarfjörður Eystri. His first commissioned works were, rather poignantly, drawings of farms for people who were emigrating, but he's most famous for his early charcoal sketches of people from the village and for his surreal landscapes. A whole beautiful building of the Reykjavík Museum of Art (Kjarvalsstaðir) is named for him.

Sculpture is also very well represented in Iceland, with works dotting parks, gardens and galleries across the country. The most famous Icelandic sculptors all have museums dedicated to them in Reykjavík. Notable exponents include Einar Jónsson (1874–1954), whose mystical works dwell on death and resurrection, and Ásmundur Sveinsson (1893–1982), whose wide-ranging, captivating kinetic works celebrate Iceland, its stories and its people. Don't miss Reykjavík Art Museum's Ásmundarsafn, the artist's peaceful former studio that is filled with inspiring sculptures. Sigurjón Ólafsson (1908–92) specialised in busts but also dabbled in abstract forms. Gerður Helgadóttir (1928–75) made beautiful stained glass and sculpture, and has a museum dedicated to her in Kópavogur. You'll also find her work in Reykjavík's Hljómskálagarður Park, along with pieces by Gunnfríður Jónsdóttir (1889–1968), Nína Sæmundson (1892–1962), Þorbjörg Pálsdóttir (1919–2009) and Ólöf Pálsdóttir (1920–).

Iceland's most famous contemporary painter is probably pop-art icon Erró (Guðmundu Guðmundsson, 1932–), who has donated his entire collection to Reykjavík Art Museum's Hafnarhús. Danish-Icelandic artist Olafur Eliasson (1967–) creates powerful installations and also designed the facade of Reykjavík's dazzling concert hall, Harpa. Páll Guðmundsson (1959–) is a working artist in Húsafell who makes evocative sculptures and paintings, and unusual stone and rhubarb *steinharpa* (similar to a xylophone), which he has played with the band Sigur Rós.

Architecture & Design

Iceland's Viking longhouses have succumbed to the ravages of time, but traditional turf-and-wood techniques were used right up until the 19th century. There is a good example at **Glaumbær** (www.glaumbaer.is; Rte 75; adult/child 1700kr/free; ☉9am-6pm mid-May–mid-Sep, 10am-4pm Mon-Fri early May & mid-Sep–mid-Oct) in North Iceland.

Guðjón Samúelsson (1887–1950), perhaps one of Iceland's most famous 20th-century architects, worked to create a distinctive Icelandic style, and you will find his minimalist buildings all over the country, from Hallgrímskirkja and the nearby swimming pool, Sundhöllin, in Reykjavík, to Þingvallabær (farmhouse at Þingvellir) and Héraðsskólinn, formerly a school in Laugarvatn. *A Guide to Icelandic Architecture* (Association of Icelandic Architects) looks at 250 Icelandic buildings and designs.

Iceland's coterie of unique designers, artists and architects tend to be Reykjavík-based, though that trend is changing with the tourism boom. Many practitioners have formed collectives and opened shops and galleries, which are full of handmade, beautiful works: everything from striking bowls made out of radishes to cool couture. Reykjavík's **Iceland Design Centre** (Hönnunarmiðstöð; ☎771 2200; www.icelanddesign.is; Aðalstræti 2; ☉10am-6pm Mon-Sat) has loads more information, and its **DesignMarch** (www.designmarch.is) annual event opens hundreds of exhibitions and workshops to the public.

Winter in Reykjavík (p35)

Icelandic Attitudes

Centuries of isolation and hardship have instilled particular character traits in the small, homogenous Icelandic population. Their connection to their homeland, history and country is deeply felt, even if the land reciprocates that love with some cruelty. Icelanders respond to life's challenges with a compelling mix of courage, candour and creativity, edged with a dark, dry humour.

Þetta Reddast' & the National Psyche

Icelanders have a reputation as tough, hardy, elemental types, and rural communities are still deeply involved in the fishing and/or farming industries. Geographically speaking, 'rural' could be said to define most of the country outside the capital region, which is home to only 36% of Iceland's total population.

Naturally enough for people living on a remote island in a harsh environment, Icelanders are self-reliant individualists who don't like being told what to do. But these steadfast exteriors often hide a more dreamy interior world. Iceland has a rich cultural heritage and an incredibly high literacy rate, and its people have a passion for all things artistic. This enthusiasm is true of the whole country, but it's particularly noticeable in central Reykjavík,

Icelandic house

where seemingly everyone plays in a band, dabbles in art or design, makes films or writes poetry or prose – they're positively bursting with creative impulses.

This buoyant, have-a-go attitude was hit hard during the 2008 financial meltdown. Soup kitchens sprang up in the city and thousands of younger people left Iceland to try their luck in Norway. But Icelanders are resilient – within just a few years, emigration rates fell, and confidence started springing up around the country, mushrooming along with new businesses catering to the tourist boom. The country maintains its belief in the old saying *'Þetta reddast'* (roughly translated: 'It will all work out okay'). The phrase is so frequently used it has been described as the country's motto.

Icelanders are happily patriotic. Witness their Euro 2016 football (soccer) victories, with their Viking thunderclap, and the fact that approximately 10% of the country went to France for the tournament. The men's team participated in the World Cup for the first time in 2018, bringing more high spirits. Citizens who achieve international success are quietly feted: celebrities such as musicians Björk and Sigur Rós reflect prestige onto their entire homeland.

Town layouts, the former US military base, and the prevalence of hot dogs and Coca-Cola point to a heavy US influence, but Icelanders consider their relationship with the rest of Scandinavia to be more important. Although they may seem to conform to the cool-and-quiet Nordic stereotype, Icelanders are curious about visitors and eager to know what outsiders think: 'How do you like Iceland?' is invariably an early question. And an incredible transformation takes place on Friday and Saturday nights, when inhibitions fall away and conversations flow as fast as the alcohol.

Work Hard, Play Hard

In the last century the Icelandic lifestyle has shifted from isolated family communities living on scattered farms and in coastal villages to a more urban-based society, with the majority of people living in the southwestern corner around Reykjavík. Despite this change, family connections are still very strong. Though young people growing up in rural Iceland are likely to move to Reykjavík to study and work, localised tourism is bringing entrepreneurial and job options to the hinterlands once again.

Icelanders work hard (and long – the retirement age is 67 and soon to be 70), often at a number of jobs, especially in summer's peak when there is money to be made feeding, accommodating, driving and guiding thousands of tourists. The locals have enjoyed a very high standard of living in the late 20th and early 21st centuries – but keeping up with the Jónssons and Jónsdóttirs came at a price. For decades, Icelanders straight out of university borrowed money to buy houses or 4WDs and spent the rest of their days living on credit and paying off loans. Then, in 2008, the financial crash occurred, and huge amounts of debt suddenly had to be paid back. People wondered how Iceland would ever work itself ut of its economic black hole. And yet, with characteristic grit, resilience, adaptability and imagination, Icelanders have hauled their country back from economic disaster.

The Icelandic commitment to hard work is counterbalanced by deep relaxation. The bingeing in Reykjavík on Friday and Saturday nights is an example of R&R gone wild. But, also keep your eye out for the hundreds of summer houses you'll see when you're driving in the country, and the exceptional number of swimming pools, which form the social hub of Icelandic life.

Women in Iceland

In 2017 Iceland held the top spot (for the ninth consecutive year) in the World Economic Forum's Global Gender Gap Index. The index ranked 136 countries on gender equality by measuring the relative gap between women and men across four key areas: health, education, economics and politics. Iceland continues to be the country with the narrowest gender gap in the world – this means Icelandic women have greater access to health and education, and are more politically and economically empowered than women in other countries. In 2018 Iceland became the first country in the world to enact a law requiring that men and women be paid equally for the same job.

The Viking settlement of Iceland clearly demanded toughness of character, and the sagas are full of feisty women (eg, Hallgerður Höskuldsdóttir, who declines to save her husband's life due to a slap that he gave her years earlier). For centuries Icelandic women had to take care of farms and families while their male partners headed off to sea.

Though women and men struggled equally through Iceland's long, dark history, modern concepts of gender equality are a pretty recent phenomenon. Women gained full voting rights in 1920, but it wasn't until the 1970s protest movements reached Iceland that attitudes really began to change. Particularly powerful was the 'women's day off' on 24 October 1975: the country ceased to function when 90% of Icelandic women stayed away from work and stay-at-home mums left children with their menfolk for the day.

In 1980 Iceland became the first democracy to elect a female president, the much-loved Vigdís Finnbogadóttir. In 2009 the world's first openly gay prime minister, Jóhanna Sigurðardóttir, came to power. Iceland has among the highest rate of women's participation in the labour market among OECD countries, at 77%.

The social-care system is so good that women have few worries about the financial implications of raising a child alone: maternity-leave provisions are excellent; childcare is affordable; there is no sense that motherhood precludes work or study; and there's no stigma attached to unmarried mothers. The country isn't perfect – sexual harassment and violence are still issues – but Icelandic women are well educated and independent, with the same opportunities as Icelandic men.

Religious Beliefs

Norse

At the time of the Settlement Era, Iceland's religion was Ásatrú, which means 'faith in the Aesir' (the old Norse gods). Óðinn (Odin), Þór (Thor) and Freyr (Frey) were the major trinity worshipped across Scandinavia. Óðinn, their chief, is the god of war and poetry, a brooding and intimidating presence. In Iceland most people were devoted to Þór (Icelandic names such as Þórir, Þórdís and Þóra are still very popular). This burly, red-haired god of the common people controlled thunder, wind, storm and natural disaster, and was a vital deity for farmers and fishers to have on their side. Freyr and his twin sister Freyja (Freya) represent

What's in a Name?

Icelanders' names are constructed from a combination of their first name and their father's (or, more rarely, mother's) first name. Girls add the suffix -dóttir (daughter) to the patronymic and boys add -son. Therefore, Jón, the son of Einar, would be Jón Einarsson. Guðrun, the daughter of Einar, would be Guðrun Einarsdóttir.

Because Icelandic surnames only usually tell people what a person's father is called, Icelanders don't bother with 'Mr Einarsson' or 'Mrs Einarsdóttir'. Instead they use first names, even when addressing strangers. It makes for a wonderfully democratic society when you're expected to address your president or top police commissioner by their first name. And yes, trivia buffs, the telephone directory is alphabetised by first name.

fertility and sexuality. Freyr brought springtime, with its romantic implications, to both the human and the animal world, and was in charge of the perpetuation of all species.

Icelanders peacefully converted to Christianity more than a thousand years ago, but the old gods linger on. The Ásatrú religion re-emerged in the 1970s, almost simultaneously in Iceland, the USA and the UK. Whereas membership of other religions in Iceland has remained fairly constant, Ásatrúarfélagið (Ásatrú Association) is growing. It is now Iceland's largest non-Christian religious organisation, with approximately 4126 members in 2018 (an increase of 54% from 2015).

Christianity

Traditionally, the date of the decree that officially converted Iceland to Christianity is given as 1000, but research has determined that it probably occurred in 999. What is known is that the changeover of religions was a political decision. In the Icelandic Alþingi (National Assembly), Christians and pagans had been polarising into two radically opposite factions, threatening to divide the country. Þorgeir, the lögsögumaður (law speaker), appealed for moderation on both sides, and eventually it was agreed that Christianity would officially become the new religion, although pagans were still allowed to practise in private.

Today, as in mainland Scandinavia, most Icelanders (around 71%) belong to the Protestant Lutheran Church – but many are nonpractising. Church attendance is very low.

Supernatural Iceland: Ghosts, Trolls & Hidden People

Once you've seen some of the lava fields, eerie natural formations and isolated farms that characterise much of the Icelandic landscape, it will come as no surprise that many Icelanders believe their country is populated by huldufólk (hidden people) and ghosts.

In the lava live jarðvergar (gnomes), álfar (elves), ljósálfar (fairies), dvergar (dwarves), ljúflingar (lovelings), tívar (mountain spirits) and englar (angels). Stories about them have been handed down through generations, and many modern Icelanders claim to have seen them...or at least to know someone who has.

There are stories about projects going wrong when workers try to build roads through huldufólk homes: the weather turns bad; machinery breaks down; labourers fall ill. In mid-2014 Iceland's 'whimsy factor' made international news when a road project to link the Álftanes peninsula to the Reykjavík suburb of Garðabær was halted after campaigners warned it would disturb elf habitat.

As for Icelandic ghosts, they're substantial beings – not the wafting shadows found elsewhere in Europe. Írafell-Móri (móri and skotta are used for male and female ghosts, respectively) is said to need to eat supper every night, and one of the country's most amous spooks, Sel-Móri, gets seasick when stowing away in a boat. Stranger still, two hosts haunting the same area often join forces to double their trouble.

Rock stacks and weird lava formations around the country are often said to be trolls, aught out at sunrise and turned to stone. But living trolls are seldom seen today – they're more the stuff of children's stories.

Surveys suggest that more than half of Icelanders believe in, or at least entertain the possibility of, the existence of *huldufólk*. But a word of warning: many Icelanders tire of visitors asking them whether they believe in supernatural beings. Their pride bristles at the 'Those cute Icelanders! They all believe in pixies!' attitude...and even if they don't entirely disbelieve, they're unlikely to admit it to a stranger.

If you want to know more, and ask all the questions you can, join a tour in Hafnarfjörður, 0km south of Reykjavík, or sign up for a course at the **Icelandic Elf School** (Álfaskólinn; www.elfmuseum.com) in Reykjavík. Yes, there really is such a place, and it runs four-hour introductory classes most Fridays.

Icelandic Ancestry & Genetic Research

Biotech research is big in Iceland – thanks, in part, to the 12th-century historian Ari the Learned. Ari's *Landnámabók* and *Íslendingabók* mean that Icelanders can trace their family trees right back to the 9th century.

In 1996 neuroscience expert Dr Kári Stefánsson recognised that this genealogical material could be combined with Iceland's unusually homogenous population to produce something unique – a country-sized genetic laboratory. In 1998 the Icelandic government controversially voted to allow the creation of a single database, by presumed consent, containing all Icelanders' genealogical, genetic and medical records. Even more controversially, the government allowed Kári's biotech startup company deCODE Genetics to create this database, and access it for its biomedical research, using the database to trace inheritable diseases and pinpoint the genes that cause them.

The decision sparked public outrage in Iceland and arguments across the globe about its implications for human rights and medical ethics. Should a government be able to sell off its citizens' medical records? And is it acceptable for a private corporation to use such records for profit?

While the arguments raged (and investors flocked), the company set to work. The database was declared unconstitutional in 2003 and deCODE was declared bankrupt in 2010, and sold to US biotech giant Amgen in 2012. By that time, deCODE had built a research database using DNA and clinical data from more than 100,000 volunteers (one third of the population), and had done work in isolating gene mutations linked to heart attacks, strokes and Alzheimer's disease.

deCODE continues to unravel the mysteries of the human genome and has had 160,000 Icelanders volunteer their data to date. With its completed research, it has also been able to 'impute' the genetic make-up of Icelanders who have not participated at all – leading to ethical questions: should they inform carriers of dangerous gene mutations even if those people have not agreed to participate? In 2018, after much debate, deCODE created a website for informing women who've given samples whether they carry the harmful BRCA2 gene.

ANTONIO SABA/GETTY IMAGES ©

Icelandic Cuisine

If people know anything about Icelandic food, it's usually to do with a plucky population tucking into boundary-pushing dishes such as fermented shark or sheep's head. It's a pity the spotlight doesn't shine as brightly on Iceland's delicious, fresh-from-the-farm ingredients, the seafood bounty or historical food-preserving techniques finding new favour with today's New Nordic chefs.

Food Heritage

For much of its history, Iceland was a poverty-stricken hinterland. Sparse soil and cursed weather produced limited crops, and Icelandic farmer-fishers relied heavily on sheep, fish and seabirds to keep them from starving. Every part of every creature was eaten – fresh or dried, salted, smoked, pickled in whey or even buried underground (in the case of shark meat), with preserving techniques honed to ensure food lasted through lean times.

Local food producers and chefs today are rediscovering old recipes and techniques with a renewed sense of pride in the country's culinary heritage, and the results can be quite special. From the capital to select restaurants, sometimes in the most improbably remote locations, you'll find rich, imaginative Icelandic fare. The strong Slow Food Movement priorities locally grown food over imports, with restaurants proudly promoting regional treats.

Staples & Specialities

Fish, seafood, lamb, bread and simple vegetables still form the typical Icelandic diet.

Fish & Seafood

'Half of our country is the sea', runs an old Icelandic saying. Fish is the mainstay of the Icelandic diet: you'll find it fresh at market stalls and in restaurant kitchens, from where it emerges boiled, pan-fried, baked or grilled.

In the past, Icelanders merely kept the cheeks and tongues of *þorskur* (cod) – something of a delicacy – and exported the rest; but today you'll commonly find cod fillets on the menu, along with *ýsa* (haddock), *bleikja* (Arctic char) and meaty-textured *skötuselur* (monkfish). Other fish include *lúða* (halibut), *steinbítur* (catfish), *sandhverfa* (turbot; nonindigenous), *síld* (herring), *skarkoli* (plaice) and *skata* (skate). During summer you can try *silungur* (freshwater trout) and *villtur lax* (wild salmon). *Eldislax* is farmed salmon; it's available year-round and appears on countless menus in smoked form.

Harðfiskur, a popular snack eaten with butter, is found in supermarkets and at market stalls. To make it, haddock is cleaned and dried in the open air until it has become dehydrated and brittle, then it's torn into strips.

Rækja (shrimp), *hörpudiskur* (scallops) and *kræklingur* (blue mussels) are harvested in Icelandic waters; mussels are at their prime during the very beginning and the end of summer. *Humar* (or *leturhumar*) are a real treat: these are what Icelanders call 'lobster'; the rest of us may know them as langoustine. Höfn, in Southeast Iceland, is particularly well known for *humar* and even has an annual lobster festival.

Meat

Icelandic lamb (promoted here: www.icelandiclamb.is) is hard to beat. During summer, sheep roam free to munch on chemical-free grasses and herbs in the highlands and valleys, before the September *réttir* (sheep round-up), after which they are corralled for the winter. The result of this life of relative luxury is very tender lamb with a slightly gamey flavour. You'll find lamb fillets, pan-fried lamb or smoked lamb on most restaurant menus.

Beef steaks are also excellent but not as widely available, and are consequently more expensive. Horse is still eaten in Iceland, although it's regarded as something of a delicacy; if you see 'foal fillets' on the menu, you're not imagining things.

In East Iceland, wild reindeer roam the highlands, and reindeer steaks are a feature of local menus. Hunting is highly regulated; reindeer season starts in late July and runs well into September.

Tastebud Touring

Skyr Rich and creamy yoghurt-like staple (though actually cheese), sometimes sweetened with sugar and berries. You can consume it in drinks or local desserts, playing a starring role in cheesecake and crème brûlée (or even 'skyramisu') concoctions.

Hangikjöt Literally 'hung meat'; usually smoked lamb, served in thin slices (it's traditionally a Christmas dish).

Harðfiskur Brittle pieces of wind-dried haddock ('fish jerky'?), usually eaten with butter.

Pýlsur Icelandic hot dogs, made with a combination of lamb, beef and pork, and topped with raw and deep-fried onion, ketchup, mustard and tangy remoulade (ask for *'eina með öllu'* – one with everything).

Liquorice Salt liquorice and chocolate-covered varieties fill the supermarket sweets aisles.

Rúgbrauð Dark, dense rye bread. Look for *hverabrauð* in Mývatn – it's baked underground using geothermal heat.

Fiskisúpa (fish soup)

Birds have always been part of the Icelandic diet. *Lundi* (puffin) used to appear smoked or broiled in liver-like lumps on dinner plates, although it's a rarer sight these days following a worrying crash in puffin numbers. Another seabird is *svartfugl;* it's commonly translated as 'blackbird' on English-language menus, but what you'll actually get is guillemot. High-class restaurants favouring seasonal ingredients may have roasted *heiðagæs* (pink-footed goose) in autumn. Ptarmagin is a Christmas delicacy, though their numbers fluctuate.

Bread

Rye flatbread (known as *flatbraud* or *flatkökur*) has been made since settlement and is stil served, often topped with smoked lamb, salmon or trout.

Sweets & Desserts

Don't miss *skyr,* a delicious yoghurt-like concoction (though technically a cheese) made from skimmed milk. Despite its rich flavour, it's actually low in fat and high in protein. It's often mixed with sugar, fruit flavours (such as blueberry) and cream to give it an extra-special taste and texture. *Skyr* can be found in any supermarket and as a dessert in restaurants.

Icelandic *pönnukökur* (pancakes) are thin, sweet and cinnamon flavoured. Icelandic *kleinur* (twisted doughnuts) are a chewy treat, along with their offspring *ástarpungar* (love balls), deep-fried, spiced balls of dough. You'll find these desserts in bakeries, along with a amazing array of fantastic pastries and cakes – one of the few sweet legacies of the Danis occupation.

Local dairy farms churn out scrumptious scoops of homemade ice cream, often featured on menus of nearby restaurants.

Drinks

Nonalcoholic

Life without *kaffi* (coffee) is unthinkable. Cafes and petrol stations will usually have an urn of filter coffee by the counter, and some shops offer complimentary cups of it to customers. Snug European-style cafes selling espresso, latte, cappuccino and mocha are ever-more popular, popping up even in the most isolated one-horse hamlets (the coffee isn't always good, though). Tea is available, but ranks as a very poor second choice – the brand sitting on most supermarket shelves make a feeble brew, though that is slowly changing with the increase in tourist demand.

Besides all that coffee, Icelanders drink more Coca-Cola per capita than most other countries. Another very popular soft drink is Egils Appelsín (orange soda) and the home-grown Egils Malt Extrakt, which tastes like sugar-saturated beer.

It isn't a crime to buy bottled water in Iceland, but it should be. Icelandic tap water generally comes from the nearest glacier or spring, and is some of the purest you'll ever drink.

Icelandic Recipes

Peruse *Cool Cuisine: Traditional Icelandic Cuisine,* by Nanna Rögn-valdardóttir, *Taste of Iceland* by Úlfar Finnbjörnssonor, or *50 Crazy Things to Taste in Iceland,* by Snæfríður Ingadóttir (including great photos by Þorvaldur Örn Kristmundsson) for pictorials and recipes for Iceland's traditional eats.

Alcohol

For some Icelanders, drinking alcohol is not about the taste – getting drunk is the aim of the game. Particularly in Reykjavík, it's the done thing to go out at the weekend and drink till you drop.

You must be at least 20 years old to buy beer, wine or spirits, and alcohol is only available from licensed bars, restaurants and the government-run Vínbúðin liquor stores (www.vinbudin.is). There are roughly 50 shops around the country; most towns have one, and the greater Reykjavík area has about a dozen. In larger places they usually open from 11am to 6pm Monday to Thursday and on Saturdays, and from 11am to 7pm on Fridays (closed Sundays). In small communities, the Vínbúðin store may only open for an hour or two in the late afternoon or evening. Expect queues around 5pm on a Friday. The cheapest bottles of imported wine cost from 1500kr. Beer costs about a third of what you'll pay in a bar.

Petrol stations and supermarkets sell the weak and watery 2.2% brew known as pilsner, but most Icelanders would sooner not drink it at all. The main brands of Icelandic beer – Egils, Gull, Thule and Viking – are all fairly standard lager or pils brews; you can also get imported beers. In recent years a slew of good local distilleries and breweries has sprung up all over Iceland, concocting whisky, vodka and dozens of high-calibre craft beers – check our cheat sheet for your next barroom order. Look out, too, for seasonal beers – the ones brewed for the Christmas period are especially popular.

Reports of astronomical prices for boozing in Iceland arise because a pint of beer in a bar or restaurant costs around 1100kr to 1900kr. In Reykjavík many venues have early-evening happy hours that cut costs to between 700kr and 900kr per beer. Download the smartphone Reykjavík Appy Hour app to gladden your drinking budget.

The traditional Icelandic alcoholic brew is *brennivín* (literally 'burnt wine'), a potent schnapps made from fermented potatoes and flavoured with caraway seeds. It has the foreboding nickname *svarti dauði* (black death) and it's essential drinking if you're trying any tasty traditional titbits (p267). There are also other local spirits producers, especially of vodka.

Where to Eat & Drink

Restaurants

Iceland's best restaurants are in Reykjavík, but some magnificent finds have also mushroomed up beyond the capital, catering to travellers looking for authentic local flavours. These restaurants are tapping into the network of unsung local producers: barley farmers, mussel harvesters, veggie growers, sheep farmers and fishers. At many places, your meal's food miles will be very low.

Beer Day

Beer Day (1 March) dates back to the glorious day in 1989 when beer was legalised in Iceland (it was illegal for most of the 20th century). As you'd expect, Reykjavík's clubs and bars get particularly wild.

Bear in mind that the price difference between an exceptional restaurant and an average one is often small, so it can be well worth going upmarket. Often, though, in rural Iceland you may not have a huge choice – the town's only eating place may be the restaurant in the local hotel, supplemented by the grill bar in the petrol station. And in peak summer, you may struggle to get a table without a reservation, and/or face long waits.

À la carte menus usually offer at least one fish dish, one veggie choice (often pasta) and a handful of meat mains (lamb is the star). Many restaurants also have a menu of cheaper meals such as hamburgers and pizzas. Soup is a mainstay – either as a lunchtime option (perhaps in the form of a soup-and-salad buffet) or as a dinnertime starter. *Fiskisúpa* (fish soup) comes courtesy of various family recipes, while *kjötsúpa* (meat soup) will usually feature veggies and small chunks of lamb.

In Reykjavík, and to a lesser extent Akureyri, there are some ethnic restaurants, including Thai, Japanese, Italian, Mexican, Indian and Chinese. You can also stumble across some welcome surprises – Ethiopian in Flúðir and Moroccan in Siglufjörður.

Opening hours for restaurants are usually 11.30am to 2.30pm and 6pm to 10pm daily. Note that even in summer, restaurants may stop serving meals around 9pm.

Cafes & Pubs

Central Reykjavík has a great range of bohemian cafe-bars where you can happily while away the hours sipping coffee, people-watching, scribbling postcards or tinkering on your laptop. Menus range from simple soups and sandwiches to fish dishes and designer burgers. Recent years have seen cafe menus morph into more restaurant-like versions (with an attendant hike in prices). The cafe scene is spreading, too, with cool new spots scattered around the country.

Many of Reykjavík's cafes morph into wild drinking dens in the evenings (mostly on Fridays and Saturdays). DJs suddenly appear, coffee orders turn to beer, and people get progressively louder and less inhibited as the evening goes on, which is usually until sometime between 4am and 5am. Outside the capital, things are considerably more subdued, although Friday and Saturday nights do see action in Akureyri.

Hot Dog Stands & Petrol Stations

Icelanders do enjoy fast food. If you see a queue in Reykjavík, it probably ends at a *pylsur* (hot dog) stand. Large petrol stations often have good, cheap, well-patronised grills and cafeterias attached. They generally serve sandwiches and fast food from around 11am to 9pm or 10pm. Some also offer hearty set meals at lunchtime, such as meat soup, fish of the day or plates of lamb. Cafeterias at N1 service stations anywhere along the Ring Road are invariably busy.

Supermarkets & Bakeries

Every town and village has at least one small supermarket. The most expensive is 10-11, but it's generally open late hours. Bónus (easily recognised by its yellow-and-pink piggy sign) is the country's budget supermarket chain. Others include Hagkaup, Kjarval, Krónan, Nettó, and Kjörbúðin, formerly known as Samkaup-Strax. Opening times vary greatly; in Reykjavík most are open from 9am to 11pm daily, but outside the capital hours are almost always shorter. Sunday hours may be limited or nonexistent.

The old-school Icelandic *bakarí* (bakeries) can't be praised enough. Most towns have one (it may be part of a supermarket), which is generally open from 7am or 8am until 4pm on weekdays (sometimes also Saturdays). These sell all sorts of inexpensive fresh bread, buns, cakes, sandwiches and coffee, and usually provide chairs and tables to eat at.

Iceland has to import most of its groceries, so prices are steep – roughly two or three times what you'd pay in North America or Europe. Fish (tinned or smoked) and dairy products represent the best value and are surprisingly cheap. Some fruit and vegetables are grown locally, and these tend to be fresh and tasty, but imported vegetables sometimes look pretty sad by the time they hit supermarket shelves.

An Old-Fashioned Banquet

Svið Singed sheep's head (complete with eyes) sawn in two, boiled and eaten fresh or pickled.

Sviðasulta (head cheese) Made from bits of svið pressed into gelatinous loaves and pickled in whey.

Slátur ('slaughter') Comes in two forms: *lifrarpylsa* is liver sausage, made from a mishmash of sheep intestines, liver and lard tied up in a sheep's stomach and cooked. *Blóðmör* has added sheep's blood (and equates to blood pudding).

Súrsaðir hrútspungar Rams' testicles pickled in whey and pressed into a cake.

Hákarl Iceland's most famous stomach churner, hákarl is Greenland shark, an animal so inedible it has to rot away underground for six months before humans can even digest it.

Vegetarians & Vegans

Vegetarians and vegans will have no problem in Reykjavík – there are some excellent meat-free cafe-restaurants in the city, and many more eateries offer vegetarian choices (you'll probably want to eat every meal at Gló). Outside the capital most restaurants have at least one veggie item on the menu – this is routinely cheese-and-tomato pasta or pizza or a salad, though, so you could get bored. Vegans usually have to self-cater, though restaurants are becoming more aware of this food choice.

Arnarstapi, Snæfellsnes Peninsula (p13

Survival Guide

Directory A–Z

Accessible Travel

Iceland can be trickier than many places in northern Europe when it comes to access for travellers with disabilities.

For details on accessible facilities, contact the information centre for people with disabilities, **Þekkingarmiðstöð Sjálfsbjargar** (Sjálfsbjörg Knowledge Centre; 550 0118; www.thekking rmidstod.is; Hátún 12, eykjavík).

A good resource is the website **God Adgang** (www. odadgang.dk), a Danish nitiative adopted in Iceland. Follow the instructions to find Icelandic service providers that have been assessed or the accessibility label.

Particularly good for ailor-made accessible trips round the country are

All Iceland Tours (http:// alliceland.is) and **Iceland Unlimited** (www.iceland unlimited.is). **Gray Line Iceland** (www.grayline.is) and **Reykjavík Excursions** (www.re.is) run sightseeing and day tours from Reykjavík and will assist travellers with special needs, but they recommend you contact them in advance to discuss your requirements.

Reykjavík's city buses are accessible courtesy of ramps; elsewhere, however, public buses don't have ramps or lifts.

Download Lonely Planet's free Accessible Travel guide from http://lptravel.to/ AccessibleTravel.

Accommodation

Iceland has a broad range of accommodation, but demand often outstrips supply. If you're visiting in the shoulder and high seasons (from May to September), book early.

○ **Campgrounds** No requirement to book, so camping allows some

degree of spontaneity – but also exposure to the elements. Campervans are very popular.

○ **Hostels** Popular budget options, spread across the country.

○ **Guesthouses** Run the gamut from homestyle B&Bs to large hotel-like properties.

○ **Hotels** From small, bland and businesslike to designer dens with all the trimmings (and prices to match).

○ **Mountain huts** A basic option for hikers and explorers, but book ahead.

Customs Regulations

Iceland has quite strict import restrictions. For a full list of regulations, see www. customs.is.

Alcohol duty-free allowances for travellers over 20 years of age:

Sleeping-Bag Accommodation

Iceland's best-kept secret is the sleeping-bag option offered by hostels, numerous guesthouses and some hotels. For a fraction of the normal cost, you'll get a bed without a duvet; you supply your own sleeping bag.

Taking the sleeping-bag option doesn't mean sleeping in a dorm – generally you book the same private room, just minus the linen. The sleeping-bag option, which is more prevalent outside the peak summer period and in more rural places, usually means BYO towel.

- 1L spirits and 750mL wine and 3L beer, or
- 3L wine and 6L beer, or
- 1L spirits and 6L beer, or
- 1.5L wine and 12L beer, or
- 18L beer

Additionally:
- Visitors over 18 years can bring in 200 cigarettes or 250g of other tobacco products.

- You can import up to 3kg of food (except raw eggs, some meat and dairy products), provided it's not worth more than 25,000kr. This may help self-caterers to reduce costs.

- To prevent contamination, recreational fishing and horse-riding clothes require a veterinarian's certificate stating that they have been disinfected. Otherwise officials will charge you for disinfecting clothing when you arrive. It is prohibited to bring used horse-riding equipment (saddles, bridles etc). See www.mast.is.

- Many people bring their cars on the ferry from Europe. Special duty-waiver conditions apply for stays of up to one year.

Smoking

Smoking is illegal in enclosed public spaces, including in cafes, bars, clubs, restaurants and on public transport. Most accommodation is nonsmoking.

Electricity

220V/50Hz

230V/50Hz

Food

The following price ranges refer to a main course.

€ Less than 2000kr (€16)
€€ 2000–5000kr (€16–40)
€€€ More than 5000kr (€40)

Health

Travel in Iceland presents very few health problems. Tap water is safe to drink; the level of hygiene is high, and there are no endemic nasties.

Before You Go

Recommended Vaccinations

There are no required or recommended vaccinations

Health Insurance

A travel insurance policy that covers medical mishaps is strongly recommended. Always check the policy's small print to see if it covers any potentially dangerous sporting activities you might be considering, such as hiking, diving, horse riding, skiing or snowmobiling.

In Iceland

Availability & Cost of Healthcare

The standard of healthcare is very high, and English is widely spoken by doctors and medical-clinic staff.

Note, however, that there are limited services outside larger urban areas.

For minor ailments, pharmacists can dispense valuable advice and over-the-counter medication; pharmacies can be identified by the sign *apótek*. Pharmacists can also advise as to when more specialised help is required.

Medical care can be obtained by visiting a primary healthcare centre, called *heilsugæslustöð*. Find details of centres in greater Reykjavík at www.heilsugaeslan.is; in regional areas, ask at a tourist office or your accommodation or advice on the closest healthcare centre.

Citizens of Nordic countries need only present their passport to access healthcare. Citizens of the European Economic Area (EEA) are covered for emergency medical treatment on presentation of a European Health Insurance Card (EHIC). Apply online for a card via your government health department's website. Holders of an EHIC are charged the same fee as locals.

Citizens from other countries can obtain medical assistance but must pay in full (and later be reimbursed by their insurance provider, if they have one). A standard consultation costs around 20,000kr. Travel insurance is advised. For more detailed information on healthcare for visitors, see www.sjukra.is/english/tourists.

Practicalities

Newspapers & Magazines

Morgunblaðið (www.mbl.is) is a daily paper in Icelandic; it has local news in English at www.icelandmonitor.mbl.is/news.

Iceland Review (www.icelandreview.com) has news and current affairs, including tourist-related news.

Reykjavík Grapevine (www.grapevine.is) has excellent tourist-oriented and daily-life articles about Iceland, plus listings of what's on. A paper copy of the *Grapevine* is widely available and free.

Radio

RÚV (Icelandic National Broadcasting Service; www.ruv.is) has three radio stations: Rás 1 (news, weather, cultural programs), Rás 2 (pop music, current affairs) and Rondó (classical music).

Hypothermia & Frostbite

The main health risks are caused by exposure to extreme climates; proper preparation will reduce the risks. Even on a warm day in the mountains, the weather can change rapidly – carry waterproof outer gear and warm layers, and inform others of your route.

Acute hypothermia follows a sudden drop of temperature over a short time. Chronic hypothermia is caused by a gradual loss of temperature over hours. Hypothermia starts with shivering, loss of judgement and clumsiness. Unless rewarming occurs, the sufferer deteriorates into apathy, confusion and coma. Prevent further heat loss by seeking shelter, wearing warm, dry clothing, drinking hot, sweet drinks and sharing body warmth.

Frostbite is caused by freezing and the subsequent damage to bodily extremities. It is dependent on wind chill, temperature and the length of exposure. Frostbite starts as frostnip (white, numb areas of skin), from which complete recovery is expected with rewarming. As frostbite develops, however, the skin blisters and becomes black. Loss of damaged tissue eventually occurs. Your should wear adequate clothing, stay dry, keep well hydrated and ensure you have adequate kilojoule intake to prevent frostbite. Treatment involves rapid rewarming.

Tap water

Iceland has some of the cleanest water in the world and tap water is completely safe to drink. Locals find it amusing to see travellers buying bottled water when the same quality of water is available from the tap.

Geothermal hot water smells of sulphur, but the cold water doesn't smell.

Insurance

Although Iceland is a very safe place to travel, theft does occasionally happen, and illness and accidents are always a possibility. A travel insurance policy to cover theft, loss and medical problems is strongly recommended.

Worldwide travel insurance is available at www.lonelyplanet.com/travel-insurance. You can buy, extend and claim online anytime – even if you're already on the road.

Internet Access

Wi-fi is common in Iceland.

● Most accommodation and eating venues across the country offer wi-fi, and often buses do too. Access is usually free for guests/customers. You may need to ask staff for an access code.

● Most of the N1 service stations have free wi-fi.

● The easiest way to get online is to buy an Icelandic SIM card with a data package and pop it in your unlocked smartphone. Other devices can then access the internet via the phone.

● To travel with your own wi-fi hot spot, check out Trawire (http://iceland.trawire.com) for portable 4G modem rental with unlimited usage from US$9 per day (up to 10 laptops or mobile devices can be connected).

● Some car- and campervan-hire companies offer portable modem devices as an optional extra.

● Most Icelandic libraries have computer terminals for public internet access, even in small towns; there's often a small fee.

● Tourist information centres often have public internet terminals, often free for brief usage.

Legal Matters

Icelandic police are generally low-key and there's very little reason for you to end up in their hands. Worth knowing is the following:

● Drink-driving laws are strict. Even two drinks can put you over the legal limit of 0.05% blood-alcohol content; the penalty is loss of your driving licence plus a large fine.

● If you are involved in a traffic offence – speeding, driving without due care and attention etc – you may be asked to go to the station to pay the fine immediately.

● Drunk and disorderly behaviour may land you in a police cell for a night; you will usually be released the following morning.

● Penalties for possession, use or trafficking of illegal drugs are strict (long prison sentences and heavy fines).

LGBTIQ+ Travellers

Icelanders have a very open, accepting attitude towards homosexuality, though the gay scene is quite low-key, even in Reykjavík.

Maps

Online maps are are indeed useful but it's better to obtain paper maps in Iceland, and don't blindly follow GPS mapping instructions (stories abound of online maps sending drivers over mountain passes in winter because it's technically the shortest distance, but definitely not the safest).

Good online maps can be found at ja.is and map.is.

In recent years Iceland has been busy building new roads and tunnels, and sealing gravel stretches. We recommend you purchase a recently updated country map – ensure it shows the re-routed Ring Road (re-routed in East Iceland in late 2017).

Tourist information centres have useful free maps of their town and region. They also stock the free tourist booklet *Around*

Iceland, which has information and town plans.

Tourist info centres, petrol stations and bookshops all sell road atlases and maps.

Map publisher **Ferðakort** (www.mapoficeland.com) sells online and has a dedicated map department at **Iðnú Bookshop** (☑ 517 7210; www.ferdakort.is; Brautarholt 8; ⊙ 10am-4pm Mon-Fri) in Reykjavík. Forlagið (Mál og Menning) is another reputable map publisher with a wide range; browse at its **shop** (☑ 580 5000; www. bmm.is; Laugavegur 18; ⊙ 9am-10pm Mon-Fri, 10am-10pm Sat; 🛜) in the capital or online (www.forlagid.is – click on 'landakort' in the category Bækur & Kort).

Both companies have good touring maps of Iceland (1:500,000 or 1:600,000; approximately 2000kr), useful for general driving. Ferðakort's more in-depth 1:200,000 *Road Atlas* (4000kr) includes details of accommodation, museums and swimming pools.

Both companies also produce plenty of regional maps – Forlagið has a series of eight regional maps *(landshlutakort)* at 1:200,000 (1800kr each). There are also 31 detailed topographic maps at a scale of 1:100,000, covering the entire country – ideal for hikers – plus there are themed maps (eg sagas, geology and birdwatching).

Serious hikers can request maps at local tourist information centres or at national park visitor centres,

Tax-free Shopping

The standard rate of value-added tax (VAT) in Iceland is 24%. A reduced rate of 11% applies to certain products and services, including books, food and accommodation. VAT is included in quoted prices.

Anyone who has a permanent address outside Iceland can claim a tax refund on purchases when they spend more than 6000kr at a single point of sale. Look for stores with a 'tax-free shopping' sign in the window, and ask for a form at the register.

Before you check in for your departing flight at Keflavík, go to the refund office at Arion Banki (located in the arrival hall opposite the car-rental counter) and present your completed tax-free form, passport, receipts/invoices and purchases. Make sure the goods are unused. Opening hours of the office match flight schedules.

If you're departing Iceland from Reykjavík airport or a harbour, go to the customs office before check-in.

both of which often stock inexpensive maps detailing regional walks and hikes.

Money

Iceland is an almost cash-less society where credit cards reign supreme, even in the most rural reaches. PIN required for purchases. ATMs available in all towns.

ATMs

• As long as you're carrying a valid card, you'll need to withdraw only a limited amount of cash from ATMs.

• Almost every town in Iceland has a bank with an ATM *(hraðbanki)*, where you can withdraw cash using MasterCard, Visa, Maestro or Cirrus cards.

• Diners Club and JCB cards connected to the Cirrus network have access to all ATMs.

• You'll also find ATMs at larger petrol stations and in shopping centres.

Credit & Debit Cards

• Locals use plastic for even small purchases.

• Contact your financial institution to make sure that your card is approved for overseas use – you will need a PIN for purchases.

• Visa and MasterCard are accepted in most shops, restaurants and hotels. Amex is usually accepted, Diners Club less so.

• You can pay for the Flybus from Keflavík International Airport to Reykjavík using plastic – handy if you've just arrived in the country.

• If you intend to stay in rural farmhouse accommodation or visit isolated villages, it's a good idea to carry enough cash to tide you over.

Currency

The Icelandic unit of currency is the króna (plural krónur), written as kr or ISK.

• Coins come in denominations of 1kr, 5kr, 10kr, 50kr and 100kr.

• Notes come in denominations of 500kr, 1000kr, 2000kr, 5000kr and 10,000kr.

• Some accommodation providers and tour operators quote their prices in euros to ward against currency fluctuations, but these must be paid in Icelandic currency.

Tipping & Bargaining

• As service and VAT taxes are always included in prices, tipping isn't required in Iceland.

• Rounding up the bill at restaurants or leaving a small tip for good service is appreciated.

• Bargaining is not an accepted practice. You are expected to pay advertised rates.

Opening Hours

Opening hours vary throughout the year (some places are closed outside the high season). In general hours tend to be longer from June to August, and shorter from September to May. Standard opening hours:

Banks 9am–4pm Monday to Friday

Cafe-bars 10am–1am Sunday to Thursday, 10am to between 3am and 6am Friday and Saturday

Cafes 10am–6pm

Offices 9am–5pm Monday to Friday

Petrol stations 8am–10pm or 11pm (automated pumps open 24 hours)

Post offices 9am–4pm or 4.30pm Monday to Friday (to 6pm in larger towns)

Restaurants 11.30am–2.30pm and 6pm–9pm or 10pm

Shops 10am–6pm Monday to Friday, 10am–4pm Saturday; some Sunday opening in Reykjavík malls and major shopping strips

Supermarkets 9am–9pm

Vínbúðin (government-run liquor stores) Variable; many outside Reykjavík only open for a couple of hours per day

Seasonal hours

Some regional attractions and tourist-oriented businesses in Iceland are only open for a short summer season, typically from June to August. Reykjavík attractions and businesses generally run year-round.

As tourism is growing at a rapid pace, some regional businesses are vague about opening and closing dates; increasingly, seasonal restaurants or guesthouses may open sometime in May,

or even April, and stay open until the end of September or into October if demand warrants it.

With the growth of winter tourism, an increasing number of businesses (especially on the Ring Road) are feeling their way towards year-round trading. Note that many Icelandic hotels and guesthouses close from Christmas Eve to New Year's Day.

Check websites and/or Facebook pages of businesses, and ask around for advice.

Note that many museums outside the capital only have regular, listed opening hours during summer (June to August). From September to May they may advertise restricted opening hours (eg a couple of hours once a week), but many places are happy to open for individuals on request, with a little forewarning – make contact via museum websites or local tourist offices.

Post

The Icelandic postal service (www.postur.is) is reliable and efficient, and rates are comparable to those in other Western European countries.

A letter to Europe costs 225kr; to places outside Europe it costs 285kr. A full list of rates, branches and opening hours is available online.

Public Holidays

Icelandic public holidays are usually an excuse for a family gathering or, when they occur on weekends, a reason to head to the countryside and go camping. If you're planning to travel during holiday periods, particularly the Commerce Day long weekend, you should book mountain huts and transport well in advance.

National public holidays in Iceland:

New Year's Day 1 January

Easter March or April. Maundy Thursday and Good Friday to Easter Monday (changes annually)

First Day of Summer First Thursday after 18 April

Labour Day 1 May

Ascension Day May or June (changes annually)

Whit Sunday and Whit Monday May or June (changes annually)

National Day 17 June

Commerce Day First Monday in August

Christmas 24 to 26 December

New Year's Eve 31 December

School Holidays

The main school holiday runs from the first week of June to the third week of August; this is when most of the Edda and summer hotels open.

The winter school holiday is a two-week break over the Christmas period (around 21 December to 3 January).

There is also a spring break of about a week, over the Easter period.

Safe Travel

Iceland has a very low crime rate and in general any risks you'll face while travelling here are related to road safety, the unpredictable weather and the unique geological conditions.

○ A good place to learn about minimising your risks is **Safetravel** (www.safetravel.is). The website is an initiative of the Icelandic Association for Search and Rescue (ICE-SAR).

○ The website also provides information on ICE-SAR's 112 Iceland app for smartphones (useful in emergencies), and explains procedures for leaving a travel plan with ICE-SAR or a friend/contact.

Road Safety

○ Specific hazards (p287) exist for drivers, such as livestock on the roads, single-lane bridges, blind rises and rough gravel roads.

○ The numerous F roads are suitable only for 4WDs, often involve fording rivers, and are often only open for a few months each year in summer.

○ For road conditions, see www.road.is or call ☎1777.

Weather Conditions

○ Never underestimate the weather. Proper clothing and equipment is essential.

○ Visitors need to be prepared for inclement conditions year-round. The weather can change without warning.

○ Hikers must obtain a reliable forecast before setting off – call ☎902 0600 for a recorded forecast (press 1 after the introduction) or visit www.vedur.is/english for a forecast in English. Alternatively, download the weather app of the Icelandic Meteorological Office (IMO), called Vedur.

○ Emergency huts are provided in places where travellers run the risk of getting caught in severe weather.

○ If you're driving in winter, carry food, water and blankets in your car.

○ In winter, rental cars are fitted with snow or all-weather tyres.

Geological Risks

○ When hiking, river crossings can be dangerous, with glacial run-off transforming trickling streams into raging torrents on warm summer days.

○ High winds can create vicious sandstorms in areas where there is loose volcanic sand.

• Hiking paths in coastal areas may only be accessible at low tide; seek local advice and obtain the relevant tide tables.

• In geothermal areas, stick to boardwalks or obviously solid ground. Avoid thin crusts of lighter-coloured soil around steaming fissures and mudpots.

• Be careful of the water in hot springs and mudpots – it often emerges from the ground at 100°C.

• In glacial areas beware of dangerous quicksand at the ends of glaciers, and never venture out onto the ice without crampons and ice axes (even then, watch out for crevasses).

• Snowfields may overlie fissures, sharp lava chunks or slippery slopes of scoria (volcanic slag).

• Always get local advice before hiking around live volcanoes.

• Only attempt isolated hiking and glacier ascents if you know what you're doing. Talk to locals and/or employ a guide.

• It's rare to find warning signs or fences in areas where accidents can occur, such as large waterfalls, glacier fronts, cliff edges, and beaches with large waves and strong currents. Use common sense, and supervise children well.

Telephone

• Public payphones are extremely elusive in Iceland, but you may find them outside larger bus stations and petrol stations. Many accept credit cards as well as coins.

• To make international calls from Iceland, first dial the international access code ☏00, then the country code, the area or city code, and the telephone number.

• To phone Iceland from abroad, dial your country's international access code, Iceland's country code (☏354) and then the seven-digit phone number.

• Iceland has no area codes.

• Toll-free numbers begin with ☏800; mobile (cell) numbers start with 6, 7 or 8.

• The online version of the phone book with good maps is at http://en.ja.is.

• Useful numbers: directory enquiries ☏118 (local), ☏1811 (international).

Mobile Phones

Mobile (cell) coverage is widespread. Visitors with GSM phones can make roaming calls; purchase a local SIM card if you're staying a while.

• As of mid-2017, the EU has ended roaming surcharges for people who travel periodically within the EU. Under the 'roam like at home' regulations, residents of the EU and European Economic Area (EEA, which includes Iceland) can use mobile devices when travelling in the EU and EEA, paying the same prices as at home.

• For non-EU folks, the cheapest and most practical way to make calls at local rates is to purchase an Icelandic SIM card and pop it into your own mobile phone (tip: bring an old phone from home for that purpose).

• Before leaving home, make sure that your phone isn't locked to your home network.

• Check your phone will work on Europe's GSM 900/1800 network (US phones work on a different frequency).

• Buy prepaid SIM cards at bookshops, grocery stores and petrol stations throughout the country, and also on Icelandair flights. Top-up credit is available from the same outlets.

• Iceland telecom **Síminn** (www.siminn.is/prepaid) provides the greatest network coverage; **Vodafone** (http://vodafone.is/english/prepaid) isn't far behind. Both have voice-and-data starter packs including local SIM cards; Síminn's costs 2900kr (including either 10GB data, or 5GB and 50 minutes of international talk

me). **Nova** (www.nova.
) is a third player, and is
heap but lacks country-
ide coverage.

Phonecards

The smallest denomina-
ion phonecard (for use in
ublic telephones – which
re very rare) costs 500kr,
nd can be bought from
rocery stores and petrol
tations. Low-cost interna-
onal phonecards are also
vailable in many shops and
osks.

Time

Iceland's time zone is
he same as GMT/UTC
London).

There is no daylight
aving time.

From late October to late
March Iceland is on the
ame time as London, five
ours ahead of New York
nd 11 hours behind Sydney.

In the northern hemi-
phere summer, Iceland is
ne hour behind London,
ur hours ahead of New
ork and 10 hours behind
ydney.

Iceland uses the 24-hour
lock system, and all
ransport timetables and
usiness hours are posted
ccordingly.

Toilets

It may surprise you to
learn that public toilets are
newsworthy in Iceland – the
shortage of them hits the
headlines every so often,
and stories of tourists doing
their business in public, in
inappropriate places (eg
car parks and cemeteries),
are guaranteed to madden
the locals. Many Icelanders
view the increase in human
waste being found in nature
as being directly linked to
campers and campervan
travellers who shun camp-
grounds, and this has led to
new laws prohibiting such
camping.

Reykjavík and larger
towns have public rest-
rooms, but natural sights
often have too few facilities
for the increasing number
of visitors. Long queues can
form at the small number of
toilets available, especially
when buses pull in. There
are also long stretches of
road with few facilities.

The authorities have built
a few new restrooms along
the Ring Road (look for blue
roadside signs of a black
door), but our advice: plan
your trip well; stop at facilities wherever you see them
(eg N1 petrol stations); and
be prepared to fork out a
small fee (eg 200kr) for the
use of some facilities. Do not
do your business in public
because you'd rather not

pay. If there's an emergency,
find an appropriate place
(do not dig up fragile land)
and do not leave your toilet
paper behind.

Tourist Information

Official tourism sites for the
country:

Visit Iceland (www.visiticeland.
com)

Inspired by Iceland (www.
inspiredbyiceland.com)

Each region also has its own
useful site/s:

Reykjavík (www.visitrey
kjavik.is)

Southwest Iceland (www.
visitreykjanes.is; www.south.is)

West Iceland (www.west.is)

The Westfjords (www.
westfjords.is)

North Iceland (www.north
iceland.is; www.visitakureyri.is)

East Iceland (www.east.is)

Southeast Iceland (www.
south.is; www.visitvatnajokull.
is)

Smartphone Apps

Useful and practical smartphone apps include the
vital 112 Iceland app for safe
travel, Vedur for weather,
and apps for bus companies
such as **Strætó** (540 2700;
www.bus.is) and **Reykjavík
Excursions** (580 5400;
www.ioyo.is). Offline maps
come in handy.

There are plenty more apps that cover all sorts of interests, from history and language to aurora-spotting, or walking tours of the capital. *Reykjavík Grapevine's* apps (Appy Hour, Appetite and Appening Today) deserve special mention for getting you to the good stuff in the capital.

Visas

The visa situation for Iceland is as follows:

○ Citizens of EU and Schengen countries – no visa required for stays of up to 90 days.

○ Citizens or residents of Australia, Canada, Japan, New Zealand and the USA – no visa required for tourist visits of up to 90 days.

○ Note that the total stay within the Schengen area

must not exceed 90 days in any 180-day period.

○ Other countries – check online at www.utl.is.

Volunteering

A volunteering holiday is a worthwhile (and relatively inexpensive) way to get intimately involved with Iceland's people and landscapes. As well as the options below, a stint at the **Arctic Fox Center** (Melrakkasetur; ☑ 456 4922; www.arcticfoxcenter.com; Eyrardalur) in the wilds of the Westfjords is also possible.

Iceland Conservation Volunteers (www.ust.is/the-environment-agency-of-iceland/volunteers)

SEEDS (www.seeds.is)

Volunteer Abroad (www.volunteerabroad.com)

WWOOF (www.wwoofindependents.org)

Transport

Getting There & Away

Iceland has become far more accessible in recent years, with more flights arriving from more destinations. Ferry transport (from northern Denmark) makes a good alternative for Europeans wishing to take their own car.

Flights, cars and tours can be booked online at lonelyplanet.com/bookings.

Air

Airports & Airlines

Keflavík International Airport (KEF; ☑ 425 6000; www.kefairport.is; Reykjanesbraut; ◔ 24hr) Iceland's main international airport is 48km southwest of Reykjavík.

Reykjavík Domestic Airport (Reykjavíkurflugvöllur; www.isavia.is; Innanlandsflug) Internal flights and those to Greenland and the Faroes use this small airport in central Reykjavík.

A growing number of airlines fly to Iceland (including budget carriers) from destinations in Europe and North America. Some airlines have services only from June to August. Find a list of airlines serving the country at www.

Climate Change & Travel

Every form of transport that relies on carbon-based fuel generates CO_2, the main cause of human-induced climate change. Modern travel is dependent on aeroplanes, which might use less fuel per kilometre per person than most cars but travel much greater distances. The altitude at which aircraft emit gases (including CO_2) and particles also contributes to their climate change impact. Many websites offer 'carbon calculators' that allow people to estimate the carbon emissions generated by their journey and, for those who wish to do so, to offset the impact of the greenhouse gases emitted with contributions to portfolios of climate-friendly initiatives throughout the world. Lonely Planet offsets the carbon footprint of all staff and author travel.

isiticeland.com (under Plan
Your Trip/Flights).

Icelandair (www.icelandair.
com) The national carrier has
an excellent safety record.

Air Iceland Connect (☑570
8030; www.airicelandconnect.is;
Reykjavík Domestic Airport) The
main domestic airline (not to be
confused with Icelandair). Also
flies to destinations in Greenland and the Faroe Islands.

Eagle Air (☑562 2640; www.
eagleair.is; Reykjavík Domestic
Airport) Scheduled domestic
flights to small airstrips.

WOW Air (www.wowair.com)
Icelandic low-cost carrier,
serving a growing number of
European and North American
destinations.

Sea

Smyril Line (www.smyril
line.com) operates a pricey
but well-patronised weekly
car ferry, the *Norröna,* from
Hirtshals (Denmark) through
Tórshavn (Faroe Islands) to
Seyðisfjörður in East Iceland.
It operates year-round,
although winter passage is
weather-dependent – see
website for more.

Fares vary greatly, de-
pending on dates of travel,
what sort of vehicle (if any)
you are travelling with, and
cabin selection. Sailing
time is around 36 hours
from Denmark to the Faroe
Islands, and 19 hours from
the Faroes to Iceland.

It's possible to make a
stopover in the Faroes. Contact Smyril Line or see the
website for trip packages.

Getting Around

Air

Iceland has an extensive
network of domestic flights,
which locals use almost
like buses. In winter a flight
can be the only way to get
between destinations, but
weather at this time of
year can play havoc with
schedules.

Domestic flights depart
from the small Reykjavík Domestic Airport, *not* from the
major international airport
at Keflavík.

A handful of airstrips offer
regular sightseeing flights
(eg Mývatn, Skaftafell, and
Reykjavík and Akureyri
domestic airports) and
helicopter sightseeing is
increasingly popular.

A list of local airports
and useful information
about them is found at
www.isavia.is.

Airlines in Iceland

Air Iceland Connect Not to
be confused with international
airline Icelandair. Destinations
covered: Reykjavík, Akureyri,
Grímsey, Ísafjörður, Þórshöfn,
Vopnafjörður and Egilsstaðir.
Offers some fly-in day tours.

Eagle Air Operates scheduled
flights to five small airstrips
from Reykjavík: Vestmannaeyjar, Húsavík, Höfn, Bíldudalur
and Gjögur. Also runs a number
of fly-in day tours.

Bicycle

Cycling is an increasingly
popular way to see the
country's landscapes, but
cyclists should be prepared
for harsh conditions.

Gale-force winds, driving
rain, sandstorms, sleet and
sudden flurries of snow are
possible year-round. We recommend keeping your plans
relatively flexible so you can
wait out bad weather if the
need arises.

You'll be forced to ride
closely alongside traffic on
the Ring Road (there are
no hard shoulders to the
roads).

The large bus companies
carry bikes, so if the weather
turns bad or your highlands
bike trip isn't working out as
planned, consider the bus.
Note that space can't be
reserved. It's free to take a
bike on **Strætó** (☑540 2700;
www.bus.is) services; other
companies, such as **SBA-
Norðurleið** (☑550 0700;
www.sba.is) and **Reykjavík
Excursions** (☑580 5400;
www.ioyo.is), charge 4000kr,
and it's advisable to contact
them regarding rules and
space.

Puncture-repair kits and
spares are hard to come
by outside Reykjavík; bring
your own or stock up in the
capital. On the road, it's
essential to know how to do
your own basic repairs.

If you want to tackle the
interior, the Kjölur route
has bridges over all major
rivers, making it fairly accessible to cyclists. A less-
challenging route is the

4

F249 to Þórsmörk. The Westfjords also offers some wonderful, challenging cycling terrain.

Hire

Various places rent out mountain bikes, but in general these are intended for local use only, and often aren't up to long-haul travel.

If you intend to go touring, it's wise to bring your bike from home or purchase one when you arrive; alternatively, **Reykjavík Bike Tours** (www.icelandbike.com) has touring bikes for rent.

Resources

Cycling Iceland (www.cyclingiceland.is) Online version of the brilliantly detailed *Cycling Iceland* map, published annually.

Icelandic Mountain Bike Club (http://fjallahjolaklubburinn.is) The English-language pages of this website are a goldmine of information.

The Biking Book of Iceland There is a series of cycling books by Ómar Smári Kristinsson, but only one has been translated into English; it covers trails in the Westfjords.

Boat

Several year-round ferries operate in Iceland. Major routes all carry vehicles, but it's worthwhile booking ahead for car passage.

Herjólfur (www.seatours.is) Connecting Landeyjahöfn in South Iceland to Vestmannaeyjar islands.

Sævar (www.hrisey.is) Frequent, easy connections from Árskógssandur in North Iceland,

north of Akureyri, to the island of Hrísey.

Baldur (www.seatours.is) Connecting Stykkishólmur in West Iceland to Brjánslækur in the Westfjords, via the island of Flatey.

Sæfari (www.saefari.is) Connecting Dalvík in North Iceland to Grímsey island on the Arctic Circle.

From June to August, regular boat services run from Bolungarvík and Ísafjörður to points in Hornstrandir (Westfjords).

Bus

Iceland has a shrinking network of long-distance bus routes, with services provided by a handful of main companies. The free *Public Transport in Iceland* map has an overview of routes; pick it up at tourist offices or view it online at www.publictransport.is.

From roughly June to August, regular scheduled buses run to most places on the Ring Road, into the popular hiking areas of the Southwest, and to larger towns in the Westfjords and Eastfjords, and on the Reykjanes and Snæfellsnes Peninsulas. The rest of the year, services range from daily, to a few weekly, to nonexistent.

In summer 2018, there was no service linking Egilsstaðir in the east with Höfn in the Southeast, making it nearly impossible to complete the Ring Road by bus.

In summer, 4WD buses run along some F roads

(mountain roads), including the highland Kjölur, Sprengisandur and Askja routes (inaccessible to 2WD cars).

Many bus services can be used as day tours: buses spend a few hours at the final destination before returning to the departure point, and may stop for a half-hour at various tourist destinations en route.

Bus companies may operate from different terminals or pick-up points. Reykjavík has several bus terminals; in small towns, buses usually stop at the main petrol station or campground, but it pays to double-check.

Many buses are equipped with free wi-fi.

Many buses have GPS tracking, so you can see when your bus is approaching your stop.

Companies

Main bus companies:

Reykjavík Excursions (580 5400; www.ioyo.is) Departs from BSÍ Bus Terminal in Reykjavík.

SBA-Norðurleið (550 0700; www.sba.is) Departs from BSÍ Bus Terminal in Reykjavík.

Sterna (551 1166; www.icelandbybus.is) Departs from Harpa in Reykjavík; stops at Reykjavík Campsite.

Strætó (540 2700; www.bus.is) Main terminal for long-distance buses is at Mjódd.

Trex (587 6000; www.trex.is) Hiker transport; has a few departure points in Reykjavík (including the main tourist office and Reykjavík Campsite).

Car & Motorcycle

Driving in Iceland gives you unparalleled freedom to discover the country and, thanks to (relatively) good roads and (relatively) light traffic, it's all fairly straightforward.

• The Ring Road (Rte 1) circles the country and is paved.

• Beyond the Ring Road, fingers of sealed road or gravel stretch out to most communities.

• Driving coastal areas can be spectacularly scenic, and incredibly slow as you weave up and down over mountain passes and in and out of long fjords.

• A 2WD vehicle will get you almost everywhere in summer (note: *not* into the highlands, or on F roads).

• In winter heavy snow can cause many roads to close; mountain roads generally only open in June and may start closing as early as September. For up-to-date information on road conditions, visit www.road.is.

• Don't be pressured into renting a GPS unit – if you purchase a good, up-to-date touring map, and can read it, you should be fine without GPS. If you are planning to take remote trails, a GPS will be worthwhile.

Bringing Your Own Vehicle

Car hire in Iceland is expensive, so bringing your own vehicle may not be as crazy

as it sounds. The Smyril Line ferry from Denmark is busy in summer bringing vehicles to Iceland from all over Europe (book passage well ahead).

For temporary duty-free importation, drivers must carry the vehicle's registration documents, proof of valid insurance (a 'green card' if your car isn't registered in a Nordic or EU-member country) and a driving licence.

Permission for temporary duty-free importation of a vehicle is granted at the point of arrival for up to 12 months, and is contingent upon agreeing to not lend or sell your vehicle. For more information, contact the **Directorate of Customs** (www.customs.is).

Winter visitors should have winter tyres fitted (studded tyres are permitted from November to mid-April).

If you're staying for a long period, you might consider shipping your own vehicle via **Eimskip** (www.eimskip.com) shipping services. Be aware that this is far from cheap, and involves heavy paperwork, but it may be useful for long-stayers who have lots of gear or a well set-up camper/4WD. Eimskip has five shipping lines in the North Atlantic.

Driving Licences

You can drive in Iceland with a driving licence from the USA, Canada, Australia, New Zealand and most European countries. If your licence

is not in Roman script, you need an International Driving Permit (normally issued by your home country's automobile association).

Fuel & Spare Parts

• Petrol stations are regularly spaced around the country, but in the highlands you should check fuel levels and the distance to the next station before setting off.

• At the time of research, unleaded petrol and diesel cost about 220kr (€1.80) per litre.

• Some Icelandic roads can be pretty lonely, so carry a jack, a spare tyre and jump leads just in case (check your spare when you pick up your rental car).

• In the event of a breakdown or accident, your first port of call should be your car-hire agency.

• Although the Icelandic motoring association **Félag Íslenskra Bifreiðaeigenda** (FÍB; www.fib.is) is only open to locals, if you have breakdown cover with an automobile association affiliated with ARC Europe you may be covered by the FÍB – check with your home association.

• FÍB's 24-hour breakdown number is ☏511 2112. Even if you're not a member, it may be able to provide information and phone numbers for towing and breakdown services.

Car Hire

Travelling by car is the only way to get to some parts of Iceland. Although car-hire rates are very expensive by international standards, they compare favourably to bus or internal air travel, especially if there are a few of you to split the costs. Shop around and book online for the best deals.

To rent a car you must be 20 years old (23 to 25 years for a 4WD) and hold a valid licence.

The cheapest cars, usually a small hatchback or similar, cost from around 8000kr per day in high season (June to August). Figure on paying around 10,000 to 12,000kr for the smallest 4WD that offers higher clearance than a regular car but isn't advised for large river crossings, and 15,000kr to 20,000kr for a larger 4WD model.

Rates include unlimited mileage and VAT (a hefty 24%), and usually collision damage waiver (CDW).

Weekly rates offer some discount. From September to May you should be able to find considerably better daily rates and deals.

Check the small print, as additional costs such as extra insurance, airport pick-up charges, and one-way rental fees can add up.

In winter you should opt for a larger, sturdier car for safety reasons, preferably with 4WD (ie absolutely *not* a compact 2WD).

In the height of summer many companies run out of rentals. Book ahead.

Many travel organisations (eg Hostelling International Iceland, Hey Iceland) offer package deals that include car hire.

Most companies are based in the Reykjavík and Keflavík areas, with city and airport offices. Larger companies have extra locations around the country (usually in Akureyri and Egilsstaðir). Ferry passengers arriving via Seyðisfjörður should contact car-hire agencies in nearby Egilsstaðir.

Car-hire companies:

Átak (www.atak.is)

Avis (www.avis.is)

Budget (www.budget.is)

Cars Iceland (www.carsiceland.com)

Cheap Jeep (www.cheapjeep.is)

Europcar (www.europcar.is) The biggest hire company in Iceland.

Geysir (www.geysir.is)

Go Iceland (www.goiceland.com)

Hertz (www.hertz.is)

SADcars (www.sadcars.com)

Saga (www.sagacarrental.is)

Campervan Hire

Combining accommodation and transport costs into campervan rental is a booming option – and has extra appeal in summer, as it allows for some spontaneity (unlike every other form of accommodation,

campsites don't need to be prebooked). Campervanning in winter is possible, but we don't recommend it – there are fewer facilities open for campers at this time, and weather conditions may make it unsafe.

Large car-hire companies usually have campervans for rent, but there are also more offbeat choices, offering from backpacker-centric to family-sized, or real 4WD set-ups for highland exploration. Some companies offer gear rental to help your trip go smoothly (GPS, cooking gear and stove, barbecue, sleeping bags, camping chairs, fishing equipment, portable wi-fi hot spots etc).

There are dozens of companies that can help you get set up. As with rental cars, prices vary depending on size and age of the vehicle, length of rental period, high/low season, added extras etc. Shop around, and read the fine print. Prices for something small and basic can start around 12,000kr per day.

Camp Easy (www.campeasy.com)

Camper Iceland (www.campericeland.is)

Go Campers (www.gocampers.is)

Happy Campers (www.happycampers.is)

JS Camper Rental (www.jscamper.com) Truck campers on 4WD pick-ups.

Rent Nordic (www.rent.is)

Insurance

A vehicle registered in Nordic or EU-member countries is considered to have valid automobile insurance in Iceland. If your vehicle is registered in a non-Nordic or non-EU country, you'll need a 'green card', which proves that you are insured to drive while in Iceland. Green cards are issued by insurance companies in your home country; contact your existing insurer.

When hiring a car, check the small print; most vehicles come with third-party insurance and CDW to cover you for damage to the car. Also check the excess (the initial amount you will be able to pay in the event of an accident) as this can be surprisingly high.

Hire vehicles are not covered for damage to tyres, headlights and windscreens, or damage caused to the car's underside by driving on dirt roads, through water or in ash- or sandstorms. Many companies will try to sell you additional insurance to cover these possibilities. You need to consider whether this is appropriate for you and your plans, and how prepared you are to cough up in the event of such occurrences (and the cost of the insurance versus factors such as the length of your rental and what regions you plan to visit). There is no way of predicting what climatic conditions you might meet on your trip.

Road Conditions & Hazards

Good main-road surfaces and light traffic (especially outside the capital and Southwest region) make driving in Iceland relatively easy, but there are some specific hazards. Watch the 'Drive Safely on Icelandic Roads' video on www.drive. is for more.

Livestock Sheep graze in the countryside over the summer, and often wander onto roads. Slow down when you see livestock on or near roadsides.

Unsurfaced roads The transition from sealed to gravel roads is marked with the warning sign 'Malbik Endar' – slow right down to avoid skidding when you hit the gravel. Most accidents involving foreign drivers in Iceland are caused by the use of excessive speed on unsurfaced roads. If your car does begin to skid, take your foot off the accelerator and gently turn the car in the direction you want the front wheels to go. Do not brake.

Blind rises In most cases, roads have two lanes with steeply cambered sides and no hard shoulder; be prepared for oncoming traffic in the centre of the road, and slow down and stay to the right when approaching a blind rise, marked as 'Blindhæð' on road signs.

Single-lane bridges Slow down and be prepared to give way when approaching single-lane bridges (marked as 'Einbreið Brú'). Right of way is with the car closer to the bridge.

Sun glare With the sun often sitting low to the horizon, sunglasses are recommended.

Winter conditions In winter make sure your car is fitted with winter tyres, and carry a shovel, blankets, food and water.

Ash- & sandstorms Volcanic ash and severe sandstorms can strip paint off cars; strong winds can even topple your vehicle. At-risk areas are marked with orange warning signs.

F roads Roads suitable for 4WD vehicles only are F-numbered.

River crossings Few highland roads have bridges over rivers. Fords are marked on maps with a 'V'.

Tunnels There are a number of tunnels in Iceland – a couple are single lane, and a little anxiety-inducing! Before you enter such tunnels, a sign will indicate which direction has right of way. There will be a couple of pull-over bays inside the tunnel (signed 'M'). If the passing bay is on your side in the tunnel, you are obliged to pull in and let oncoming traffic pass you.

Road Rules

- Drive on the right.

- Front and rear seatbelts are compulsory.

- Dipped headlights must be on at all times.

- Blood alcohol limit is 0.05%.

- Mobile phone use is prohibited when driving except with a hands-free kit.

- Children under six years must use a car seat.

○ Do not drive off-road (ie off marked roads and 4WD trails).

Speed Limits

○ Built-up areas: 50km/h

○ Unsealed roads: 80km/h

○ Sealed roads: 90km/h

Roundabout Rules

There are many large roundabouts, especially in Reykjavík. Drivers need to know that the *inside lane* of a two-lane roundabout always has priority over traffic in the outer lane. This is a law that is not common outside of Iceland, and causes some confusion (and accidents!).

Off-Road Driving

Off-road driving is illegal, and hugely destructive to the fragile environment. It is a surefire way to anger the locals. Roads with numbers count as on-road, so please stick to them.

Hitching

Hitching is never entirely safe, and it's not recommended. Travellers who hitch should understand that they are taking a small but potentially serious risk. Nevertheless, we met scores of tourists who were hitching their way around Iceland and most had positive reports. Single female travellers and couples tend to get a lift the quickest.

Patience is a prerequisite of hitching, and logic is important too – be savvy about where you position yourself. Try standing at junctions, near petrol stations or even by Bónus supermarkets.

When you arrive at your accommodation it can't hurt to let people know where you're aiming for the next day. There may be another traveller going that way who can give you a ride.

Check out **Carpooling in Iceland** (www.samferda.is) for rides – note there is an expectation that passengers will contribute to fuel costs.

Local Transport

Bus

Reykjavík has an extensive network of local buses connecting all the suburbs, and running to Akranes, Borgarnes, Hveragerði and Selfoss. There are now night services on some routes, running from around 1am to 4.30am on Saturday and Sunday. See www.straeto. is for information on routes, fares and timetables.

Local bus networks operate in Akureyri, Ísafjörður, and the Reykjanesbær and Eastfjords areas.

Taxi

Most taxis in Iceland operate in the Reykjavík area, but many of the larger towns also offer services. Outside of Reykjavík, it's usually wise to prebook.

Taxis are metered and can be pricey. Tipping is not expected.

At the time of research, there were no app-based ride-sharing services (such as Uber and Lyft) in Iceland.

Language

Icelandic belongs to the Germanic language family, which includes German, English, Dutch and all the Scandinavian languages except Finnish. It's related to Old Norse, and retains the letters 'eth' (ð) and 'thorn' (þ), which also existed in Old English. Be aware, especially when you're trying to read bus timetables or road signs, that place names can be spelled in several different ways due to Icelandic grammar rules.

Most Icelanders speak English, so you'll have no problems if you don't know any Icelandic. However, any attempts to speak the local language will be much appreciated.

Basics

Hello.	*Halló.*	ha·loh
Good morning.	*Góðan daginn.*	gohth·ahn dai·in
Goodbye.	*Bless.*	bles
Good evening.	*Gott kvöld.*	khot kverld
Good night.	*Góða nótt.*	gohth·ah noht
Thank you	*Takk./Takk fyrir*	tak/tak fi·rir
Excuse me.	*Afsakið.*	af·sa·kidh
Sorry.	*Fyrirgefðu.*	fi·rir·gev·dhu
Yes.	*Já.*	yow
No.	*Nei.*	nay

How are you?
Hvað segir þú gott? kvadh say·yir thoo got

Fine. And you?
Allt fínt. En þú? alt feent en thoo

What's your name?
Hvað heitir þú? kvadh hay·tir thoo

My name is ...
Ég heiti ... yekh hay·ti ...

Do you speak English?
Talar þú ensku? ta·lar thoo ens·ku

I don't understand.
Ég skil ekki. yekh skil e·ki

It will be OK.
Þetta reddast. the·tah re·dahst

Directions

Where's the (hotel)?
Hvar er (hótelið)? kvar er (hoh·te·lidh)

Can you show me (on the map)?
Geturðu sýnt mér (á kortinu)? ge·tur·dhu seent myer (ow kor·ti·nu)

What's your address?
Hvert er heimilisfangið þitt? kvert er hay·mi·lis·fown·gidh thit

Eating & Drinking

What would you recommend?
Hverju mælir þú með? kver·yu mai·lir thoo medh

Do you have vegetarian food?
Erud þið með grænmetisrétti? er·udh thidh medh grain·me·tis·rye·ti

I'll have a ...
Ég ætla að fá ... yekh ait·la adh fow ...

Cheers!
Skál! skowl

Emergencies

Help!	*Hjálp!*	hyowlp
Go away!	*Farðu!*	far·dhu
Call ...!	*Hringdu á ...!*	hring·du ow ...
a doctor	*lækni*	laik·ni
the police	*lögregluna*	leukh·rekh·lu·na

I'm lost.
Ég er villtur/villt. (m/f) yekh er vil·tur/vilt

Where are the toilets?
Hvar er snyrtingin? kvar er snir·tin·gin

Transport

Can we get there by public transport?
Er hægt að taka rútu þangað? er haikht adh ta·ka roo·tu thown·gadh

Where can I buy a ticket?
Hvar kaupi ég miða? kvar keuy·pi yekh mi·dha

Is this the ... to (Akureyri)?	*Er þetta ... til (Akureyrar)?*	er the·ta ... til (a·ku·ray·rar)
boat	*ferjan*	fer·yan
bus	*rútan*	roo·tan
plane	*flugvélin*	flukh·vye·lin

I'd like a taxi ...	*Get ég fengið leigubíl ...*	get yekh fayn·gidh lay·khu·beel ...
at (9am)	*klukkan (níu fyrir hádegi)*	klu·kan (nee·u fi·rir how·day·yi)
tomorrow	*á morgun*	ow mor·gun

How much is it to ...?
Hvað kostar til ... ? kvadh kos·tar til ...

Please stop here.
Stoppaðu hér, takk. sto·pa·dhu hyer tak

Behind the Scenes

Acknowledgements

Climate map data adapted from Peel MC, Finlayson BL & McMahon TA (2007) 'Updated World Map of the Köppen-Geiger Climate Classification', *Hydrology and Earth System Sciences*, 11, 1633–44.

This Book

This 1st edition of Lonely Planet's *Best of Iceland* guidebook was curated by Paul Harding. It was researched and written by Alexis Averbuck, Carolyn Bain, Jade Bremner and Belinda Dixon.

This guidebook was produced by the following:

Destination Editor Clifton Wilkinson

Senior Product Editor Genna Patterson

Regional Senior Cartographer Valentina Kremenchutskaya

Product Editor Jenna Myers

Book Designer Jessica Rose

Assisting Editors Judith Bamber, Pete Cruttenden, Bruce Evans, Gabrielle Innes, Kate Morgan, Monique Perrin

Assisting Book Designer Clara Monitto

Cover Researcher Naomi Parker

Thanks to Hannah Cartmel, Mark Griffiths, Corey Hutchison, Chris LeeAck, Anne Mason, Kirsten Rawlings, Vicky Smith, Diana Von Holdt

Send Us Your Feedback

We love to hear from travellers – your comments keep us on our toes and help make our books better. Our well-travelled team reads every word on what you loved or loathed about this book. Although we cannot reply individually to postal submissions, we always guarantee that your feedback goes straight to the appropriate authors, in time for the next edition. Each person who sends us information is thanked in the next edition, the most useful submissions are rewarded with a selection of digital PDF chapters.

Visit lonelyplanet.com/contact to submit your updates and suggestions or to ask for help. Our award-winning website also features inspirational travel stories, news and discussions.

Note: We may edit, reproduce and incorporate your comments in Lonely Planet products such as guidebooks, websites and digital products, so let us know if you don't want your comments reproduced or your name acknowledged. For a copy of our privacy policy visit lonelyplanet.com/privacy.

ndex

Symbols & Map Key

Look for these symbols to quickly identify listings:

- ◉ Sights
- 🟢 Activities
- 🟢 Courses
- 🟢 Tours
- 🟢 Festivals & Events
- ❌ Eating
- 🟢 Drinking
- ⭐ Entertainment
- 🟢 Shopping
- ❶ Information & Transport

These symbols and abbreviations give vital information for each listing:

🌿 Sustainable or green recommendation

FREE No payment required

- 🕿 Telephone number
- ⏱ Opening hours
- 🅿 Parking
- 🚭 Nonsmoking
- ❄ Air-conditioning
- @ Internet access
- 🛜 Wi-fi access
- 🏊 Swimming pool
- 🚌 Bus
- ⛴ Ferry
- 🚋 Tram
- 🚆 Train
- 📖 English-language menu
- 🌱 Vegetarian selection
- 👪 Family-friendly

Find your best experiences with these Great For... icons.

- Art & Culture
- Beaches
- Budget
- Cafe/Coffee
- Cycling
- Detour
- Drinking
- Entertainment
- Events
- Family Travel
- Food & Drink
- History
- Local Life
- Nature & Wildlife
- Photo Op
- Scenery
- Shopping
- Short Trip
- Sport
- Walking
- Winter Travel

Sights
- Beach
- Bird Sanctuary
- Buddhist
- Castle/Palace
- Christian
- Confucian
- Hindu
- Islamic
- Jain
- Jewish
- Monument
- Museum/Gallery/ Historic Building
- Ruin
- Shinto
- Sikh
- Taoist
- Winery/Vineyard
- Zoo/Wildlife Sanctuary
- Other Sight

Points of Interest
- Bodysurfing
- Camping
- Cafe
- Canoeing/Kayaking
- Course/Tour
- Diving
- Drinking & Nightlife
- Eating
- Entertainment
- Sento Hot Baths/ Onsen
- Shopping
- Skiing
- Sleeping
- Snorkelling
- Surfing
- Swimming/Pool
- Walking
- Windsurfing
- Other Activity

Information
- Bank
- Embassy/Consulate
- Hospital/Medical
- Internet
- Police
- Post Office
- Telephone
- Toilet
- Tourist Information
- Other Information

Geographic
- Beach
- Gate
- Hut/Shelter
- Lighthouse
- Lookout
- Mountain/Volcano
- Oasis
- Park
- Pass
- Picnic Area
- Waterfall

Transport
- Airport
- BART station
- Border crossing
- Boston T station
- Bus
- Cable car/Funicular
- Cycling
- Ferry
- Metro/MRT station
- Monorail
- Parking
- Petrol station
- Subway/S-Bahn/ Skytrain station
- Taxi
- Train station/Railway
- Tram
- Tube Station
- Underground/ U-Bahn station
- Other Transport

Our Story

A beat-up old car, a few dollars in the pocket and a sense of adventure. In 1972 that's all Tony and Maureen Wheeler needed for the trip of a lifetime – across Europe and Asia overland to Australia. It took several months, and at the end – broke but inspired – they sat at their kitchen table writing and stapling together their first travel guide, *Across Asia on the Cheap*. Within a week they'd sold 1500 copies. Lonely Planet was born.

Today, Lonely Planet has offices in Franklin, London, Melbourne, Oakland, Dublin, Beijing, and Delhi, with more than 600 staff and writers. We share Tony's belief that 'a great guidebook should do three things: inform, educate and amuse'.

Our Writers

Paul Harding

As a writer and photographer, Paul has been travelling the globe for the best part of two decades, with an interest in remote and offbeat places, islands and cultures. He's an author and contributor to more than 50 Lonely Planet guides to countries and regions as diverse as India, Belize, Vanuatu, Iran, Indonesia, New Zealand, Iceland, Finland, Philippines and – his home patch – Australia.

Alexis Averbuck

Alexis has travelled and lived all over the world, from Sri Lanka to Ecuador, Zanzibar and Antarctica. In recent years she's been living on the Greek island of Hydra and exploring her adopted homeland; sampling oysters in Brittany and careening through hill-top villages in Provence; and adventuring along Iceland's surreal lava fields, sparkling fjords and glacier tongues.

Carolyn Bain

A travel writer and editor for more than 20 years, Carolyn has lived, worked and studied in various corners of the globe, including Denmark, London, St Petersburg and Nantucket. She has authored more than 50 Lonely Planet titles, with her all-time favourite research destination being Iceland.

Jade Bremner

Jade has been a journalist for more than a decade. She has lived in and reported on four different regions. Wherever she goes she finds action sports to try, the weirder the better, and it's no coincidence many of her favourite places have some of the best waves in the world.

Belinda Dixon

Only happy when her feet are suitably sandy, Belinda has been (gleefully) travelling, researching and writing for Lonely Planet since 2006. It has seen her navigating mountain passes and soaking in hot-pots in Iceland's Westfjords, marvelling at Stonehenge at sunrise; scrambling up Italian mountain paths; horse riding across Donegal's golden sands; gazing at Verona's frescoes; and fossil hunting on Dorset's Jurassic Coast.

STAY IN TOUCH LONELYPLANET.COM/CONTACT

AUSTRALIA The Malt Store, Level 3, 551 Swanston St, Carlton, Victoria 3053
☎03 8379 8000, fax 03 8379 8111

IRELAND Digital Depot, Roe Lane (off Thomas St), Digital Hub, Dublin 8, D08 TCV4

USA 124 Linden Street, Oakland, CA 94607
☎510 250 6400, toll free 800 275 8555, fax 510 893 8572

UK 240 Blackfriars Road, London SE1 8NW
☎020 3771 5100, fax 020 3771 5101

 twitter.com/lonelyplanet   facebook.com/lonelyplanet   instagram.com/lonelyplanet   youtube.com/lonelyplanet   lonelyplanet.com/newsletter